THE GARDEN OF LIFE IS abundant, prosperous and magical. ❦ In this garden, there is enough for everyone. ❦ Share the fruit and the knowledge ❦ Our brothers and we are in this lush, exciting place together. ❦ Let's show others the way. ❦ Kindness. Generosity. ❦ Hard work. ❦ God's care.

Targeting
THE JOB
You Want

Kate Wendleton

**author of *Through the Brick Wall:
How to Job-Hunt in a Tight Market***

with Wendy Alfus Rothman,
Patricia Kitchen, Lydia Bronte, C.B. Bowman,
Harriet Greisser, Michael Wheeler, and Russ Schundler

Five O'Clock Books / New York / 1996

The
Five
O'Clock
Club

For my parents
who had the strength to impose their own terms upon life
—with generosity and caring

Copyright © 1996 by Kate Wendleton and The Five O'Clock Club

Published in the United States by Five O'Clock Books, a division of The Five O'Clock Club, New York.

Some of the contents of this work appeared previously in somewhat different form in *The Job-Changing Workbook, The Five O'Clock News, Through the Brick Wall: How to Job-Hunt in a Tight Market* and *Through the Brick Wall: Job Finder*

The Five O'Clock Club and Workforce America are registered trademarks.

Library of Congress Cataloging-in-Publication Data

Wendleton, Kate.
  Targeting the job you want : for job hunters, career changers, consultants and freelancers / Kate Wendleton.
    p.   cm.
  Includes bibliographical references and index.
  ISBN 0-944054-08-0

  1. Job hunting. 2. Career changers. I. Title
HF5382.7.W46 1996   650.14
                          QBI95-20648

For information, address The Five O'Clock Club,
300 East 40th Street - 6L, New York, New York 10016

FIRST EDITION
FIRST PRINTING

Manufactured in the United States of America

9 8 7 6 5 4 3 2 1

If you haven't the strength
to impose your own terms upon life,
then you must accept the terms it offers you.

T. S. Eliot,
The Confidential Clerk

Preface

Dear Member or Prospective Member of The Five O'Clock Club:

Have you ever asked yourself the question, "What should I be doing with my life?" This book will help you find the answer. It is the first in a three-part series for job hunters, career changers, freelancers and consultants who want some guidance about what to do in this changing economy. None of us can depend on our employers to help us through this—we have to figure it out for ourselves. And if we do, we will all be better off.

Learning how to manage our own careers is the only job security we can expect from now on. And this book will show you how to do it. *Targeting the Job You Want* is the most extensive and thorough book on the subject. It is important to do the exercises in this book. The results are the only things that will keep you calm and secure in this stormy market.

Taken together, the books in this series prepare you to deal with the continuous change we are all experiencing, figure out where you fit in, and help you to get what you want.

The books present the strategies we use at The Five O'Clock Club, our national job-search strategy program. *The Five O'Clock Club* series is the result of fourteen years of research into how successful people plan and manage their careers, and land the best jobs—whether on payroll or on assignment—at the best pay. These books provide the most sophisticated and most detailed explanation of the process:

- *Targeting the Job You Want* helps you figure out what to do with your professional life.
- *Job-Search Secrets* presents the targeted, strategic approach to career development and job search that we use at The Five O'Clock Club. It tells you how to get more interviews in your target areas, turn those interviews into offers, and get the best compensation package—whether for full-time, part-time, freelance or consulting work. It contains dozens of cover letters, follow-up letters, and letters to search firms and for answering ads.
- *Building a Great Résumé* uses a case-study approach. You will find out why a perfectly good "before" résumé did not work for a job hunter. When you read about the situation that job hunter was facing, you will see why the "after" résumé was more effective.

Running The Five O'Clock Club is the most gratifying thing I do. Those who head up and coach job hunters at our Affiliates agree that nothing gives them more satisfaction than helping someone figure out a career path, and then coaching that person to land a great job at a great salary.

Even those who have been unemployed a long time find help in our groups. Do not become discouraged if you have been in search a long time. You may be doing something wrong. Some of our best stories are about people who had been unemployed two years or longer, and found the job that was perfect for them at just the right salary. All of the case studies in this and our other books are of actual people.

All of this information is based on the highly successful methods used at The Five O'Clock Club, where the average, regularly attending member finds a job within ten weeks. For a packet of information on joining the Club and subscribing to *The Five O'Clock News*, call 1-800-538-6645 ext. 600, or see the Application Form in the last section of this book.

We are guided by the original Five O'Clock Club, where the leaders of Old Philadelphia met regularly to exchange ideas and have a good time. Today's members are the same—they exchange ideas, operate at a high level, brain-storm to help each other, and truly enjoy each other's company.

I hope these books will assist you as they have so many others. Thank you for supporting The Five O'Clock Club through your purchase of this book. Because of people like you, we can keep the program going and spread to new cities so we'll be there when you need us. Our goal is, and always has been, to provide the best affordable career advice. And—with you as our partners—we will continue to do this.

Cheers and good luck!

Kate Wendleton
New York City, 1996

Acknowledgements

With appreciation to the entire Dobbs Family, of which I am the eldest, for being dependable cheerleaders. To Nancy O'Shea Mercante, my friend and partner at The Main Club. To my key advisors: Kay Shadley, friend and attorney, who has helped me start Affiliates in other cities; Dr. George Barrister, a steady, astute businessman and friend, who is also very funny; and Bob Riscica, a new friend, who is helping us to take this adventure even further.

I appreciate all Five O'Clock Club members, old and new, some of whose stories are contained herein: Members provide feedback on our techniques, which allows our approach to evolve continually with the changing job market. Members also give us information for our database, so we can track trends and know what is going on.

I thank our Affiliates, which have brought this high-quality program to other cities with enthusiasm and dedication to our members. Special mention to the following Affiliate heads: Barbara Bruno (Chicago, IL), Sylvia Gaffney (Rockford, IL), Phil Gittings (Philadelphia, PA), Fred Hopkinson (Toronto, Canada), Robert Maher (Cleveland, OH), Bobbie Rich (Fairfield, CT), Amy Rust (Cincinnati, OH), George Jung and Victoria McLaughlin (Long Island, NY), and C.B. Bowman, Ellis Chase, Deborah Brown, Jim Butler and Bill Stanley (NY, NY).

I thank the excellent staff of The Five O'Clock Club, especially Sharon Williams, who keeps our office running smoothly. Our warmest thanks to Norman and Lillian Cohen, who have been devoted and attentive volunteers for years. I am especially grateful to the staff of the Main Club, who have worked with me for so many years. The original counselors included: Ellis Chase, Roy Cohen, Barbara Earley, Shelli Kanet, John Leonard, Wendy Rothman, and Gloria Waslyn. Our present counselors include Michael Aronin, Fredi Balzano, Jim Borland, C.B. Bowman, Roy Cohen, Stacy Feldman, John Leonard, and Ed Witherell. In addition, I would like to acknowledge Patricia Kelly, whose artwork, *Fruytagie*, hangs in our offices and appears in our publications—including this one.

We are all especially proud of Workforce America, which runs The Five O'Clock Club program in Harlem. It was started with the help of the Reverend James Russell, and is headed by Debbie Brown with George Lumsby. The initial funding for this program was provided by Deirdre Cavanagh, my friend, and The Brick Church. My deepest appreciation to them both. We also appreciate the help of Tracy Balzano, Tara Stevens, Hank Williams and Deirdre Cavanagh.

Since I came to New York in 1985, I have gotten a number of big breaks from people who believed in me. Edith Wurtzel at The New School for Social Research encouraged me to speak there. Three hundred and fifty people attended, and I later became director of their career center. Abe Fiss at Barnes & Noble agreed to carry my first self-published book in 1986, then my second, and kept reordering them for five years. Many, many others have befriended me, and have helped me to bring you what we have today.

Finally, my deepest appreciation and fondest gratitude go to my trusted editor, Cordelia Jason, for her clarity, creativity, and caring.

K.W.
New York City, 1996

Table of Contents

NOTE: CHAPTERS IN BOLDFACE ARE THE MOST IMPORTANT.

Preface

PART ONE—The Changing Job Market:
How It Works Today
(IF YOU ARE IN A HURRY TO DO THE EXERCISES, GO TO PART TWO.)

- You and the New Job Market 5
- How to Change Careers 9
- Job Hunting versus Career Planning 11
- Targeting the Jobs of the Future 17
- Case Studies: Targeting the Future 25
- Learning to Track Trends: The Electric Power Industry 29
- Career Makeovers: Five Who Did It 32
      (in Sports, Animals, Small Business, Cosmetics, Teaching)
- What Longevity Means to Your Career 45

PART TWO—Deciding What You Want:
Start by Understanding Yourself
(IF YOU ARE ALREADY IN A FIELD YOU LOVE, GO TO PART FOUR.)

- How to Find Your Place in the World 51
- How to Decide What You Want 57
- Deciding What You Want: Selecting Your Job Targets 59
- Exercises to Analyze Your Past and Present:
    - **The Seven Stories Exercise** **63**
    - Your Current Work-Related Values 72
    - Other Exercises: Interests, Satisfiers, and Bosses 73
    - Your Special Interests 74
    - Satisfiers and Dissatisfiers in Past Jobs 75
    - Your Relationship with Bosses 76
    - Getting Feedback From Others 77
- Looking Into Your Future: 81
    - **Your Forty-Year Plan** **83**
    - The Ideal Scene 86
    - Howard: Developing a Plan 91
    - Self-Assessment Summary 94
- Take a Breather 95

PART THREE—How to Select Your Job Targets:
Brainstorming Possible Jobs

- Brainstorming Possible Jobs 99
    - Chiron: Finding a Future 103
    - Life Takes Time 110
- How to Decide What You Want to Offer 111
- Jobs/Industries Worth Exploring:
    Preliminary Target Investigation 114
- Targeting: The Start of an Organized Search 116

- How to Target the Job You Want 118
- **Target Selection** **123**
  - **Measuring Your Targets** **124**
- A Job Well Done 125
- Elizabeth Ghaffari: A Résumé Case Study 126
- Research (DO NOT SKIP THIS STEP.)
  - **Researching Your Job Targets.** **133**
  - List of Companies to Contact 137
  - Research Resources for an Effective Job Search 139

PART FOUR—Advanced Career Planning: How to Manage Your Future

- Having a Balanced Life 151
- Deborah: Developing a Detailed Plan 153
- What You Can Do in Your Present Situation 160
- The Eight-Word Message 161
- Two Simultaneous Careers: An Interim Step 166
- How Companies Are Helping Employees to
  Manage Their Own Careers 169
- A Reminder of Some Basic Career Principles 172
- How to Keep Your Life Course in Mind 173
- Congratulations! 177

PART FIVE—Career and Job-Search Bibliography

Introduction 180
Section One: Materials in Print 181
1. Guide to Guides, Directories, and
      Business Information Sources 181
2. General: Industry Trends, Forecasts, and Outlooks 182
3. General: Company Information Guides and Directories 183
4. Specific Industry Trends and Company Information 185
      A. Advertising and Public Relations 185
      B. Environment 185
      C. Finance 186
      D. Health Care 188
      E. High Technology 188
      F. Human Resources 189
      G. Importing / Exporting / Trading 189
      H. Information Industry 190
      I. International Markets 191
      J. Law and Government 195
      K. Media 195
      L. Not-for-Profit / Fund-Raising 196
      M. Public Relations 197
      N. Publishing 198
      O. Sales and Marketing 198
      P. Services 199

Q. Small / Private Business 199
R. Special Events / Trade Shows 200
S. Transportation.. 200
T. Travel and Hospitality 200
U. Real Estate 200
V. Education 201
5. Information on Executives and Management 201
Section Two: CD-ROM Databases 202
General Reference Information /
        General Financial Information 202
Newspaper Articles and Abstracts 203
Magazines, Trade Journals, and Abstracts................... 204
Science, Engineering, and Technology 204
Health Care (also check Science,
        Engineering, and Technology) 205
Government and Law.. 205
Academia 205
Services 206
Miscellaneous Creative: Music, Art, Architecture,
        Graphics, and Religion 206
Section Three: On-Line Databases... 206
Big Picture / Trends 206
General News/Trade/Business Articles 207
Engineering 207
Finance Industry 208
Financial Information about Companies 208
General Company Information 208
Advertising 208
Health Care 209
High Technology 209
Insurance 209
International Markets 209
Law 209

PART SIX—Join The Five O'Clock Club
"For busy, career-minded people"
• How to Join the Club 212
• **Questions You May Have About the Weekly**
    Job-Search Strategy Group 214
• The Way We Are 217
• Lexicon Used at The Five O'Clock Club 218
• Application for Club Membership and Subscription to
    The Five O'Clock News.. 219

Index 220

Targeting
THE JOB
You Want

PART ONE

THE CHANGING JOB MARKET

HOW IT WORKS TODAY

You and the New Job Market

I'm going to fight hard.
I'm going to give them hell.
Harry S. Truman
Remark on the presidential campaign,
August 1948

Your Employer Has Got to be Sharper— and So Do You

In a growing economy, the market favors the job hunter. There are more jobs than there are job applicants. Sloppy job-hunting techniques work "well enough." Companies can hire more people than they need and hope someone will do the job right.

In today's economy, job hunters face greater competition for the jobs that are available. Everyone has to be sharper. Just as your employer cannot be sloppy when competing in world markets, you cannot be sloppy when competing in job markets. Your prospective employers have to be more serious about every position they fill. You, too, must take your job hunt more seriously.

Don't Be Scared by the Headlines

Labor is the superior of capital, and
deserves much the higher consideration.
Abraham Lincoln

Job hunters are starting to realize that a large number of people may be laid off in one part of a company, while different kinds of people are hired in other parts of the same company. In the news, you will hear about the layoffs, but you will not hear about the hiring—the company would be deluged with résumés.

Get used to the headlines. Companies must react quickly to changing world circumstances, and they no longer have time to figure out where the laid-off people could fit into other parts of the same company. Some companies now allow laid-off employees to job-hunt both inside and outside the company. It can be an efficient way for the company to change direction, and save perhaps 10 percent of the laid-off employees who can fit into the new direction.

The laid-off employee is usually able to find a position outside more quickly because, by definition, there are more positions outside. No matter how big the old company is, it is small compared to the outside world. A smart employee would devote 10 percent of his efforts to an inside search, and 90 percent outside.

A Changing Economy

Today, we know that doing a good job is not enough. Our career prospects can now change for reasons that have nothing to do with our personal job performance, but with the performance of our employers. It's a new economy—a world economy—and the changes are not going to slow down. Not only will things not return to the way they were, the amount of change will increase.

Government statistics show the impact of change on job hunters:

The average American has been in his or her job only four years.

The average American getting out of college today can expect to have five careers during his or her lifetime—that's not five jobs, but five separate careers!

We will probably have twelve to fifteen jobs in the course of those five careers.

Ten years from now, half the working population will be in jobs that have not yet been invented. Let's make that more personal: ten years from now, half the people reading this book will be in jobs that do not exist today. That's okay. We'll tell you where some of the new jobs are, but you'll have to do research as well.

Ten years from now, half the working population will be in non-traditional forms of employment. This means that half of us will not be working full-time, on payroll, for one employer—a wrenching change in our mindsets. Some of us may work two days a week on payroll for one employer, and three days a week for another. Or three days a week on payroll, with consulting or freelance work on the other days. Or we may be paid by one company that farms us out to another. The variations are endless—and changing.

The situation is unsettling—to say the least. However, we cannot fight it. In this time of dramatic change, few companies really know where they are heading, but some are learning what kind of workers they need: flexible, self-aware ones who continually improve their skills. Gone are the days when it was good enough for employees to simply do their assigned jobs well. America wants and needs a new kind of workforce.

Employees too are learning that they must take care of themselves and remain marketable so they are not dependent on one employer. They are proactively figuring out what they bring to the party, while finding out—and fitting into—the new directions their companies and industries are taking.

A few smart companies have wisely embraced a process of helping employees take charge of their own careers. Most of us, however, will have to develop career plans on our own, and this book can help you do just that.

Continual Career Development —An Enlightened Approach

All of this fits in with what we have taught at The Five O'Clock Club since 1978: It is best for both the employee and the employer if "job hunting" is seen as a continual process—and not just something that happens when a person wants to change jobs. Continual job search means continually being aware of market conditions both inside and outside of our present companies, and continually learning what we have to offer—to both markets.

With this approach, workers are safer because they are more likely to keep their present jobs longer: they learn to change and grow as the company and industry do. And if they have to go elsewhere, they will be more marketable. Companies are better off because employees who know what is going on outside their insular halls are smarter, more sophisticated and more proactive, and make the company more competitive.

Every industry is going through dramatic change—and hence needs a more aware and flexible workforce. Read what Russ Schundler and Harriet Greisser of Right Associates write in the chapter about the apparently stable electric utilities industry. Even as a consumer, you will be surprised and intrigued by what is happening in that industry.

The economy is changing too fast for you to use

People are always blaming their circumstances for what they are.
I don't believe in circumstances. The people who get on in this world are the people
who get up and look for the circumstances they want, and if they can't find them, make them.
George Bernard Shaw

---

the same old career planning techniques or the same old attitudes about job hunting.

Technology is the Most Pervasive

Probably no change will affect our careers more than technological change. It's not like a stock market crash, or tearing down the Berlin Wall. It doesn't make the headlines, because it's happening everywhere—every day. When you want money from a bank, you can go to a machine. The human—the middleman doing the drudgery—is no longer required in that job. People are required in *new* jobs—to design and make the machines, service them, sell them, and so on—jobs that did not exist a few years ago.

Computers are part of the reason companies have been able to cut the ranks of middle management. Companies no longer need layers of management to pass information up and down. The reports and studies and controls that were the domain of these managers are now that of computers.

As a result of technology, new industries are possible, such as direct marketing and the express-mail industry. Desktop publishing has affected the publishing, typesetting, and printing industries.

Professions are changing. Many artists now work at a computer keyboard instead of a drawing board. Their jobs did not exist ten years ago. Accountants are no longer needed to do compounded-growth rates and other complex calculations. Their jobs are changing. Salespeople are being replaced by computers and the UPC codes you see on packages. Musicians are being replaced by electronic synthesizers, which can replicate virtually every instrument.

Whether you are talking about manufacturing or hospital technology, artists or accountants, salespeople or teachers—virtually every industry and profession has or will be affected. There are no secure jobs because the jobs themselves are changing. If you think your industry or profession is not being affected, think again.

The Good Old Days—People Were Stuck

I remember the "good old days"—the days of one employer and one career. It used to be that when you found a job, you had found a home. You expected to get in there, do what the company wanted, learn to play the game, rise through the ranks, and eventually retire. People had secure jobs with large, stable employers.

People may have had job security, but the downside is that they were often stuck. Changing jobs was frowned upon. For every satisfied person, there was someone stifled, who knew he or she had made a dreadful mistake.

Today, many of us might fear losing our jobs—even from week to week—but *no one—absolutely* no one—needs to feel stifled, deadened, or stuck in a career they no longer find satisfying. *Everyone has an opportunity to do something that is better.*

What we see now is that many of the people pushed out of companies after twenty years are actually relieved to get out of jobs they'd found deadening. Some decide to think about what they really want to do and make the second phase of their lives much more fulfilling than the first.

In this book you will learn how to take more control of your life, how to plan for your own future and not be at the mercy of others. Many people who are laid off say, "This will never happen to me again. I will never again be caught off guard and unprepared."

A New Definition of Job Hunting

Job hunting in our changing economy is a *continuous* process and requires a new definition. Job hunting now means continually becoming aware of market conditions both inside and outside of our present companies, and learning what we have to offer—to both markets. This new definition means we must develop new attitudes about our work lives, and new skills for doing well in a changing economy.

Today's economy requires job hunters to be more proactive, more sophisticated, and more willing to go through brick walls to get what they want. Employers no longer plan your career for you. You must look after yourself, and know what you want and how to get it.

---

*If you haven't the strength
to impose your own terms upon life,
then you must accept the terms it offers you.*
T. S. Eliot, *The Confidential Clerk*

Understanding How the Job-Hunting Market Works

Knowing why things work the way they do will give you flexibility and control over your job hunt. Knowing how the hiring system works will help you understand why things go right and why they go wrong—why certain things work and others don't. Then you can modify the system to fit your own needs, temperament, and the workings of the job market you are interested in.

It is overly simplistic to say that only one job hunting system works. The job selection process is more complicated than that. Employers can do what they want. You need to understand the process from their point of view. Then you can plan your own job hunt, in your own industry. You will learn how to compete in this market.

Always remember, the best jobs don't necessarily go to the most qualified people, but to the people who are the best job hunters. You'll increase your chances of finding the job you want by using a methodical job-hunting approach.

Even if you have worked for the same employer for many years, learn how to job-hunt in a changing economy. At first it will seem strange. It's a new skill, but one you can use for the rest of your life. For a while you may feel as though things will never be the same. And they won't. No job is secure. At the same time, we now know that no one has to be locked into one job, one boss, one employer. Skilled job hunters have a real ability to plan their careers.

The Only Port in This Storm: You

"They" cannot offer you job security. They cannot offer you loyalty in exchange for your own loyalty. The rules have changed very quickly, and they expect you to adapt very quickly.

If you don't plan your own path through all of this, you will continue to be thrown around by the turbulence. The better you understand yourself—your motivations, skills, and interests—the more solid your foundation will be.

In our world of revolving bosses—whether you are on payroll or not—you will come across as a shallow, rough person who does not understand your value. But if you have done the exercises in this book—especially the Seven Stories—you will understand your own value, and your self-esteem is more likely to remain intact. You will keep yourself on course and continue to follow your plan.

The better you are at plotting out your own future, the more you will get out of each of your jobs or assignments. Each one will fit in with your long-term plan, and you will not get so ruffled by corporate politics and pettiness. You will be following your own vision.

They say we will all adapt to this new world, and I am sure we will. I must admit that Five O'Clock Clubbers are a heartier and more resilient bunch than I am sometimes. Every week, I see people land great new jobs and assignments in this exciting new world. They have created their own career paths, have let go of the old fields that they loved and had worked in for so long, and are having fun—sometimes even more fun—in the new fields. Like these other Five O'Clock Clubbers, you can do it too. You will have help from the head of The Five O'Clock Club Affiliate in your area, as well as from the Five O'Clock Club counselor who heads your small group. You can read more about The Five O'Clock Club at the end of this book.

Changes Mean New Opportunities

The world is changing. What's hot today is not tomorrow. You can use these changes to your advantage. You can choose to head your career in the direction that's right for you.

You can impose your own terms upon life. You don't have to accept the terms it offers you. Read on, and see what others have done.

*Alice said nothing: she had sat down with her
face in her hands, wondering if anything would ever
happen in a natural way again.*
Lewis Carroll, *Alice in Wonderland*

How to
Change Careers

If an idea, I realized, were really a valuable one,
there must be some way of realizing it.
Elizabeth Blackwell
(the first woman to earn a medical degree)

When a large American steel company began closing
plants in the early 1980's, it offered to train the displaced
steelworkers for new jobs. But the training never "took;"
the workers drifted into unemployment and odd jobs
instead. Psychologists came in to find out why,
and found the steelworkers suffering from acute identity
crises. "How could I do anything else?"
asked the workers. "I am a lathe operator."
Peter Senge, *The Fifth Discipline*

Ted had spent ten years in marketing and finance with a large cosmetics company. His dream was to work in the casino industry. He selected two job targets: one aimed at the cosmetics industry, and one aimed at his dream.

All things being equal, finding a job similar to your old one is quicker. A career change will probably take more time. What's more, the job-hunting techniques are different for both.

Let's take Ted's case. The casino industry was small, focused in Atlantic City and Las Vegas. Everyone knew everyone else. The industry had its special jargon and personality. What chance did Ted have of breaking in?

Ted had another obstacle. His marketing and finance background made him difficult to categorize. His hard-won business skills became a problem.

It's Not Easy to Categorize Job Hunters

The easier it is to categorize you, the easier it is for others to see where you fit in their organizations, and for you to find a job. Search firms, for example, generally will not handle career changers. They can more easily market those who want to stay in the same function in the same industry. Search firms that handled the casino industry would not handle Ted.

You Must Offer Proof of
Your Interest and Competence

Civility is not a sign of weakness,
and sincerity is always subject to proof.
John F. Kennedy
Inaugural Address, January 20, 1961

Many job changers essentially say to a prospective employer, "Give me a chance. You won't be sorry." They expect the employer to hire them on faith, and that's unrealistic. The employer has a lot to lose. First, you may lose interest in the new area after you are hired. Second, you may know so little about the new area that it turns out not to be what you had imagined. Third, you may not bring enough knowledge and skill to the job and fail—even though your desire may be sincere.

The hiring manager should not have to take those risks. It is the job hunter's obligation to prove that he or she is truly interested and capable.

How You As a Career Changer Can Prove Your Interest and Capability
- Read the industry's trade journals.
- Get to know the people in that industry or field.
- Join its organizations; attend the meetings.
- Be persistent.
- Show how your skills can be transferred.
- Write proposals.
- Be persistent.
- Take relevant courses, part-time jobs, or do volunteer work related to the new industry or skill area.
- Be persistent.

Ted, as a career changer, had to offer proof to make up for his lack of experience. One proof was that he had read the industry's trade newspapers for more than ten years. When he met people in his search, he could truthfully tell them that he had followed their careers. He could also say he had hope for himself because he knew that so many of them had come from outside the industry.

Another proof of his interest was that he had sought out so many casino management people in Atlantic City and Las Vegas. After a while, he ran into people he had met on previous occasions. Employers want people who are sincerely interested in their industry, their company, and the function the new hire will fill. Sincerity and persistence count, but they are usually not enough.

Another proof Ted offered was that he figured out how to apply his experience to the casino industry and its problems. Writing proposals to show how you would handle the job is one way to prove you are knowledgeable and interested in an area new to you. Some people prove their interest by taking courses, finding part-time jobs, or doing volunteer work to learn the new area and build marketable skills.

Ted initially decided to "wing it," and took trips to Atlantic City and Las Vegas hoping someone would hire him on the spot. That didn't work and took two months and some money. Then he began a serious job hunt—following the system which will be explained in the pages that follow. He felt he was doing fine, but the hunt was taking many months and he was not sure it would result in an offer.

After searching in the casino industry for six months, Ted began a campaign in his old field—the cosmetics industry. Predictably, he landed a job there quickly. Ted took this as a sign that he didn't have a chance in the new field. He lost sight of the fact that a career change is more difficult and takes longer.

Ted accepted the cosmetics position, but his friends encouraged him to continue his pursuit of a career in the casino industry—a small industry with relatively few openings compared with the larger cosmetics industry.

Shortly after he accepted the new position, someone from Las Vegas called him for an interview, and he got the job of his dreams. His efforts paid off because he had done a thorough campaign in the casino industry. It just took time.

Ted was not unusual in giving up on a career change. It can take a long time, and sometimes the pressure to get a paycheck will force people to take inappropriate jobs. That's life. Sometimes we have to do things we don't want to. There's nothing wrong with that.

What *is* wrong is forgetting that you had a dream. What *is* wrong is expecting people to hire you on faith and hope, when what they deserve is proof that you're sincere and that hiring you has a good chance of working. *What is wrong is underestimating the effort it takes to make a career change.*

In the future, most people will have to change careers. Your future may hold an involuntary career change, as new technologies make old skills obsolete. Those same new technologies open up new career fields for those who are prepared—and ready to change. Know what you're up against. Don't take shortcuts. And don't give up too early. Major career changes are normal today and may prove desirable or essential tomorrow.

Job Hunting versus Career Planning

Most people say their main fault is a lack of discipline.
On deeper thought, I believe that is not the case.
The basic problem is that their priorities have not
become deeply planted in their hearts and minds.
> Stephen R. Covey,
> *The Seven Habits of*
> *Highly Effective People*

Afoot and light-hearted
I take to the open road,
Healthy, free, the world before me,
The long brown path before me,
leading wherever I choose.
> Walt Whitman,
> *Complete Poetry and Collected Prose*

You are probably reading this because you want a job. But you will most likely have to find another job after that one, and maybe after that. After all, the average American has been in his or her job only four years. To make smoother transitions, learn to plan ahead.

If you have a plan and keep it in mind, you can continually "position" yourself for your long-range goal by taking jobs and assignments that lead you there. Then your next job will be more than just a job. It will be a stepping stone on the way to something bigger and better.

When faced with a choice, **Select the job that fits best with your Forty-Year Plan--the job that positions you best for the long term.**

It takes less than an hour to make up a rudimentary Forty-Year Plan. But it is perhaps the single most important criterion for selecting jobs. Do the plan quickly. Later, you can refine it and test it against reality. Do the Forty-Year Plan using the worksheet in this book. This is exactly what helped the people in the following case studies. **All of the people described are real people and what happened to them is true.**

CASE STUDY: BILL
Bypassing the "Ideal" Offer

For most of his working life, Bill had been a controller in a bank. He was proud of the progress he had made, given his modest education. Now he was almost fifty years old. It was the logical time to become a chief financial officer (CFO), the next step up, ideally in a company near home, since his family life was very important to him. At just this point, he lost his job.

Following The Five O'Clock Club method, Bill got three job offers:

1) as CFO for a bank only ten minutes from home —the job of his dreams.

2) as controller for a quickly growing bank in a neighboring area—still a long commute.

3) as controller for the health-care division of an insurance company—but it was 200 miles from home.

Bill wisely selected the job that would put him in the strongest position for the long term, and would look best in his next job search. He selected job #3 because it would allow him to include two new industries on his résumé. Health care was growing, and insurance would broaden his financial-services experience.

Bill wanted to hedge his bets, and not uproot his family. So he got an apartment close to the new company, and went home on weekends. After a year and a half, the company was taken over, an unpredictable event. The new management brought in their own people. He was out.

But this time, Bill was not worried. Since he now had valuable new experience on his résumé, he was sought after. He was offered and took a key post in a consulting firm that served the health-care and financial industries.

CASE STUDY: CHARLOTTE
Positioning over Money

Charlotte, a marketing manager, received three offers:

1) with a credit-card company in a staff marketing position dealing with international issues.

2) with a major music company as head of marketing for the classical-music division.

> *A man may not achieve everything he has dreamed,*
> *but he will never achieve anything great without having dreamed it first.*
> William James

3) with a non-profit research organization as head of marketing.

The first two positions paid about the same, let's say $90,000. The position with the not-for-profit offered $75,000, and there was no room for moving the salary higher.

How did Charlotte decide which position to take? The music company was not a good fit for her: she was not compatible with the people, and she would probably have failed in that job. The credit-card job would have been easy but boring, and she would not have learned anything new.

Charlotte selected the not-for-profit position, the lowest-paid job. In her Forty-Year Plan, she saw herself as the head of a not-for-profit someday. Since she was only thirty-five, she did not now need a position with a not-for-profit. But she felt good when she interviewed there. So she took the job that best fit with her long-term plan.

Charlotte loved the people, and her position put her in contact with some of the most powerful business people in America. Top management listened to her ideas, and she had an impact on the organization.

After one and a half years, there was a reorganization. Charlotte was made manager of a larger department. She received a pay increase to match her new responsibilities, which brought her salary higher than the salaries of the other two job offers. But, best of all, Charlotte's job was a good fit for her, and made sense in light of her Forty-Year Plan.

CASE STUDY: HARRY
Stuck in a Lower-Level Job

Harry was a window-washer for the casinos, earning an excellent hourly salary. The pay was high because the building was slanted, making the job more dangerous.

Harry did a great job, was responsible and well-liked. He was offered a supervisory position, which could lead to other casino jobs. But the base pay was less than his current pay including overtime, and allowed for no overtime pay. Harry decided he could not afford to make the move and stayed as a window-washer paid by the hour. Today, several years later, he still cleans windows.

There's nothing wrong with washing windows, or any other occupation. But if you make this kind of choice based on short-term gain, be aware that you may be closing off certain options for your future.

Sometimes we have to make short-term sacrifices to get ahead—if indeed we *want* to get ahead.

Selecting the Right Offer

Doing the exercises will give you some perspective when choosing among job offers. I hope that you will attempt to get six to ten job possibilities in the works (knowing that five will fall away through no fault of your own). Then most likely you will wind up with three offers at approximately the same time.

If you have three offers, the one to choose is the one that positions you best for the long run.

People Who Have Goals Do Better

A study of Harvard students, ten years after graduation, shows that **those who had specific goals made salaries three times greater than the salary of the average** Harvard graduate. **Those with *written* goals made ten times the average!**

Money is not the only measure of success. When you have a clear, long-term goal, it can affect everything: your hobbies and interests, what you read, the people to whom you are attracted. Those who have a plan do better at reaching their goals, no matter what those goals are. A plan gives you hope and direction. It lets you see that you have plenty of time—no matter how young or how old you are.

CASE STUDY:
BILL CLINTON
A Clear Plan

Bill Clinton is a good example of the power of having a vision. A small-town boy, Bill decided in his teens that he wanted to become President. He developed his plan, and worked his entire life to make that dream come true.

Optimism Emerges as Best Predictor to Success in Life

"**Hope has proven a powerful predictor of outcome in every study we've done so far,**" said Dr. Charles R. Snyder, a psychologist at the University of Kansas. . . . "**Having hope means believing you have both the will and the way to accomplish your goals, whatever they may be. . . . It's not enough to just have the wish for something. You need the means, too. On the other hand, all the skills to solve a problem won't help if you don't have the willpower to do it.**"

Dr. Snyder found that people with high levels of hope share several attributes:

• **Unlike people who are low in hope, they turn to friends for advice on how to achieve their goals.**

• **They tell themselves they can succeed at what they need to do.**

• **Even in a tight spot, they tell themselves things will get better as time goes on.**

• **They are flexible enough to find different ways to get to their goals.**

• **If hope for one goal fades, they aim for another. Those low on hope tend to become fixated on one goal, and persist even when they find themselves blocked. They just stay at it and get frustrated.**

• **They show an ability to break a formidable task into specific, achievable chunks. People low in hope see only the large goal, and not the small steps to it along the way.**

People who get a high score on the hope scale have had as many hard times as those with low scores, but have learned to think about it in a hopeful way, seeing a setback as a challenge, not a failure.

Daniel Goleman,
The New York Times,
December 24, 1991

CASE STUDY: BRUCE
Plenty of Time

Bruce—young, gifted, and black—was doing little to advance his career. Like many aspiring actors, he worked at odd jobs to survive and auditioned for parts when he could.

But, in fact, Bruce spent little time auditioning or improving his craft because he was too busy trying to make ends meet. What's more, he had recently been devastated by a girlfriend.

Using The Five O'Clock Club assessment, Bruce realized he was going nowhere. His first reaction was to attempt to do everything at once: quit his part-time jobs, become a film and stage director, and patch things up with his girlfriend. With the help of the Forty-Year Plan, Bruce discovered that his current girlfriend was not right for him in the long run, and that he had plenty of time left in his life to act, direct, and raise a family.

Because of his plan, Bruce knew what to do next to get ahead. He was prompted to look for a good agent (just like a job hunt), and take other steps for his career. Six months later, Bruce landed a role in *Hamlet* on Broadway. He is on tour with another play now.

CASE STUDY: SOPHIE
Making Life Changes First

Sophie, age twenty-two, had a low-level office job, wanted a better one, and did the assessment.

She did her Forty-Year Plan, but was depressed by it. Like many who feel stuck, Sophie's "plan" seemed to be the same uninspiring situation from year to year. It seemed her life would never change.

With encouragement and help, she did her plan again, and let her dreams come out, no matter how implausible they seemed. She saw herself eventually in a different kind of life. Although she initially did the plan because she wanted to change jobs, she saw she needed to change other things first.

She moved away from a bad situation at home, got her own apartment, broke up with the destructive boyfriend she had been seeing for eight years, and enrolled in night school. It took her two years to take these first steps.

She is now working toward her long-term goal of becoming a teacher and educational film maker. She says that she is off the treadmill and effortlessly making progress.

CASE STUDY: DAVE
A New Life at Sixty-two

After Dave had worked for his company for over twenty-five years, they eliminated his job. He still had a lot of energy and a lot to offer, and he wanted to work. But he was depressed by his prospects until he did his Forty-Year Plan.

His dream plan for his new life included: working two days a week developing new business for a small company, volunteering on the Board of a not-for-profit, heading a state commission, and consulting for an international not-for-profit. Instead of slowing down, Dave became busier and happier than he had been on his old job. He was able to quickly implement most of his plan.

CASE STUDY: BOB
Sticking With His Vision

Bob was feeling restless about his career. This prompted him to do a Forty-Year Plan. He wanted to end up at age eighty having done something significant for the community, and having earned a good living doing it. At age forty-three, he was offered a substantial promotion at his curent job—but it was at odds with his community-service goal. After much soul-searching, Bob turned down the promotion, and took steps to implement his plan. He ended up starting his own not-for-profit that eventually will impact communities across America.

CASE STUDY: KAREN
Our Values Change Over Time

Karen had been a high-powered executive, earning over $300,000 a year. When she took time off to have her first baby, she was surprised by how much she loved taking care of her daughter. After Karen had stayed at home for two years, her husband lost his job. She had to look for work.

At first, her plan was to "have it all." She assumed she needed another $300,000-a-year job to keep up their lifestyle, yet she also wanted time with her child. The assessment helped her see that she had never really enjoyed the grueling hours she had to work before, and she now imagined a better balance between work and family.

Karen received three offers: one for $300,000; one for $200,000, which required a lot of travel; and one for $125,000, which she knew fit into her Forty-Year Plan. Although she was at first embarrassed by having taken a lower-level position, she grew to love it and her new lifestyle.

Over time, our values change. As her daughter grow older, Karen may decide again that a higher-powered job is fine for her.

Men experience value changes too--easing up a little when they want to spend time with the kids, for example, and focusing more on their careers at other times.

CASE STUDY: HANK
Thinking Too Small

Hank, a senior executive who lost his job, chose a new field, just because it was lucrative. But the assessment showed it would not position him well for the job *after* that one.

Instead, Hank became a senior executive with a major company in his old field. The quick route to financial success no longer appealed to him. He took a more sure road that would position him well for the future. In fact, the job he took paid well enough to make his family very comfortable.

Thinking Big; Thinking Small

A Forty-Year Plan gives you perspective. Without one, you may think too small or too big. Writing it down makes you more reasonable, more thoughtful, and more serious. **Having a plan also makes you less concerned about the progress of others because you know where *you* are going.**

CASE STUDY: JIM
Objective vs. Subjective

Jim had to choose between two job offers, one

paying $350,000 and another at $500,000. The thought process is the same regardless of salary. To prove it, let's pretend the positions were paying $35,000 and $50,000. Which should he take?

Jim's wife wanted him to take the $50,000 job. It paid more and had a better title.

Jim liked the people at the $35,000 job, and they appreciated him and listened to his suggestions. But they could pay no more than $35,000. He delayed the start date while we talked, and listed the pros and cons of each position. He *still* could not decide. After all, $15,000 is a big difference.

Finally, I said to Jim: "I'm going to make it easy for you. The $35,000 a year job no longer exists. Let's not talk about it. You will take the $50,000 a year job, have a very nice commute, make your wife happy, have a title you can be proud of, and make $50,000."

Jim sat in silence. Then he said: "The thought of going there depresses me. I think the job is not do-able. They may be offering me an impossible job."

Sometimes objective thinking alone is not enough. The exercise helped Jim find out what his gut was telling him. During the interview process, things had turned him off about the $50,000 company—but not enough to turn down the extra $15,000. It wasn't logical.

When Jim finally made up his mind to take the "$35,000" job, he was so happy, he bought presents for everyone. Even his wife was pleased. He had made the right choice.

Consider Objective and Subjective Information

If you tend to pay too much attention to subjective information, balance it by asking: "What is the logical thing for me to do regardless of how I feel?"

If you tend to be too objective, ask: "I know the logical thing to do, but how do I really feel about it?"

CASE STUDY: DEAN
Expect to Be Paid Fairly

Dean had been making $60,000. He lost his job and uncovered two choices: one at $75,000 and one at $100,000. He asked to meet with me.

Dean was not worth $100,000 at this stage in his career, and I told him so. In addition, that company was not a good fit for him.

The $75,000 job seemed just right for Dean. He had an engineering degree, and the work dealt with high-tech products.

Yet he took the $100,000 position. Within four months, he was fired.

Dean met with me again to discuss two more possibilities: another position for $100,000 and one at a much lower salary. Since he had most recently been making $100,000, interviewers thought perhaps he was worth it. Again, he opted for the $100,000 position--he liked making that kind of money. Again he could not live up to that salary, and again he was fired.

Life Skills, Not Just Job-Hunting Skills

A plan helps people see ahead, and realize that they can not only advance in their careers, but they can change their life circumstances-- such as who their friends are and where they live.

Your career is not separate from your life. If you dream of living in a better place, you have to earn more money. If you would like to be with better types of people, you need to **become a better type of person yourself.**

The Forty-Year Plan cannot be done in a vacuum. Research is the key to *achieving* your plan. Without research, it is difficult to imagine what might be out there, or to imagine dream situations. Be sure to read the two chapters on research in this book.

Whatever your level, to get ahead you need:

- **exposure** to other possibilities and other dreams;
- **hard facts** about those possibilities and dreams (through networking and research);
- the **skills** required in today's job market;
- **job-search training** to help you get the work for which you are qualified.

In 1991, nearly 1 out of 3 American workers had been with their employer for less than a year, and almost 2 out of 3 for less than 5 years.
The United States contingent workforce—consisting of roughly 45,000,000 temporaries, self-employed, part-timers, or consultants—has grown 57% since 1980.
Going, if not yet gone, are the 9-5 workdays, lifetime jobs, predictable hierarchical relationships, corporate culture security blankets, and, for a large and growing sector of the workforce, the workplace itself (replaced by a cybernetics "workspace").
Constant training, retraining, job-hopping, and even career-hopping, will become the norm.

Mary O'Hara-Devereaux and Robert Johansen,
Global Work: Bridging Distance, Culture and Time

Since 1983, the U.S. work world has added 25,000,000 computers. The number of cellular telephone subscribers has jumped from zero in 1983 to 16,000,000 by the end of 1993.
Close to 19,000,000 people now carry pagers, and almost 12,000,000,000 messages were left in voice mailboxes in 1993 alone.
Since 1987, homes and offices have added 10,000,000 fax machines, while E-mail addresses have increased by over 26,000,000.
Communications technology is radically changing the speed, direction, and amount of information flow, even as it alters work roles all across organizations. As a case in point, the number of secretaries is down 521,000 just since 1987.

Rich Tetzeli, "Surviving Information Overload," *Fortune*, July 11, 1994

The Department of Labor estimates that by the year 2000 at least 44% of all workers will be in data services—for example, gathering, processing, retrieving, or analyzing information.
As recently as the 1960's, almost one-half of all workers in the industrialized countries were involved in making (or helping to make) things.
By the year 2000, however, no developed country will have more than one-sixth or one-eighth of its workforce involved in the traditional roles of making and moving goods.
Already an estimated two-thirds of U.S. employees work in the services sector, and "knowledge" is becoming our most important "product."
This calls for different organizations, as well as different kinds of workers.

Peter F. Drucker, *Post-Capitalist Society*

The factory of the future will have only two employees, a man and a dog. The man will be there to feed the dog. The dog will be there to keep the man from touching the equipment.

Warren Bennis

Less than half the workforce in the industrial world will be holding conventional jobs in organizations by the beginning of the 21st century.
Those full-timers or insiders will be the new minority. Every year more and more people will be self-employed. Many will work temporary or part-time—sometimes because that's the way they want it, sometimes because that's all that is available.

John Handy, *The Age of Unreason*

The
Five
O'Clock
Club®

Targeting the Jobs
of the Future

Less than half of the workforce in the industrial world will be in "proper" full-time jobs in organizations by the beginning of the twenty-first century.
Charles Handy

The time is not far off when you will be answering your television set and watching your telephone.
Raymond Smith, chairman and chief executive of the Bell Atlantic Corporation, *The New York Times*, February 21, 1993

---

*There is guidance for each of us,
and by lowly listening,
we shall hear the right word.*
Ralph Waldo Emerson

The psychic task which a person can and must set for himself is not to feel secure, but to be able to tolerate insecurity, without panic and undue fear.
Erich Fromm, *The Sane Society*

All our lives we are engaged in the process of accommodating ourselves to our surroundings; living is nothing else than this process of accommodation.
When we fail a little, we are stupid. When we flagrantly fail, we are mad. A life will be successful or not, according as the power of accommodation is equal to or unequal to the strain of fusing and adjusting internal and external chances.
Samuel Butler, *The Way of All Flesh*

Note: In this article, fields and industries buried in the text are underlined to help you locate them later.

The Times are Changing

Ten years from now, half the working population will be in jobs that do not exist today. Positions and industries will disappear almost completely—edged out by technological advances or new industries. When was the last time you saw a typewriter repairman? When was the last time you saw a typewriter? There are few TV or radio repair jobs either. They have been replaced by new jobs.

Some industries retrench—or cut back—slowly and trick us into thinking they are solid and dependable. At the turn of the last century, there were literally thousands of piano manufacturers. A few still remain, but that industry was affected by new industries: movies, TV, radio, and other forms of home entertainment.

At the time, most people probably thought: "But we'll *always* need pianos." People today think the same way about the industries they are in.

Experts say the traditional advertising industry has permanently retrenched. Those who want to stay in that industry often must go to small U.S. cities or abroad. Or they work for corporations rather than advertising agencies.

Peter Drucker said: "Network television advertising is in a severe crisis. . . . None of the mass advertisers—Procter & Gamble, Coca-Cola—none of them knows what to do about it."

A study by Lee Hecht Harrison, a major outplacement firm (as reported by Patricia Kitchen in *The American Banker*, March 1993), showed that 47 percent of laid-off bankers found their next job outside the industry. They moved, for example, to the technology, health-care and not-for-profit industries. Most bankers believe banking is permanently retrenching—and changing at the same time because of technology and the international marketplace.

Being a bank teller, for example, used to be a good entry-level position. But many tellers have been replaced by ATMs. There is a new industry that has created jobs to manufacture, sell and

If you succeed in judging yourself rightly,
then you are indeed a man of true wisdom.
Antoine de Saint-Exupéry, *The Little Prince*

service these machines.

Some promising new industries don't last at all, so great is the impact of the ever-quickening pace of technological and global change. Data entry until very recently seemed like a relatively safe new field. However, some studies say that data-entry jobs will be virtually non-existent in the United States five years from now. Much of that work is now being farmed out to low-paying countries, such as Russia and India. Job seekers focusing on data-entry jobs in the United States will find it more difficult as time goes on.

Temporary Setbacks

Further, some industries and occupations ebb and flow with supply and demand. When there is a shortage in a well-paid field, such as nursing, engineering, or law, school enrollments increase, creating an excess. Then people stop entering these fields, creating a shortage. So sometimes it's easy to get jobs and sometimes it isn't.

The overall economy may also temporarily affect a field or industry. Real estate, for example, may suffer in a down economy and pick up in a strong one.

Ahead of the Market

When the Berlin Wall came down, there was a rush of companies wanting to capitalize on the potential market in Eastern Europe. Given all they were reading in the papers, job hunters thought it would be a good market for them to explore as well. They were ahead of the market. It took a few years before the market caught up with the concept. Now many people are employed in Eastern Europe or in servicing that market.

The same may be true for the area that you are in or are trying to get into: The market may not be there because it has not yet developed.

Another growth area is the "new media." This is such a rapidly changing area that it is hard to define. As of this writing, it can include cable stations, a number of which are devoted to home shopping; "imaging" of medical records and credit card receipts; supermarket scanners and other

devices that promote items or record what you buy; multi-media use of the computer (sound, motion and color instead of just text); virtual reality; interactive TV; telephone companies (with cable already going into every home); CD/ROM (compact disk containing "read-only memory") which puts materials such as games and encyclopedias on CD's; and the increasingly important Internet.

Two years ago, a client at The Five O'Clock Club believed that the "new media" would be in much demand in the industry she has long followed. But she believed the demand would not happen for a few years—she was then ahead of the market. So she found a job with a small company that was *developing* the new media (as opposed to using it).

She has worked for that company for two years. With this marketable experience under her belt, she plans to move on to the industry she is most interested in--it is now ready for her.

What About *Your* Industry or Profession?

Is your industry or field growing, permanently retrenching, or in a temporary decline because of supply and demand or other economic conditions? If you are lucky, your company is ahead of the market, and the industry will pick up later. However, this is unlikely unless you are on the cutting edge of high tech.

Most people in permanently retrenching industries, including the leaders, incorrectly think the decline is temporary. You have to decide for yourself. You could perhaps gain insight and objectivity by researching what those outside your industry have to say.

It has been predicted that if things continue as they are going, there will soon be a great divide in America, with technologically and internationally aware workers making fine salaries, while the unaware and unskilled earn dramatically lower wages. (Even high-level executives can be unaware and unskilled, and thus face reductions in their salaries as they become less useful.) If this does come to pass, the best I can do as a career counselor is to encourage people to try to be on the winning side of that divide. You could hedge your bets, as Debbie did.

*One doesn't discover new lands without consenting
to lose sight of the shore for a very long time.*
André Gide

CASE STUDY: DEBBIE
Hedging Her Bets for the Future

Debbie had been an account manager in advertising for fifteen exciting years. She loved learning everything she could about her shampoo or detergent account, or whatever she was assigned. Debbie was reluctant to change industries despite some negatives: She had a long commute. (Those who want to stay in a retrenching industry often must commute long distances or relocate.) And her job was not as much fun as it used to be. (Companies that survive in retrenching industries tend to experience greater pressure on their bottom line. Thus employees have to work longer hours with smaller rewards.)

She decided to stay on, but took proactive steps to better insure her future in two ways:

1.) She asked to be assigned to a high-tech account. She knew that if she learned that business, she could someday get a job in the marketing or advertising department of a high-tech company in an industry that is growing.

2.) In addition to proposing traditional advertising solutions for her clients' problems, she also began to investigate and propose that they take advantage of the new media, such as home shopping and the Internet. This would help her clients, but would also give Debbie experience in the way companies market their goods in the nineties, and give her an edge over those who know only traditional advertising.

Debbie continues to hold her own as her colleagues get squeezed out of advertising. Some are forced to commute longer distances or relocate just so they can stay in the industry. Although many have lost their jobs, or work for half what they used to, there are still enough people making good money to create the illusion that things are the same as they were.

Traditional advertising may revive and prove the doomsayers wrong, but at least Debbie has hedged her bets: she can either stay in the industry or be valuable outside.

You can be like Debbie: you can position yourself for the future by gaining new experience on the job you are now in, or by doing volunteer work or taking a course to learn the new skills you need to remain competitive.

Retrenching Markets Are All Alike

When an industry retrenches, the results are predictable. A retrenching market, by definition, has more job hunters than jobs. The more that market retrenches, the worse it gets.

Those who want to stay in the field have increasingly longer searches as more people chase fewer jobs. They will also tend to stay less time in their new jobs as companies in the retrenching industry continue to downsize or go out of business.

Profit margins get squeezed as companies compete for a slice of a shrinking pie. Those companies become less enjoyable to work for because there is less investment in training and development, research, internal communications, and the like. Of course, salaries are cut.

Most laid-off workers target only their current industry at the start of their search. They consider other targets only after they have difficulty getting another job in their present field. They would probably have found something faster if they had looked in other fields from the beginning.

<u>Those in retrenching industries who also target new industries have a shorter search time.</u>

Expanding Your Search Geographically; Targeting Small Companies

Census Bureau data show that more than 90% of all new jobs in the '80s were created in the suburbs (a Harvard University study as reported by Leon E. Wynter in The Wall Street Journal, May 3, 1993). Oops! It's good to know the facts, because you can conduct your search accordingly. If you have been ignoring the suburbs, think about them.

Job growth has been in smaller companies. Large companies do most of the downsizing. In New York City, for example, there are 193,000 companies. Only 270 of them employ 1000 people or more. James Brown, economist for the Department of Labor, specializing in the New York City labor market, advised members of the mid-Manhattan Five O'Clock Club to look to the other

192,730 companies—those that employ fewer than 1,000 employees.

Think about your geographic area, and think about the companies you are targeting. Most jobs hunters naturally think about the big companies that are in the news, but perhaps you should think about the new "hidden job market": the suburbs, and companies with fewer than 1000 employees.

The Bad News Is Good News
—If You Are *FLEXIBLE*

Virtually every industry and field has been and will continue to be affected by technological changes. Whether you are in <u>education</u>, work for the <u>Post Office</u>, or <u>sell books</u>, your field will be affected. As Alice said about Wonderland: It takes all the running you can do to stay in the same place.

The good news is that many fields are much easier to enter today than they were in times when careers were more stable. There is room for you if you target properly and stay flexible. If you continue to learn in the field you are now in, and get to know the areas you are pursuing, you will be able to make changes as the world changes.

If your current industry or profession is retrenching (and you expect to be working more than five or ten more years), it makes sense to investigate some of the growing fields.

Even if you end up back in your old retrenching industry, the time you have spent exploring a new industry is not wasted, because you will probably have to search again.

Examples of
Growth Occupations

U.S. Department of Labor projections are a fine place to start. Listed below are the fastest-growing occupations, as well as the ones with largest job declines, projected for 1995 - 2005.

Growing: registered nurse; systems analyst/computer scientist; nursing aide and home-health aide; physical therapist; operations-research analyst; psychologist; computer programmer; restaurant cook and food-preparation worker; marketing, advertising and public relations manager; accountant and auditor; lawyer; and teacher—secondary and elementary.

Declining: directory-assistance operator; farmer; bookkeeper, accounting and auditing clerk; electrical and electronic assembler; central-office operator; child- care worker—private household; statistical clerk; telephone-station installer; typist and word processor.

The National Business Employment Weekly projected these employment opportunities, based on executive recruiting activity in managerial and professional areas:

• <u>Consumer Goods:</u> strong demand for senior marketing executives, especially with direct-mail experience.

• <u>Retailing:</u> need for merchandisers remains strong.

• <u>Information systems and technology:</u> demand is strong if your skills are current, and you have some business know-how.

• <u>Publishing:</u> is looking for business-oriented executives and database marketers.

• <u>Insurance:</u> needs senior-level marketers, especially with direct-mail experience.

If I venture to displace, by even the billionth part of an inch,
the microscopical speck of dust
which lies now upon the very point of my finger,
what is the character of that act upon which I have ventured?

I have done a deed which shakes the moon in her path,
which causes the sun to be no longer the sun,
and which alters forever the destiny
of the multitudinous myriads of stars that roll and glow
in the majestic presence of their Creator.

Edgar Allen Poe? (If you know the author, please let me know. I memorized this when I was very young.)

• Banking: is looking for credit-card marketers, corporate and retail product specialists, senior relationship managers, and multi-discipline managers. International experience is a major plus.

• Pharmaceuticals: no growth expected overall, but there is opportunity in small biotech firms that are partnering with big firms.

• Health care: demand for workers in hospitals is slowing, as managed care health systems emphasize outpatient and in-home care; therefore, home care and outpatient clinics will have growth.

• Engineering: continues to have problems in defense and export-related areas but opportunities are increasing in manufacturing related to the general increase in consumer demand. Opportunities continue to be good in software engineering.

**The new fields
are new to everyone.
An outsider has a chance of
becoming an insider.**

Predictions 1995 to 2005

Harriet Greisser, director of Executive Employment Research for Right Associates, had this to say in *The Five O'Clock News* (July, 1995):

The Bureau of Labor Statistics predicts that service-producing jobs will account for 93% of all job growth during the period. Health services and business services (which includes computer and data processing services) will be among the fastest-growing areas. Education, child day-care, and residential care will also grow, driven primarily by demographics. Financial services, such as banking and insurance, will continue to lose jobs due to the consolidation of functions and increased productivity from the application of technology.

Manufacturing employment is projected to decline due to technology-based productivity increases, and the composition of manufacturing jobs will shift as production jobs decrease and managerial jobs increase. Construction is expected

to increase substantially, and growth in agricultural services will help fuel modest growth in the agricultural, forestry and fishing sector.

Projections for occupational groups show the fastest growth rates for those requiring higher levels of education or training: 1) professional specialty; 2) technicians and related support; and 3) executive, administrative, and managerial. These occupational groups are also those that have the highest earnings.

Since demographics drives employment growth overall, the aging of the baby boomers over the 1995 to 2005 period will create a glut of highly experienced workers competing for the best jobs. On a regional basis, the U.S. Bureau of the Census projects that the West (24%) and the South (16%) will continue to be the fastest-growing regions, while the Midwest will grow 7% and the Northeast will grow only 3%.

Getting More Sophisticated

If you have been working awhile, think past the obvious and think more deeply about the changes that are occurring.

Listed below are a few of the industries business experts project will grow in the next decade. Try to discover other areas that may be affected by these or how your own job may be affected by growth in these areas. Each is huge and changing, and should be better defined by your investigation through networking and library research.

Here is the list of some of the industries expected to grow:

• Computer software, not hardware.
• Anything high-tech, or the high-tech aspect of whatever field or industry you are in.
• The international aspect of the field/industry you are in.
• The environmental area; waste management.
• Telecommunications, the new media and global communications (movie studios, TV networks, cable companies, computer companies, consumer-electronics companies, and publishers).
• Health care, or anything having to do with it.

Ideas are like rabbits. You get a couple and learn how to handle
them, and pretty soon you have a dozen.
John Steinbeck

Even if health care's growth slows down, it will change dramatically, which means there will be room for new people. Health care is still considered a sure bet because of the aging population and the advances being made in medical technology.

•   Education in the broadest sense (as opposed to the traditional classroom, including computer-assisted instruction. (Researchers have found that illiterates learn to read better with computer-assisted instruction than they do in a classroom.)

Because all of us will have to keep up-to-date in more areas in order to do our jobs well, technology will play an important part in our continuing education. Further, with America lagging so far behind other countries educationally, both the for-profit and not-for-profit sectors are working hard to revamp our educational system.

•   The alternative means of distributing goods. Instead of retail stores, think not only about direct mail, which may already be a bit out-of-date, but about purchasing by TV—or the World Wide Web.

•   Anything serving the aging population, both products and services.

In studying the preceding list, think of how you can combine different industries to come up with areas to pursue. For example: combine the aging population with education, or the aging population with telecommunications, or health care with education, and so on. The more you research, the more sophisticated your thoughts will get.

If you combine education with the new media, you will be thinking like many experts. They seem to agree that students in schools will soon learn from interactive multi-media presentations on computers—presentations that will be as exciting as computer games and MTV combined, and almost as up-to-date as the morning news (most textbooks are years out-of-date). Teachers will do what computers cannot do: facilitate the groups, encourage, reinforce learning.

The National Gallery of Art has put its entire collection of 2,600 works of American painting and sculpture on laser video disk for use in schools. 700 disks were distributed free to schools in poor neighborhoods. "Thanks to digitized computer

imaging technology, the quality of the images is extremely sharp, perhaps 10 times clearer than pictures produced by the earlier video disks . . . approaching magazine quality. . . . In most cases, there are five or six detailed close-ups for children to study. Some of the detail pieces are so clear that brush strokes can be examined and the warps and weaves of the canvases are clearly visible." (Irvin Molotsky, The New York Times, June 6, 1993)

A computer-based approach can be used to train and update the knowledge of America's workers: employees can learn when they have the time and at their own pace, rather than having large numbers of workers leave their jobs to learn in a classroom situation.

When you read predications that there will be a huge growth in home health care workers, personal and home care aides, and medical assistants, medical secretaries, radiology technologists and technicians, and psychologists, you may think: "I don't want to be any of those." Think more creatively. Companies will have to spring up to supply and train those workers. (Some of the training could even be done on multi-media.) People will be needed to manage the companies, regulate the care given, coach patients on how to select and manage such workers, and so on.

When you read about the tremendous growth in the temporary help business, you may become a temporary worker yourself, or you could go to work running one of the temporary help companies.

Your Own Field or Industry

Think about the field you are in now, and how it is being affected by technology. People say: "Not my field. I'm a salesperson. They'll always need salespeople." Wrong. The sales-person's job has been affected by technology —the UPC bar codes on the sides of packages now allow computers to take inventory—something the salesperson used to do. Stores no longer need a salesperson to ask for the reorder.

Virtually every job and industry—whether it is publishing, entertainment, manufacturing, finan-

*When I examined myself and my methods of thought,
I came to the conclusion that the gift of fantasy has meant more to me
than my talent for absorbing positive knowledge.*
Albert Einstein

cial services, or farming— is being impacted by technology, and by the global marketplace. If you are not aware , you will be blind-sided.

For example, a photographer noticed that digital imaging was affecting her industry, so she bought a computer. Now she can do digital imaging herself rather than being left out of the market. Musicians are learning to use electronic synthesizers; artists are drawing on computers.

Peter Drucker said: "I see the disappearance of the computer market as the computer becomes an accessory. That's already happening. Look at all the medical instrumentation that has become computerized. We are at the point where telecommunications, television, copying and computers are becoming incorporated into one instrument. You don't sell an automobile engine separately. This will soon be the same for computers." (*Forbes ASAP*, March, 1993)

Your Age: How Much Longer Do You Want to Work?

If you want to work only two more years, it may not be worth investing the time to learn a new area. (This is assuming you can get a job in your old area if it is retrenching.)

If you want to work another ten years, learn new things—if only to keep up with what is happening in your present field.

Some Areas Are Safer Bets

The rate of change is so fast that by the time this is published, some of the technologies discussed here will be replaced with new developments. However, some areas are safer bets than others. "Hard skills" are more marketable than "soft skills." For example, a person who wants to get a job as a general writer will have more difficulty than someone who can bring more to the party—such as doing layout on the Macintosh.

We publish *The Five O'Clock News*™ to keep you up-to-date on market information and changing techniques for managing your career. Look at the order form in the back of this book, and consider becoming a member. We'll keep you informed.

Figure It Out

It's your job to figure out how your industry or field is being impacted by technology and global competition. Think where you fit into the future. Do research.

When I started out as a computer programmer in 1966, I believed I was on the ground floor of this amazing industry. Computers are still on the ground floor, and there's room for those who are interested. In fact, we are now on the ground floor of many industries, and at an exciting time for those who choose to take advantage of the revolutionary changes that are taking place.

Remember the new definition of job-hunting (which The Five O'Clock Club developed in 1986):

**Job-hunting in a changing economy
means continuously becoming aware of
market conditions inside as well as outside
your present company, and learning more
about what you have to offer—both inside
and outside your company.**

A New Way of Thinking

Any assignment (or job) you get, is a temporary one. You're doing work, but you don't have a permanent job. It's like an actor who lands a part. He or she does not really know how long it may last. Furthermore, actors tend to worry about whether or not a role will typecast them and potentially cause them to lose future roles. Or they may intentionally decide to be typecast, hoping it will increase their chances going forward. Actors understand that they will most likely have to land another role after this one, and they constantly think about how a certain role will position them going forward. And so must you. Your next job is only a temporary assignment.

Work today is not just doing;
it is, more than ever, thinking.
Today's corporation needs thinking, flexible,
proactive workers. It wants creative problem
solvers, workers smart and skilled enough
to move with new technologies and with the
ever-changing competitive environment.
It needs workers accustomed to collaborating
with co-workers, to participating in quality
circles, to dealing with people high and low.
Communication skills and people skills have
become parts of the necessary repertoire
of the modern worker.

Hedrick Smith, *Rethinking America*

The line between
the self-employed condition
and working for an "employer"
has become unclear:
Communications technology and flextime
arrangements allow official, full-time employees
to telecommute and to do their
forty hours a week without leaving home.
At the same time, self-employed people may get
contracts that not only require them to perform
the tasks that used to be done by a jobholder,
but also give them an in-house office,
membership on a task force within the
organization, and even a discount at the
employee store.

William Bridges, *JobShift: How to Prosper in a*
Workplace Without Jobs

Strangely enough, this is the past that somebody
in the future is longing to go back to.

Ashleigh Brilliant

Executives have often been hired
with contracts that specify some compensation
if the arrangement is terminated sooner than
planned, and such clauses will
become available to other workers as well.
All of us are going to move toward
some kind of contract with the organization
that pays for our services.

William Bridges, *JobShift: How to Prosper in a*
Workplace Without Jobs

Today's workers need to forget jobs
completely and look instead for work that needs
doing—and then set themselves up as the best
way to get that work done.

William Bridges, *Ibid.*

The trouble with the future is that it usually
arrives before we're ready for it.

Arnold H. Glasow

Enjoy yourself. If you can't enjoy yourself,
enjoy somebody else.

Jack Schaefer

I was going to buy a copy of The Power of
Positive Thinking, *and then I thought:*
What the hell good would that do?

Ronnie Shakes

Progress might have been all right once,
but it has gone on too long.

Ogden Nash

Case Studies:
Targeting the Future

While your basic emotional temperament may not change much during your lifetime, you can make significant day-to-day adjustments in the way you perceive events and respond to them. When you face an emotionally trying situation, guard against exaggerating or over-generalizing, and focus instead on your specific options for taking direct action. Avoid putting yourself down by doing something that will exercise your good traits. And seek the company of others, whether it's to gather more rational views on the situation or simply to change your mood.

Jack Maguire,
Care and Feeding of the Brain

---

*The person who fears to try
is thus enslaved.*
Leonard E. Read

---

*Fighting futility is a waste of energy, Samantha.
Either do something or quit fretting.*
Celebra Tueli

---

*Cato learned Greek at eighty; Sophocles
Wrote his grand Oedipus, and Simonides
Bore off the prize of verse from his compeers,
When each had numbered more than four-score years...
Chaucer, at Woodstock with the nightingales,
At sixty wrote the Chaucer Tales;
Goethe at Weimar, toiling to the last,
Completed Faust when eighty years were past.*
Henry Wadsworth Longfellow,
Morituri Salutamus

Within the next decades education will change more than it has changed since the modern school was created by the printed book over three hundred years ago. An economy in which knowledge is becoming the true capital and the premier wealth-producing resource makes new and stringent demands on the schools for education performance and educational responsibility . . . How we learn and how we teach are changing drastically and fast—the result, in part, of new theoretical understanding of the learning process, in part of new technology.
Peter Drucker, *The New Realities*

What About Your Field, Industry or Geographic Area?

As I define it in *Job Search Secrets*, "a job target is a clearly selected geographic area, an industry or company size, and function within that industry." An accountant, for example, may target a certain industry (such as telecommunications or hospitals), or may see himself in the accounting function and may not care which industry he is in but prefer instead to focus on "company size." This means he wants to target a small, medium, or large company, regardless of industry.

Examine your target to see how each is doing. Perhaps, for example, your industry is okay, but the large companies are not doing well, while smaller companies are hiring. In this case, target the smaller companies.

What changes are taking place in your industry or function? If you think your industry or function will continue to retrench, find a "new horse to ride": an industry or function that is on a growth curve, or one that will give you transferrable skills.

CASE STUDY: ED
The Benefit of Targeting

Ed and Steve were both administrative managers in the retail industry. Both had lost their jobs. Each had spent twenty years—their entire working lives—in retail. Both wanted to work in health care.

Steve actually had hands-on health-care experience. A few years earlier, his company had lent him to a major hospital to serve as the interim administrative head for a full year. He loved that assignment, did very well at it, and swore he would get a job like that again someday.

But Steve decided to be "practical": "All my contacts are in retail, and I need a job *now*. It's true I would like to move into a growth area, but I don't have time to learn a new industry. I have no choice but to focus on the retail industry."

Ed, on the other hand, targeted health care, and had retail as a separate target. Ed joined health-care associations that dealt with administration, read all the health-care administration trade magazines, and became knowledgeable about the industry. He met with lots of people, largely through the associations. He was even willing to take a temp job doing data entry in the administrative area of hospitals so he could see what was happening from the inside. His ego did not get in the way.

A job came up: exactly the same hospital job Steve had worked in for a full year. Both Ed and Steve heard about the job, and interviewed extensively.

Who got the job? Ed did—because he sounded more believable, more committed to the industry. Even though he had never held a job in that industry, Ed had *proven* by all his activities that he was sincerely interested in health care.

Steve sounded like all the other job-hunters: He wanted this job just because there happened to be an opening.

He had nothing to talk about except the fact that he had held that job before and that they had liked him. Of course, he tried to maximize that experience. But what was noticed was that he had given no recent indication that he was committed to hospital work—he had not interviewed at other hospitals, etc.

This story is a vivid example of the benefits of thoroughly targeting an industry. It is also encouraging proof that people can enter new industries with no prior experience.

"People in that industry won't let me in."

Job-hunters always say it's hard to change from one industry to another. "Hiring managers don't believe I want to get into that field." I don't believe those job-hunters either because they never read anything about the field, and don't know anyone in the field who would serve as a reality check for them. How do you prove to the hiring managers that you are truly interested? As we say in the chapter "How to Change Careers:"

- Read the industry's trade journals.
- Get to know people in that industry or field.
- Join its organizations; attend its meetings.
- Be persistent.
- Write proposals.
- Be persistent.
- Take relevant courses, part-time jobs, or do

volunteer work related to the new industry or skill area.
- Be persistent.

If you want to get into an industry or field, learn about it.

It's Time to Take Control of Your Own Career

Get in the habit of reading the papers and noticing what news may affect the industry or field you are in. Learn about some of the industries of the future.

Even if all you want is a job right now, instead of a career, do the exercises in this section. Be sure to include at least the Seven Stories Exercise, Interests, Values, and Forty-Year Plan. They won't take a long time to do, and they will shorten the length of your search.

CASE STUDY: SCOTT
What Should I Be When I Grow Up?

Scott is thirty-eight, a lawyer with a varied background. He had worked for the DA's office, a stock exchange, and writing for a magazine. With his diverse past, he didn't know what to do next.

I know only one way to figure out what a person should be, and it's to use the methodology in this book. So that's what I did with Scott—a shortened version of the exercises.

Seven Stories Exercise

First, we did The Seven Stories Exercise. I said: "Tell me something you've done that you really enjoyed doing, know you did well, and felt a sense of accomplishment about. It doesn't matter what other people thought, how old you were, whether or not you earned money doing it. You may want to start with: 'There was the time when I ...'"

Scott said: "There was the time when I argued my first case before a jury."

I asked him to tell me the details and what he enjoyed about it.

"I liked being independent, I was calling the shots. I had to plan the whole thing myself ..."

To tend, unfailingly, unflinchingly, towards a goal, is the secret of success.
Anna Pavlova, Russian Ballerina, Franks, *Pavlova*

I asked for another story.

Scott said: "I wrote an exposé for a magazine."

I asked Scott to tell me more. He said he enjoyed the same things: being independent, calling the shots, etc. Seemingly, the only time Scott enjoyed a bureaucratic environment was when he broke away from it.

Scott thought that he had a scattered background, and that everything was different. To my mind, those two stories were alike, so I had enough to go on. (If the stories had been in conflict, I would have asked him for as many as seven stories.)

Values Exercise

"Scott, tell me the things that are important to you." He replied, "Money is important, and independence."

Interests Exercise

"Scott, what are your interests?" Languages were very important to him; he had command of a few. The international area was central to his interests.

Scott's exercise results will serve as a template. He can make sure that his next job will allow him to be independent, to earn the money he wants, to enjoy the international area, and so on.

The Forty-Year Plan

Then I guided him through an abbreviated version of the Forty-Year Plan. I don't know how to help people unless I know where they are heading. If all I know is their past, their future will be more of the same. We spent only five minutes on this exercise.

I start with the present to get people grounded in the present. If I simply ask: What do you want to be? it doesn't work. They have nothing to base it on.

"Tell me what your life is like right now. What is your relationship with your family, however you define family? Where do you live? What is it physically like? What are your hobbies and interests? How is your health? What do you do for exercise? How would you describe the job you have right now? And tell me anything else you want to about your life today."

Next, I asked Scott to tell me about his life at age forty-three. Then I asked about his life at age fifty-three. In part, he said:

"I am living in the suburbs. I have a wife and four kids. The oldest is sixteen; the youngest is nine. (It is helpful to put down how old your kids are at each stage so you feel yourself getting older.) I have a small consulting firm, with perhaps four employees who do research and support me in what I am doing. I do a lot of business in Europe. Whatever I am doing is 'at the center of the world'—I feel I'm on top of the important things that are happening."

From my point-of-view, there were no conflicts in the results of his exercises. They all showed him in an independent situation.

Scott seemed to me to be the stereotypical entrepreneur. I do think he should have his own business, but not right now. Having people work for him sounded right because he seemed disorganized. As he himself suggested, one person could keep him in line and clean up after him. His business might have to do with international business, and also with high-tech. He wants to be at the center of what's happening.

Scott needs to *focus* on something that is a growth area and also satisfies his other needs. There are lots of areas that could fulfill him. The danger is that he may spend twenty years never selecting something to focus on. If a person like Scott is always exploring, like Scott, it may be best to just arbitrarily pick something because there is no one correct answer. Other people, who are in a rut, may need to spend more time exploring.

Scott happens to have contacts in the telecommunications industry. If he can get into the telecommunications field, he should try to learn what he can, and develop a business plan while he is there.

Scott now has a plan. He can follow the plan, or not. If he continues to try out every field he comes across, he will be in constant turmoil. He will simply go from job to job, and wind up in his sixties with a lot of experiences but no career, and never reach his dream.

It's the same for you. Figure out the things you enjoy doing and also do well. Do your Forty-Year

First say to yourself what you would be; and then do what you have to do.
Epictetus

Plan. These exercises will serve as your anchor as well as your guide. You won't get as irritated in your next job, because you'll know what you're getting out of it. You will keep up your research and your knowledge of the field. You will gain the skills you need to go forward.

Retraining Is For Everybody
—Even Executives

When people talk about retraining in America, they are usually talking about lower-level workers who don't have computer skills. Retraining is necessary at all levels. Do research to learn the terminology of the industry you want to enter so you can be an insider, not an outsider.

By definition, new industries must hire people from outside the industry. If a job-hunter studies the field, and develops a sincere interest in it, he or she has a good chance of being hired.

Careful research is a critical component, and will become a central part of every sophisticated person's job search.

If you just think off the top of your head about the areas you should be targeting, your ideas will probably be superficial—and outdated.

The Rate of Change

Change is happening at an increasingly faster rate. Industries disappear, and new ones spring up quickly. Instead of simply hunting for the next job, think about your long-range career.

You can pick the "right horse to ride" into your future rather than hanging on for dear life in a declining market. If you pick the right horse, you'll have a much easier ride.

Achieving Stability in a Changing World

How can you keep yourself stable in a constantly changing economy? If the world is being battered, and companies are being battered, and even CEO's cannot keep their jobs, what are you going to do?

The benefit of doing the following exercises is that they give you confidence and a sense of stability in a changing world. You will learn to know yourself and become sure of exactly what you can take with you wherever you go.

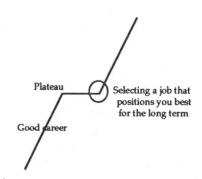

Plateau

Selecting a job that positions you best for the long term

Good career

The Result of Assessment Is Job Targets

If you go through an assessment with a career counselor or vocational testing place, and do not wind up with tentative job targets, the assessment has not helped you very much. You must go one more step, and decide what to *do* with this information.

The Result of Assessment Is Power

The more you know about yourself, the more power you have to envision a job that will suit you. The exercises give you power.

People find it hard to believe that I went through a period of about thirty years when I was painfully shy. In graduate school, I was afraid when they took roll because I obsessed with whether I should answer "here" or "present." When I had to give a presentation, the best I could do was read the key words from my index cards. (Today, my throat is actually hoarse from all the public speaking I do.) I will be forever grateful for the kindness of strangers who told me I did well when I knew I was awful.

The only thing that ultimately saved me was doing the Seven Stories Exercise. When I was little, I had led groups of kids in the neighborhood, and I did it well. It gave me strength to know that I was inherently a group leader regardless of how I was behaving now. (I was in my thirties at the time.)

The Seven Stories Exercise grounds you, and the Forty-Year Plan guides you. When people said: "Would you like to lead groups?" I said to myself, "Well, I led groups when I was ten. Maybe I can do it again." The transition was painful, and took many years, but my Seven Stories Exercise kept me going. And my Forty-Year Plan let me know there was plenty of time in which to do it.

The Five O'Clock Club

Learning to Track Trends:
The Electric Power Industry

by: Russ Schundler (with Harriet Greisser,
Director of Executive Employment
Research, Right Associates)

Virtually every industry is in turmoil. For just one example, read about the electric power industry. Then think about—or research—the industry you are in now. What are the trends? What outside forces are affecting *your* industry? How might you be affected? How can you prepare for the future?

If you are targeting other industries, research them to see how you fit in with their new directions. This research and planning will keep you more prepared—and more stable—in this unstable world.

C an you imagine if every company and every home had its own power-generator? Believe it or not, the day when this picture becomes a reality is fast approaching. That's the trend projected by the economics of power-generation technology, combined with changing government regulations. If things keep going in this direction, what would happen to power plants? What would happen to the people who work there? What kind of people will be needed in the electric power industry? Perhaps somebody like you.

If this is your present industry—or one that you want to get into—you need to be aware of the changes taking place.

External Factors Driving Change

Since the Energy Policy Act of 1992, the government has encouraged deregulation of the electric power industry. Alternate sources of power have been promoted, and recently they have become extremely cost-effective. Consider the dilemma of those who own fossil fuel and nuclear power generating plants, which can deliver power at the cost per kwt of $0.06 to $0.08, when they need to compete with a modern fuel cell or gas turbine generator, which can deliver power at the cost per kwt of $0.01 to $0.02.

To make matters worse, utilities are expected, in the near future, to be required by law to open their power lines to any producer, a practice known as "retail wheeling." What this means is that theoretically anybody—including you and me—can go out and buy a power generator and sell to anybody who wants to buy power at a fraction of the cost they would pay a large utility. This scenario suggests that factories, shopping centers, and multi-unit apartment complexes will be using small stand-alone power generators to supply their own needs.

Of even greater concern to power companies and their employees is the likelihood that excess capacity will be sold on the open market at very low prices.

Future Organizational Structures

The power industry's initial response to this competitive cost pressure is to lobby the regulatory commission to slow the pace of change by breaking up the large monolithic power companies.

They can be divided into: natural monopolies (the power lines and distribution grids); competitive power suppliers (the generating facilities); and competitive services. (Competitive services include power plant engineering and maintenance, facilities management, meter reading and billing, sales and customer service, line maintenance, and demand management consulting.) This action by the regulatory commission will transform a large monolithic power company into many focused organizations.

The unbundling of the industry is likely to take place in incremental steps, moving from increasingly autonomous divisions to profit centers to subsidiary companies within a large holding company and finally to stand-alone independent businesses. Much like the Baby Bells, each independent business will "live or die" based on its ability to provide valuable and differentiable products and services.

An example of this kind of thinking comes

Since college, I'd always worked at top speed. From a demanding law practice, I'd gone to work in Richard Nixon's White House. Days began at six a.m., and I seldom was home before ten at night. Suddenly there was a vacuum in my life. I had nothing productive to do.
John Ehrlichman, former White House domestic policy coordinator

from Illinois Power, where stockholders have created a holding company to serve as a parent company for the original power company and several non-utility subsidiaries. Chairman Larry Haab says "a holding company will give us greater flexibility to start new ventures and it will satisfy the desire to have a formal structure separating our regulated from our non-regulated business." In a similar manner, Duke Power, based in North Carolina, has reorganized into two divisions: the Duke Power Company, which will assume responsibility of the company's regulated business, and Associated Enterprises Group, which will conduct supervision of the non-regulated businesses in energy and diversified areas. (Edison Electric Institute, Economics & Planning Department: Issues & Trends Briefing Paper, December 1994.)

Skills for Tomorrow's Electric Utility Industry
- Marketing • Partnering • Outsourcing
  • Consulting
- International business development

The traditional skills that caused one to be successful in the electric power industry included being good at negotiating with regulatory agencies, large-project management, long-range planning, power generation engineering, power transmission engineering, and managing a vertical organization. This is an industry that has barely changed in thirty years. But if you want to work for the power industry of the future, you should consider the following trends:

• Marketing:

Selling power as a commodity in an unregulated market will be extremely competitive, with little means to sustain profitable margins. To overcome this problem, today's utilities will need to be able to determine unique customer needs for power and services. Considerations should be the customer's size, operating hours, demand patterns, and technology base. Are the

customer's needs met by a fuel cell, a gas-fired co-generation plant, or a tie into a conventional grid? Does a customer have resources to run private power generators or would a facility management package be more cost effective? What about maintenance services? Should private generation capability be ensured by a backup power plan? How much more can one charge for instant backup power?

This is just a sampling of the many difficult questions which utility companies will be asking their newly created or newly emphasized marketing departments. For example, Pennsylvania Power & Light has begun reorganization plans which will create a Marketing & Economic Development Department. William F. Hecht states: "The new structure is geared to providing high quality, consistent and cost-competitive services to our customers." (Edison Electric Institute, Economics & Planning Department: Issues & Trends Briefing Paper, December 1994.)

• Partnering:

In their annual report, Florida Power & Light states they have formed "energy partnerships with commercial and industrial customers to help them operate more efficiently and to become more competitive." An example of this initiative was their energy-saving teamwork with a school system to help design "energy conservation standards in all new construction and renovations."

Union Electric talks in their annual report of a partnership with Shell Oil called QUEST. They have formed a quality team that "meets regularly to review Shell's energy use and UE's service quality." The "team members have used each other's expertise and feedback to improve their respective businesses."

Team leadership skills and the ability to see "win-win" opportunities between supplier and customer in this industry will be sought by power companies to develop value-added relationships which transcend price as the only means for competing.

• Outsourcing:

Larry Ellis, senior vice president of energy services at Virginia Power, says "We have learned from our customers that they need and want new products and services to help them be more competitive. If Virginia Power can manage a customer's energy operations, that customer can concentrate on its core business and therefore be more viable in its marketplace." (Energy Daily, July 6, 1995.) These words reflect a need which is just beginning to be evident among large customers of the electric utilities. As the number of power-generating options increases and as their cost decreases, many more customers, large and small, will have "make or buy" options when considering how to acquire power. As more and more opt for the "make" decision, the electric power industry will need to build the skills to service this expanding need for outsourcing.

• Consulting:

Union Electric recently commented that they "provide expertise about a variety of electrotechnologies with problem-solving applications (support) for industrial, medical and governmental customers." Virginia Power's Larry Ellis says his unit will "provide new products and services ... to Virginia Power's large industrial, commercial and government customers." These comments suggest that by providing a total solution that includes consulting on the application of power, an electric power company can reinforce its valued customer relationships.

Another form of consulting will be that of selling—and training customers in the use of—computerized optimization models which manage, in real time, the most cost-effective sourcing of power. These models will take into account spot pricing from multiple vendors, demand levels, time of day, quality of power, and a company's own internal generation capacity and costs.

Quantitative analysis and operations research modeling skills will be increasingly in demand.

These consulting skills may be provided by power companies themselves or by independent organizations such as LCG Consulting, based in Los Altos, California, that provides consulting services on utility planning, operations, pricing, and power industry strategies.

• International Business Development:

The lead line in a recent article in Energy Daily states: "Dominion Energy Inc. and Energy Initiatives Inc. continued their international expansion last week, winning bids for control of state-owned electric generating facilities being privatized by the government of Bolivia." In that article, Thomas Chewning, president and chief executive officer of Dominion Energy, stated: "This is consistent with our plans to increase our presence as an energy company serving the Southern Cone." Dominion Energy will be capitalizing on their current experience in Argentina. Energy Initiatives, which has several projects under development in Latin America and the Far East, is building on experience in Nova Scotia and Colombia.

This international expansion highlights an approach that energy companies are using to diversify their risks associated with deregulation. More important, it suggests that anyone with skills in international trade, contracting and negotiations, and foreign languages might be able to define new and expanding markets.

Change Means Opportunity

Dramatic change is here to stay in the electric power industry. The industry's needs are evolving continuously—and shifting abruptly. However, if you recognize the forces of change, you will be positioned for exciting new opportunities in the future.

Russell D. Schundler is vice president, Client Services, for Right Associates in Parsippany, New Jersey. Russ has provided management consulting services in the area of change management, with a focus on the electric power industry.

The
Five
O'Clock
Club®

Career Makeovers:
Five Who Did It

Fortune sides with him who dares.
Virgil, Aeneid

The following stories on career changers were written by Patricia Kitchen, a staff writer for *Newsday*, a large New York newspaper. The Five O'Clock Club worked with Patricia to provide this valuable information for their readers.

A variety of people wrote to *Newsday* telling them that they wanted to make a career change. The newspaper chose several who represented goals or situations common to many readers. I worked with them weekly, in a group, to help them refine their goals and develop plans to make their career dreams come true.

As Patricia said in her introductory article: "While the recareering process is similar for most, each person profiled has a different plan and is starting from a different place. One man had been laid off, several feared it and one woman is re-entering the workplace after twenty years at home raising a family—and boy, has the workplace changed."

Read how these regular, everyday folks made their dreams come true. The process worked for them. It can work for you.

These five articles are followed by one for those over fifty years of age. Lydia Bronte tells us how longevity is affecting all of our careers.

The articles written by Patricia Kitchen are reprinted with permission from *Newsday*.

The Five O'Clock Club

Case Study:
Trying to Make a Winning Move

By Patricia Kitchen, Staff Writer for *Newsday*

Rich Kier caught baseball fever when he was seven years old, watching the 1956 World Series with his dad and his grandfather, who were both rooting for the Brooklyn Dodgers. For Kier, it was the beginning of his lifelong worship of Mickey Mantle and, like many boys, he started dreaming of playing centerfield for the New York Yankees. "'Rock and roll was in its infancy, Mickey was our hero and the Yankees were on top. You couldn't ask for more than that," says Kier.

At age forty-five, he knows he's never going to play centerlield. But after logging 20 years in the credit and collection business—and, like many others, laid off from his job—Kier is resurrecting his dream of working in the sports industry. He's one of a group of readers chosen by this newspaper to work with counselor Kate Wendleton, director of The Five O'Clock Club, a Manhattan-based job search and career strategy network, to refine their career goals and embark on short- and long-term plans to make them happen.

"The process is the same, no matter what your level. People need a plan. Without one, they're not successful," Wendleton told the group at their first meeting last fall. She helped each person list, analyze and prioritize the seven most satisfying paid, or unpaid, experiences of their lives, to help guarantee their vision of a new profession is realistic, not just based on glamorized media images or pressures from society.

Richard Kier, a career-makeover participant, has always dreamed of working for the New York Yankees in their business or legal operations.

She also asked each to write a Forty-Year Plan, imagining where they would be and what they would be doing at ten-year intervals. After a little thought, it only took most people a couple of hours to actually write their plans. This long-range view will help them break down their pursuit into the small steps that will comprise a campaign. This way they don't feel intimidated at the thought of making a giant leap right away. "People with a longer perspective are more successful. Plus, you can keep your pay up if you look for ways to segue into a new career," Wendleton says.

Members of the group helped one another brainstorm ideas for careers, companies or agencies to approach in doing research to further test the feasibility of their dream careers. Wendleton emphasized the need to define their targets, and for research. This way they can avoid the "I don't know what it is, but I'll know it when I see it" approach.

As for Kier, he's well into his research of the sports industry, and where he might fit in. After he was laid off, he took another job in the collection industry, but hated it. His wife encouraged him to go back to school to become a paralegal. Going into this career makeover project, his dream job was to work in the business operations or legal area of a professional baseball team, preferably the Yankees. Here's how he refined that dream, and a sketch of his game plan now:

Major lesson learned

One team, or even one sport, is just too narrow a target. Without even going into the woes of professional baseball, it's not realistic to hitch your wagon to only one star. "The numbers have to be on your side," says Wendleton, who suggests targeting enough employers to represent 200 appropriate positions, even if they may be filled at this time. As she points out, "Sports is a huge industry."

So, with the help of the other group members, Kier brainstormed the possibilities to broaden his horizons. He's now researching football, hockey and minor league affiliates, law firms with sports specialties, college athletic departments, sporting arenas like Madison Square Garden and the Nassau Coliseum, as well as organizations like the New York Mets, the National Football League and USA Baseball, the group that governs amateur baseball. One member of the group tossed out the idea of the media end of the business, and gave him a contact at *Golf* magazine. But when someone suggested sports equipment and manufacturing companies, Kier nixed that idea. "It just doesn't appeal to me. A baseball glove is just a baseball glove. It's a thing. There's no interaction."

If you really want to advise me, do it on Saturday afternoon between 1 and 4
o'clock. And you've got 25 seconds to do it, between plays. Not on Monday.
I know the right thing to do on Monday.
Alex Agase, Northwestern football coach

Wrong turn

When Kier started his research, he jumped the gun. At the second counseling session, he told the group he had sent résumés to the people he was calling. "Wrong," said Wendleton. "That's the activity of a sprinter. This is a long-distance run." Kier is still an outsider, and as such, getting a job so soon in his campaign is a long shot. His goal now is to gather information on how things work. "You need to get to know a critical mass of people and get to the point where you give as much information as you take away. That makes you a contributor, an insider, and at that stage, getting a job is more realistic," says Wendleton, who is also the author of The Five O'Clock Club series of career books.

Resources and research

So Kier adjusted his approach. "I'm finding out the value of research," he told the group. Now when he calls contacts, he says he is a career changer who wants to combine his legal experience with a sports career and just wants information on that process. "I let them know I have a definite idea about what I want. If you sound like you have no plan, they just say, 'Send a résumé,' and that's that. So far, no one has been discouraging."

Now when he reads publications like *Sporting News* and *Baseball America*, he sees them through the eyes not just of a fan, but of a career changer, looking for names, sources and organizations. And he plans to attend an upcoming conference at Hofstra University on Babe Ruth. "I can make some good contacts there," he says.

Short-term plan

"I anticipate it takes about a year to establish contacts and figure out what you want to do, can do and won't do," says Kier. So, as he continues his research, he's now looking for a full-time paralegal job that hopefully will take him in the direction of his goal. He's completed an internship at a Garden City law firm and is now working part-time. As for salary, he anticipates taking a financial hit from the $41,000 he was making before he was laid off.

Entry-level paralegals start out as low as $25,000, but he says there's potential to double that in two to three years. Fortunately, he has a supportive wife, who works full-time as a nurse.

Smart move

Going into this project, Kier knew to build on the skills he's developing as a paralegal. It's unrealistic to plunge into a new industry cold, saying you'll take just anything. As Wendleton says, "The goal is to capitalize on skills you already have so you don't have to start at the bottom getting coffee for people. It's a way to keep your salary up."

What sports experts say

"Kier is definitely on the right track," says David Sussman, general counsel for the Yankees. "You can't look at it as one move [into the sports industry], but as two or three. You need to look for businesses that overlap."

To help flesh out his résumé, Kier can volunteer at corporate and nonprofit sports events, says Sylvia Allen, who's teaching an upcoming seminar at New York University called "Starting a Career in Sports and Special Events."

As for job targets, Kier's smartest route is to pursue those major law firms that handle cases for teams, leagues, college athletic departments or individual players, says David M. Carter, author of "You Can't Play the Game if You Don't Know the Rules — Career Opportunities in Sports Management" (*Impact*, Manassas Park, Va.). Kier should also delve into more technical sports journals and specialized newsletters. "What he's reading now is great for fans, but not for practitioners. He needs meatier information beyond who's hit the most home runs," Carter says.

One concern Carter has is Kier's age. It's easier to break into an industry when you are twenty-five years old by taking an entry-level job, such as season ticket sales. Kier knows that's true, but as he says, "I'm not going to let it stop me. It's only a deterrent if you let it be." And, as he says, a lightbulb went off in his head when Wendleton told the group, "So what if you'll be fifty by the time you make your new career happen? You're going to be fifty anyway."

"That was a wake-up call. I don't want to be stuck in a position someday of saying 'I coulda, shoulda, woulda," says Kier.

Case Study: Working With Animals Was Her First Love

By Patricia Kitchen, Staff Writer for *Newsday*

Diane Murray has nursed baby mice with an eyedropper. She's rushed a wounded seagull to the vet. She hangs "Baby Geese Crossing" signs in nesting areas. She rescued a lost Yorkshire Terrier one Christmas and had him over for a filet mignon dinner. She's taken two dream vacations—one a photo safari to Kenya, the other to swim with dolphins in the Florida Keys. Plus, at her home in Seaford, Long Island, she has four cats, a dog and two birds.

So why is Murray working as a manager at a travel agency instead of with animals? Back in 11th grade, "My guidance counselor talked me out of it. He guaranteed me I would never find a job in that career. He swayed me from animal-related fields, and I ended up going in for art education [in college]," she said.

Like many people, Murray, thirty-seven, was derailed at an early age from her true calling. She is one of a group of readers chosen to work with Kate Wendleton, director of The Five O'Clock Club, a Manhattan-based job search and career strategy network, who is helping them get back on the right career track. As part of the process, Wendleton asked each person to list his or her seven most satisfying life experiences—either paid or unpaid. Plus, everyone wrote a Forty-Year Plan, outlining at ten-year intervals how they would like to see their futures develop.

"I have been told countless times by the people I work with that I'm in the wrong profession. This is due to the fact that my 'first love' is so obvious," Murray wrote in a letter to this newspaper. So, with counsel from Wendleton and encouragement from the rest of the group, here's how she is plotting her career change into wildlife management or marine biology.

It's a process

Like many people with an eye on a different career, Murray was afraid of taking one big, dramatic leap. "That thought was overwhelming," she said. But Wendleton took the pressure off when she told the group: "You can do everything. You just can't do it all at once. That's why it's important to

have a long-term plan, so you can fit it all in."

Murray's first stage is to research jobs that involve animals, make contact with people in the field, scout out volunteer opportunities and collect information on degree programs. Stage two: to be volunteering by the spring and to start a degree program by the summer. In no way is she actually looking for a job at this point. She wouldn't be ready, said Wendleton. People need time to adjust—both emotionally and financially—to the idea of such a big change.

Diane Murray got a kiss from Winston, a beluga whale, during her dream career day at the New York Aquarium.

Murray does welcome the time to put her finances in order. She recently bought a new car, had an apartment built in her parents' home and bought some furniture. Those bills are manageable given her present salary of about $30,000. But a career change could well mean a cut, so she wants to whittle down her financial obligations before she makes a move. As for taking a lower salary, she says, "Personal satisfaction for me is more important than the money."

What about the degree?

When Murray had fantasized about working with animals, one roadblock always loomed—she had no related degree. But, she now says, "It's a roadblock I can detour around." Several people she's spoken with had no formal education in the field. One woman at an aquarium answered an ad in the paper, another was hired right out of high school and a dolphin trainer in Florida had been an air traffic controller.

Yet she knows education is important, so she's researching programs at Adelphi University, State College at Old Westbury, Hofstra University, Dowling College and Nassau Community College, with an eye to taking one evening class each semester while she keeps her job at the travel agency. But she's not going to wait for the degree itself before moving into her new career. Her plan is to start

If a cat spoke, it might say things like "Hey, I don't see the problem here."
Roy Blount, Jr.

looking for a new job two years from now, even if her degree is still in progress.

Love and marriage

Murray's career is not the only factor in her life equation. She would like to get married and start a family over the next five years, so that needs to be part of her written plan. Though Murray says she's skeptical, Wendleton told her she should use the same approach to find the right relationship that she's using to find the right career. "You have to intentionally and methodically make yourself run into the kind of people you want to meet. Most people, though, don't want to admit to the effort they put into finding a mate," Wendleton said.

Murray, a diehard romantic, maintains that "love is a little luck. The guy I'll probably fall in love with is the hunter I'm trying to stop [from killing animals]."

Research

Once she saw she could make her dream job happen, Murray plunged into research. She read books such as *Opportunities in Animal and Pet Care Careers, Careers for Nature Lovers and Other Outdoor Types* and *Careers for Animal Lovers and Other Zoological Types.* She rejected the idea of being a veterinarian or vet technician—"I just couldn't see me putting animals to sleep," she said.

To find volunteer opportunities, she called the Okeanos Ocean Research Foundation in Hampton Bays; the Aquarium for Wildlife Conservation in Coney Island; Volunteers for Wildlife in Huntington; and the Nature Conservancy in Cold Spring Harbor.

And she really got her nickel's worth out of those phone calls. Besides asking for literature to be mailed to her, she grilled everyone she spoke to about their jobs and workplaces. A night watchman talked to her for half an hour about how his daughter got a degree in zoology, found her job and met her husband in a diving class. He also gave her names of other places to call. "That really broke the

ice," Murray said. "It was so easy after that. So many people ended up telling me their personal stories."

Wendleton, who also is the author of The Five O'Clock Club series of career books, says the keys to this kind of research are discipline and enthusiasm. "You want to get people on your side—and not just people you see as high-level. Secretaries, receptionists—and night watchmen—can be tremendous sources of information."

Expert advice

Murray's approach—to volunteer while she's taking courses—is a good one, says Kevin M. Walsh, director of marine mammal training at the Aquarium for Wildlife Conservation. Too often when he's hiring, he sees people with experience and no education or with education and no experience. He also says it's important to have a view of the job that is grounded in reality: "It looks glamorous, especially when you're feeding the dolphins in mid-July in your shorts. But it can be grueling, repetitious and subject to the weather. Last February we had to shovel our way to the whales—and our hands were frozen!"

If there's one thing she's learned, she says, it's that "Anyone can reroute their future. It's never too late."

For people interested in training animals, he suggests studying biology and psychology to learn conditioning techniques. Entry-level jobs as animal keepers pay about $24,000 in the New York area but can pay half that in places like Florida, where the cost of living is lower. As further resources, he suggests two associations, the American Zoo and Aquarium Association in Wheeling, W. Va., and the International Marine Animal Trainers Association, 1720 South Shores Road, San Diego, Calif. 92109.

Walsh says there are relatively few positions available, so a job search can be frustrating. But Murray is not discouraged. If there's one thing she's learned, she says, it's that "Anyone can reroute their future. It's never too late."

Case Study: Self-Image Was the Key for this Homemaker

By Patricia Kitchen, Staff Writer for *Newsday*

Betty Oliver, Aug. 19, 1994
Age: 44
Occupation: "Just a housewife"
Confidence level: Zip

Betty Oliver, Feb. 19,1995
Age: 45
Occupation: Free-lance bookkeeper
Confidence level: Zip-plus and rising fast

Like many women who work at home raising children and managing the household for no set salary, Betty Oliver from Huntington Station, Long Island, didn't think she had much to offer in the world of "for pay" work. After years of telling people she was a housewife, to the resounding reaction of "Oh," she didn't see her home-management skills as valuable or transferable. But, in spite of a lack of confidence, she somehow did find the courage to write to this newspaper late last summer to ask for a career makeover.

She is one of nine readers chosen to work as a group with Kate Wendleton, director of The Five O'Clock Club, a national job search and career strategy network.

To help make sure their career dreams stemmed from deep-rooted values and motivation, the participants had to list and prioritize their seven most rewarding life experiences—whether paid or not. Plus, each wrote a Forty-Year Plan, describing at five- and ten-year intervals how they would like to see their lives and careers develop.

Before she got married and started raising her two daughters, Oliver worked as a bank teller in Indiana and then in Garden City. When her kids came along, she was a traditional stay-at-home mom, helping teachers with field trips, holiday celebrations and fund-raising bake sales.

But, being someone who gets a real thrill from balancing a checkbook to the penny, she also took over the family's money management duties.

Besides reconciling the household accounts, she also researches and manages the family's mutual funds, IRAs and insurance policies. Plus she prepares the annual taxes. She pores over the financial pages of two daily newspapers and checks out

books from the library like *Bond and Money Market Investments*. Yet Oliver didn't see these skills as marketable in the outside world. "I just thought I was doing these things so my household would survive," she says.

Oliver is now considering several career avenues within the money management field. She thinks she could get good experience working in the bookkeeping department of a small company. Plus, she wants to learn more about providing money management services to senior citizens and young people who are just starting out. Here's a look at her progress:

Easy entry

Some professions call for formal training and licensing. But others, such as public relations, career counseling and freelance bookkeeping, are what Wendleton calls easy entry. "You can do it just by tagging along with an expert and learning the ropes," she told the group. "You can start by volunteering to help out as you're learning, and then once you have some experience, you can start charging."

She's applying her organizational skills to bookkeeping jobs

But Oliver skipped the "tag along" approach and proceeded directly to get a "for-pay" assignment. She mentioned to her local banker that she wanted to do bookkeeping or money management work. "Do we have a client for you," said the banker, referring to a customer, a small rock 'n roll memorabilia company, that had not balanced its books in 12 months.

So in early January, at her dining room table, Oliver spent nine hours sorting and re-sorting a hill of checks and deposit tickets, getting the books balanced to the penny.

To calculate her own fee, she took into consideration the minimum wage, the fact that this was her first job, plus her low overhead. Her first in-

*As a general rule, you have to accept that no matter where you work, you are
not an employee; you are in a business with one employee—yourself.*
Andrew S. Grove, president of Intel, as quoted in *Fortune*, September 18, 1995

voice was for $72, at a charge of $8 an hour. "This was probably too low, but I wanted the experience to put on my résumé, she says.

Short-term plan

Oliver knew she needed computer skills, so she's already taken a course in Windows at a local computer store. And she'll be getting involved with some of the volunteer programs she tracked down at schools, libraries and religious institutions. She's also researching certificate programs in accounting and tax preparation at local colleges.

She knows her networking skills are not up to snuff, so she needs to push herself to join professional associations, especially those with members involved in money management.

Betty Oliver, who is making the transition to becoming a freelance bookkeeper, works on improving her computer skills.

And, because down the road she may find herself actually leading seminars, she needs to develop public speaking skills. This means looking into local chapters of Toastmasters, a group that helps people learn to give speeches.

The C-factor

To say Oliver was apprehensive about coming to the career makeover group is an understatement.

"I was petrified," she says. "I didn't think I would fit in. I knew everyone else had jobs. I thought I would be the last one in line. I kept saying to myself: 'Get a grip, Betty. Give this a chance.' " And, if it hadn't been for encouragement from her husband and daughters, she might not have come back for the second session.

But she's learning that confidence is not something you're born with. It develops over time if you look for ways to nurture it. She's been reading biographies of successful people to learn that process, the most recent being *Henry & Clare: An Intimate Portrait of the Luces.*

"I've learned I have to focus, build up steam

and keep pushing. It's like *The Little Engine That Could,*" she says, referring to a popular children's book.

Stepping outside the comfort zone is not easy, but it's essential. "You have to do it anyway, even if you feel awful and you're up all night throwing up," says Wendleton, who learned to overcome her own shyness.

"I now have no shame," she says, attributing that to the fact she believes God put her here with a job to do, and who is she to say to an authority like that, "No, I'm not confident enough"? "When you see yourself as part of a grander scheme, it gives you the courage you need," she says.

As a further confidence-booster, she points to the "seven stories" life experience exercise she did with the group. That calls for people to list their seven most satisfying experiences—things they did particularly well and enjoyed doing—reaching all the way back to childhood.

"When you see a pattern and can say you've been good at doing such-and-such your whole life, it gives you roots to hang onto and makes you feel more secure," she says.

**Oliver watched others prepare tax returns.
As a homemaker, Oliver took pride in
managing all her family's financial matters.**

A shot in the arm

Oliver started off working 35 hours a week researching her career change, which is what Wendleton prescribes. But the holidays set in, and Oliver's momentum lagged, so she's down to just 15 hours a week. And as with many people, her energy seems to give out by mid-afternoon. So, after reading about the importance of health and fitness in Wendleton's books, Oliver invested in a treadmill, on which she exercises twenty minutes a day as a way to boost her energy.

Plus, she's more careful about her diet and she's used a highlight rinse in her hair "This has nothing to do with looking younger. I just want to look and feel better," she says.

Research

Books she's found helpful for basic job descriptions, industry profiles and listings of employers: *Occupational Outlook Handbook*, published by the U.S. Department of Labor, and *Career Guide for 1995*, published by Dun & Bradstreet.

She advises anyone doing library research to take note of the publication dates of reference books. She wasted considerable time calling out-of-date phone numbers and tracking down defunct professional associations that were listed in a reference book published in 1987.

On homemaking skills

"It's no nine-to-five job. You put in twenty-four hours a day," Oliver says of the effort it takes to run a home and make sure everyone's schedule is met. "Homemakers are undervalued in this society," says Oliver, who, when people at social functions asked what she did to fill her day, used to start to say, tongue-in-cheek, "Oh, I just eat bonbons."

Advice from an expert

Because computer skills are so important, Oliver should consider taking a more extensive computer course to learn spreadsheet applications like Lotus and Excel, says Jean Carol Kunzelman, director of the Manhattan office of Accountemps, which places temporary workers in accounting and finance jobs. And Oliver definitely should jack up the fee she charges for her next free-lance bookkeeping job. That work should command at least $10 to $12 an hour, says Kunzelman, adding that Oliver's first client "really got a bargain."

Keep in mind that there is no harder work than thinking—really thinking—about who you are and what you want out of your life. Figuring out where your goals and your skills match up is a painful, time-consuming process. . . . But unless you make the effort you are no more likely to be happy in your next career than you have been in your current one. In fact, you're likely to be a good deal less happy.
Julie Connelly, *Fortune* magazine, February 6, 1995

Case Study: Looking to Make-Up a World of Opportunity

By Patricia Kitchen, Staff Writer for *Newsday*

Colleen McFarlane is one of those people you could call an adventurer. Not just because she picked up and moved to Australia for a year, crewed on a yacht in the Caribbean, and has an orange belt in karate.

But like many creative people, when it comes to committing to one career, she sees all the possibilities and—until recently—couldn't throw all her enthusiasm behind one thing. She had considered working for an advertising agency, for a fashion magazine, and in retail management. "I was scared I would miss out on something else, and end up being bored," said McFarlane, thirty-four, from Medford, Long Island.

She's one of a group of readers chosen for a career makeover with counselor Kate Wendleton, director of The Five O'Clock Club, a Manhattan-based job search and career strategy network. To pinpoint their true interests, Wendleton asked each participant to list and prioritize their seven most rewarding life experiences—whether paid or unpaid. Plus, each had to write a Forty-Year Plan, describing at ten-year intervals how they would like their life and career to develop.

Colleen McFarlane went to Revlon for an information interview to learn about cosmetics.

"I am absolutely desperate! I'm in the process of job hunting and don't want to get railroaded back into my old career," wrote McFarlane in a letter to this newspaper. Encouraged at an early age by her parents to go into medicine, she majored in biology in college, but discovered through several internships that she wasn't crazy about the idea of "looking at slide sections of the brain and grinding up people's livers. "I found it sad," she said of her experience working for the Suffolk County medical examiner. So, as she finished college, she took a job in retailing, an industry she's been in for the past 13 years, while yearning to do something more entrepreneurial.

Her goal now? To start a small business marketing cosmetics, clothing, crafts, and home prod-

ucts to women of color in South Africa, Latin America, and Australia. As she says, when you run your own shop, there's "freedom and creativity. There may be more pressure, but nobody else blows it for you. If you blow it, you blow it yourself."

Here's how she came to settle on her new career plan:

The Power of the pen

"I had dreams and a ton of ideas, but it was a mixing bowl of things. By writing the Forty-Year Plan, those dreams and ideas came together," she says. She discovered that committing to one direction did not make her feel closed in. "Expansive thinkers worry they're going to get bored or miss something, but they really miss something else if they don't focus—that is, they just don't get very far," Wendleton told the group. Her advice? Write down your ideas, decide which ones have the major elements that will make you most satisfied, know that there's not just one perfect career, and then "just shut up and pick something." You can always switch if you find out through research that it really isn't going to meet your needs after all.

Having your goals in writing can also keep you focused when temptations come your way. You may be seduced by other opportunities and end up doing "someone else's thing instead of your own," says Wendleton. "But if your plan is written—in so much detail you can taste it—it's easier to stay on track."

Finding the time

McFarlane didn't have just a nine-to-five job. During this makeover project, she worked as a personal shopper for Bergdorf Goodman's—during the holiday season, yet. Her days started at ten A.M. and lasted until seven or eight P.M. She worked six or seven days a week, and as for lunch break time, "What's that?" she asked.

This means it was just about impossible for her to log in the 15 hours a week Wendleton said career changers who are employed full-time should spend

They laughed at Joan of Arc, but she went right ahead and built it.
Gracie Allen

researching their new careers. But even though people are pressed for time, they still should struggle to make some progress—even if it's just thinking about their goal and jotting down notes, says Wendleton. It's easy to take the "all-or-nothing" approach and say, "Well, I'm too busy now. I'll start researching once this spurt of work is over." If you do that, you lose momentum and forget what it is you were planning to do.

So, at the very least, you can subscribe to trade journals. "They just arrive under your door," says Wendleton. You can also call companies to have them send you their promotional material. And you can do something simple that McFarlane caught on to—she just started talking to people about her dream. "I used to keep ideas close to the vest, but I got a lot less paranoid," she says. Simply through articulating her career wish, she learned that one friend in the restaurant business had done considerable research into the cosmetics industry, and another is a friend of a woman who is starting a new fashion magazine.

Wrong turn

McFarlane did find time to send letters to six huge cosmetics companies, asking for information interviews so she could learn more about doing business globally. But she addressed the letters to the human resources manager, which was a big mistake. Her follow-up calls generally led her to voice mail. And she ended up getting a flurry of rejection letters because they thought she was looking for a job. "I should have done research to find out who runs the appropriate department or found a contact through a friend," she says.

Short-term plan

Unlike a business that is easier to get into—like a franchise, consulting in your own industry, or buying a business that already exists, McFarlane's idea is a big one—to start a company from scratch that's global in scope. So she knows it's going to take her two years of research and planning before she's ready to take the plunge. She has a lot to learn during that time—marketing, distribution, pricing,

finance, profitability. And it's especially important for her to do her homework because starting a business that's successful is no piece of cake. More than 50 percent of new businesses fail within four years, according to the Small Business Administration.

So Wendleton suggested McFarlane get some relevant experience under her belt by working for a small- to medium-sized company where she can learn about the many facets of running a smaller firm. "Learning finance in a big company like General Motors does not translate into finance for a small business," said Wendleton. So the first step in McFarlane's plan is to find a sales or marketing job with a company that sells cosmetics in the new-business markets overseas.

Her next step will be to sign up for courses at the American Woman's Economic Development Corp., a nonprofit group in Manhattan that helps women entrepreneurs set up and manage their own businesses.

She went to the career research section of her local library.

Good research sources

So, now that her gig at Bergdorf Goodman's is over, she has her days free to target prospective employers, which she's doing at the job information center of the mid-Manhattan branch of the New York Public Library. Her goal is an ambitious one—to find a job by the time the career makeover group meets again in early March.

Among the sources she's finding helpful: *Research Your Way to Your Next Job*; InfoTrac, a CD-Rom indexing magazine and newspaper articles; *The Million Dollar Directory* published by Dun & Bradstreet; *Standard and Poor's Register of Companies*; *Hoover's Handbook of American Businesses*; and *The International Business Woman* by Marlene Rossman.

Role models

McFarlane already looks up to Anita Roddick, founder of the Body Shop, as well as an African-

American executive she heard speak at a teleconference conducted by the National Association for Female Executives. She also has developed a mentor relationship with a woman who runs a public relations firm—and a retail operation in St. Thomas. "I'm learning from them that the odds aren't so insurmountable—the key is just to keep going."

And sometimes role models can show you what not to do. Because so much can go wrong in a new business, Wendleton says McFarlane should read magazines like *Success* and *Entrepreneur* with an eye to learning what mistakes others have made so she can avoid them.

What experts say

So far, so good, says Tina Lassiter, director of training at the American Woman's Economic Development Corp. McFarlane has a clear concept of what she wants to do and is taking the right steps to get there. "That's 95 percent of the game."

One suggestion. After she's settled in a new job, she should attend functions given by groups outside her specialty—and comfort level. That means she needs to network with groups of bankers and investors, says Lassiter.

And this advice from Cindy Melk, thirty-two, founder and creative director of H2O Plus, which sells skin, bath, and bodycare products: Because doing business globally is so complex, McFarlane should consider opening a pilot store in her own backyard, one that she can "watch, nurture, and manipulate," before she ventures overseas. Doing business abroad means bilingual labels, customs clearances, government and safety regulations. McFarlane will be better off if she "defines her unique point of difference" on a smaller, close-to-home scale first.

And as for any negative feedback she'll be getting, Melk advises her to view it as a signal she needs to become better educated in that area. "Negativism can actually be quite motivating. It all depends on how you process it," she says. "Tell her to stick to her guns."

The
Five
O'Clock
Club

Case Study: Stalled Career
Opens Door for Mechanic

By Patricia Kitchen, Staff Writer for *Newsday*

He's trading his aviation tools
for teaching

Five years ago, Angel Perez, thirty-five, of Kew Gardens, Queens, thought he was living the American Dream. He had a good job as a flight mechanic with Eastern Airlines, earning $42,000 a year. He got to travel, work outdoors and have the leeway to decide whether or not a plane was fit to take off. But Eastern—and the airline industry—took a nosedive, and along with it went Perez' dream. Since 1989 he's worked for five airlines and expects to be laid off any day from his job at USAir. "I have fifteen years' experience, but I keep slipping further and further back," says Perez, who has seen his salary drop by 20 percent.

But sometimes disappointment in one career forces people to look for another— one they end up liking even better. And that was Perez's thinking when he wrote to this newspaper asking to be part of a career makeover project. Nine readers worked as a group with Kate Wendleton, director of The Five O'Clock Club, a Manhattan-based job search and career strategy network. As a preliminary step, each had to identify and prioritize his or her seven most satisfying life experiences, either paid or unpaid. All of them also had to write Forty-Year Plans describing how they want to see their lives and careers develop.

Perez had been dreaming of becoming a high school history teacher. When he was in college, he worked summers as a youth counselor, taking young people on field trips. And more recently, he has been spending time at his neighborhood baseball diamond, coaching young people in playing techniques as well as life skills. "These kids don't have a lot to look forward to. They see guns, crime and AIDS and ask 'What's the use?'" says Perez. So he talks to them about the merits of getting a steady job instead of going for drugs, which he tells them "have a heavy price tag —fear, running, hiding and death." Perez says he's living proof to kids that they can take control of their lives. Here's how he's planning to take control of his career change.

A bridge job

A move from aviation mechanic to history teacher is a big leap. Perez could chuck his aviation experience, go back to school and start all over again from scratch. But, as Wendleton asked, "Why toss away a whole industry?" She suggested he play off his strength by teaching aviation at a vocational high school. That puts him in the teaching arena, and he's then in a position to work toward a degree in history.

A move South

By writing out his Forty-Year Plan, Perez and his wife realized part of their dream was to live in Florida, where he had spent nine years working for Eastern. They knew their first step should be a move south, so when his wife, a mortgage banker, heard of an opening at her company's Miami office, she jumped at it. She'll be starting her new job next month, and Perez will follow in April. His plan is to try to find a job in aviation mechanics at the same time he's looking into teaching opportunities.

Wendleton says this two-prong job search is a must. Career changers who are relocating have a tendency to get a job in the old field first, telling themselves they'll start looking for something they really want to do after they're settled in. "Well, you know about inertia," says Wendleton. "It's hard to pick up again once the trail is cold." Perez is better off doing research and making contacts in the two industries at once. This way, if he does take a job as a mechanic, he already has a few "ins" with the teaching profession, so he won't have to start from square one.

So he's talking to some of his buddies in Florida, plus picking up the Miami *Herald* every day—not newsstand copies but discarded ones left on planes that come up daily from Miami. He looks at the help wanted ads, but Wendleton says he also needs to be reading up on the airline industry in general, as well as issues and activities at high schools, vocational schools, youth organizations and boys' clubs in the Miami area.

Learning to brag

Like many people, Perez is not comfortable tooting his own horn. Wendleton dragged out of him the fact that he routinely had been selected by his companies to attend special training programs and in turn to train other mechanics. "Some people don't want to admit how special they are—they take that for granted," says Wendleton. Perez, like many people, needs to become more comfortable identifying and talking about his strengths. As Wendleton says, it's not the brightest and most competent people who get ahead. Often it's the most feisty—the ones who are just dying to get hired and who aren't shy about sharing their accomplishments.

"Yes, but"

Perez's wife and family support his goal to become a teacher. But some friends and colleagues have pointed out all the potential obstacles to making a career change. Wendleton's response: "Some people have not seen a lot of success in their lives. When they hear about opportunities, their heads are programmed to say, "Yes, but what about . . .?" She says the key is to replace "Yes, but" with "How can I get this to work?" And generally, it's best to share your goals only with people who give encouragement and constructive suggestions.

Wrong turn

Last year Perez called the New York City Board of Education to find out how to make a move into teaching. But he wasn't specific about his specialty and was given the brush. He wishes now he had done more networking with people who specialize in aviation education. He recently spoke with the assistant principal of Aviation High School, who told Perez he would be an ideal candidate to teach there, given his experience and fluency in Spanish. "I was just barking up the wrong tree first," he says.

Research

Perez went to the Mid-Manhattan Library job information center, where a librarian helped him find names of Washington, D.C.-based education associations. He wrote away for pamphlets and received useful information from the American Association for Adult and Continuing Education and the National Council for Accreditation of Teacher Education.

Expert advice

According to Ruby Jones, an assistant principal at the George T. Baker Aviation Maintenance Technician School in Miami, Perez already meets the basic requirements to teach airplane mechanics. He has plenty of hands-on experience, plus he has the appropriate licenses required by the FAA. And his experience as a trainer is a definite plus. Perez' first step should be to get an application for employment from the Dade County Public Schools. He also can look into career days at her school and others, because volunteering to speak is a good way to get to know teachers and principal, who can be valuable contacts.

The first principle of ethical power is Purpose . . . .
By purpose, I mean your objective or intention—
something toward which you are always striving.
Purpose is something bigger. It is the picture you
have of yourself—the kind of person you want to be
or the kind of life you want to lead.
Kenneth Blanchard and Norman Vincent Peale,
The Power of Ethical Management

The
Five
O'Clock
Club®

What Longevity Means to Your Career

by Lydia Bronte, author of *The Longevity Factor*

*"When I was fifty, I thought my life was over...
Little did I know that the best years of my life
were still ahead of me."*
Evelyn Nef, 80-year-old psychotherapist
who trained in her 60's

I n every era there have been a few people who lived to be unusually old, but who kept working—and were still good at what they did. We all know that Pablo Picasso and Marc Chagall continued to paint until their deaths at 92 and 97 respectively; and that classical guitarist Pablo Casals remained a master musician until his death at 96, despite arthritis.

Usually we rationalize the accomplishments of people like these by calling them exceptions— implying that perhaps their genius was also responsible for their lasting productivity.

But we won't be able to dismiss such late-life achievements as rarities much longer. One of the most astonishing changes that has ever taken place in human life has occurred during this century, although it went relatively unnoticed until a few years ago: people are living a lot longer.

The average life expectancy today in the United States is 29 years longer than at the turn of the century. These years have been added to middle age, not old age.

Recently we have begun to focus upon one aspect of this change—aging—because of the growing numbers of older people in our society. The big news, however, is not aging. It is longevity. And as it turns out, although we tend to confuse them, they are two quite different things.

Galloping Longevity

How many times do you say to yourself, "If only I had more time"? Chances are that you'll have it: up to thirty years' worth of extra time, and maybe more. **Longevity has increased during this century more dramatically than at any other time in recorded human history.**

In less than one hundred years, the length of adult life has doubled. We've gone from an average life expectancy of 47 to one of 76, and still climbing.

Something that happens over the span of one century may seem ploddingly slow in terms of an individual's day-to-day experience. By ordinary statistical standards, however, this change has taken place with the speed of a moon rocket.

Consider: from A.D. 1 to A.D. 1900, human beings gained about **1 1/2 years** of average life expectancy per century. By contrast, from 1900 to 1994, we have added **29 years**—almost three decades—to average life expectancy.

This is a stunning change. What is even more stunning is that it is continuing; in both 1993 and 1994, average life expectancy gained one year in the U.S.A. **We are nearing the point where we may add as much average life expectancy every year as former generations added in an entire century!**

The extra time starts to click in at around the age of 50. And to make it even better, even though you will live to an older chronological age, for reasons scientists don't yet understand, that extra time for most is **not** time spent in old age.

The Second Middle Age

As lifetimes have lengthened, the physical aging process has been slowed down or postponed. The three extra decades gained through longevity have really been added to the **middle** of our lives. It amounts to a "second middle age" between the end of the old-style "first middle age," 35 to 50, and the age at which we become physically old, which varies according to the individual.

The Long Careers Study

From 1987 to 1993, I conducted detailed life-history interviews with 150 people who continued to be active and to work during the second middle age and beyond the age of 65. Their ages ranged between 65 and 102, with the majority in

"If you can feel growth and development, you don't feel old. It's when you feel you can't learn anything or do anything new that it's the end of the road."
Shirley Brussell, Founder of Operation Able
at age 55 (now 74 and still its executive director)

their 70's and 80's. These long-lived Americans can be considered the pathfinder generation for those of us in our 30's, 40's, and 50's.

We have had an image of adult life based on the lives of our parents and grandparents, assuming a relatively short lifetime. Relying on this outdated notion is a little like trying to drive across the U.S.A. using a road map that was printed in 1930: the highway system isn't the same and even the landscape is different. Today we need a new "map" when thinking about adult life,

The Long Careers Study suggests that in order to make good use of this new life stage, all of us need to change radically the way we think about work.

There's no question that the length of your life has a connection to your career. The more you know now, the better you will be able to plan ahead for your worklife. If you've followed The Five O'Clock Club's suggestion and made a Forty-Year Plan, you may live to see every aspect of it come true—even if you're 50 right now.

New Horizons in Growth

As a result of this study, I am convinced that the developmental patterns of a long lifetime are different in many respects from those of a short lifetime. And the patterns of a long career are different from those of a short one.

Americans have a widespread belief that youth and the "first middle age" are the most creative periods of one's life and career.

For many years we have been told that the most vigorous and productive period is between 30 and 45. This idea was publicized around 1950 by Harvey Lehman, a scientist who calculated creative output in scientists, philosophers, artists, writers, and musicians—without, however, taking into account the possibility that the automatic ceiling of a short lifetime might have skewed the results.

The examples cited below are drawn from the careers of well-known people because of their recognition value. But the patterns hold true for average people too.

Multiple Career Peaks

The Long Careers Study participants showed astonishing differences in their periods of high achievement. Some of them did have early peaks of achievement, while others blossomed later or several times. For example: Dr. Linus Pauling made a discovery in his early 30's for which he subsequently won a Nobel Prize; Dr. Jonas Salk invented the polio vaccine in his late 30's to early 40's.

However, most of the people who had early peaks subsequently went on to have second and third peaks later in life. Pauling, for example, went on to make other scientific discoveries, and then in his late 40's took ten years to go around the world speaking on behalf of world peace, an effort for which he won a second Nobel Prize.

Next, Pauling began his path-breaking research on human nutrition and vitamins. Ultimately he played a key role both in educating the public about the value of vitamin and mineral supplements, and in persuading government agencies to acknowledge the importance of nutrition to health and to sponsor more research on the subject.

Early Sustained Peaks

The exceptions to the multiple-peak pattern were people who stayed in the same career and turned an early peak into a lifelong high plateau, like science fiction writer Isaac Asimov. Beginning with his first successes in his early 30's, Asimov built a career which helped shape the genre itself, developing science fiction into one of the most popular forms of contemporary literature. His productivity continued unabated until shortly before his death of heart failure at 72.

The Age-50 Gateway

There was another group of participants who began an extraordinary period of productivity at about the age of 50. **Almost half of the Study participants had a major career peak after age 50.**

This was a completely unexpected finding. In this pattern, the individual seems to be serving a

46

"You can't retire from life—or from work, in a true sense. Work is something you do because you have internal needs. I can no more help working than I can help breathing."
Max Lerner, author, columnist, teacher, lecturer, active until his death at age 89

---

kind of apprenticeship during the first thirty years of working life—accumulating experience in a way that leads to a massive upward shift in achievement around 50.

Culinary expert Julia Child is a striking example. Forced to abandon her first career because she married a fellow civil servant, Paul Child, she searched for several years to find another field. Finally she discovered French cooking by chance, when her husband was assigned to France as a USIA officer.

Starting at about the age of 35, Child trained as a chef, founded her own cooking school, and worked on a cookbook, *Mastering the Art of French Cooking.* In 1960, when Child was almost 50, the couple moved back to the U.S.A., where the book was published. A chance publicity appearance on television led to her famous TV series. The peak of Child's career has lasted into her early 80's, and shows no signs of slowing down.

A slightly different pattern was that of John W. Gardner, who was president of Carnegie Corporation of New York. When he was in his late 40's, he was stimulated by the discussions of an education commission of which he was a member. Gardner started writing down his ideas. He eventually developed them into a small book, *Excellence: Can We Be Excellent and Equal Too?* Decades later the book still forms the basis for many popular business books, by Tom Peters and others.

Gardner went on to make another leap by leaving his comfortable Carnegie position in his 50's to become Secretary of HEW in Washington. Next he founded two public-interest organizations. He made his most recent career change at 79 when he accepted a professorship at the Stanford University Business School. Now in his early 80's, he is teaching students more than half a century younger than he is.

The Age-65 Gateway
<u>About one-third of the participants had major career peaks after age 65;</u> 5 percent had their **highest** peak of achievement after age 65.

Most of these people found their real vocation later in life. They had no intention or expectation of becoming prominent; they were simply following their own developmental pattern.

Take, for example, Maggie Kuhn, who had a stable and respectable career as a church organizer. What changed her life was her mandatory retirement at the age of 65. Several other women she knew were also forced out of their careers.

Kuhn and her friends were furious at the discrimination they had experienced. They felt that if they had been men, they undoubtedly would have been offered several more years of full-time work, or consulting contracts. But as women they were simply ushered out unceremoniously.

They decided to form a discussion group to figure out what to do with the rest of their lives. By a series of fortuitous circumstances, their little association ended up becoming the Gray Panthers, a nationwide activist organization.

The Long Growth Curve
Finally, there was a group of people who had "long growth curves." This means that they moved upward at a relatively steady pace throughout the first 30 or 40 years of their worklives. The progression ended in a pinnacle of achievement after age 50 or after 65.

The late Norman Cousins, for example, served for decades as the well-known and greatly loved editor of *The Saturday Review of Literature.* In his 50's he had an almost-fatal illness which stimulated him to write a book, *Anatomy of an Illness* (1979). Its tremendous popularity led him to a major career change at the age of 64: he became an adjunct professor of medicine at the UCLA Medical School.

Until his death at the age of 76, Cousins helped design experiments on the relationship of the mind to physical health. His brilliant work with his medical colleagues at UCLA laid a solid scientific foundation for mind-body health research.

Cousins' career had a steady ascent, with new periods of growth triggered by his response to experience. This proactive stance towards one's own life was displayed by most of the Study participants.

Progressive Patterns

Finally, there were other types of progressions in the careers of some Study participants. Many participants progressed from being employees, to becoming managers or administrators, to becoming entrepreneurs. This pattern suggests increased learning about administrative functions, and the growing desire to shape the course of an organization, culminating in the creation of one's own organization.

Another progression was a change in geographical order of magnitude: moving from local concerns, to state or regional, then to national and finally to an international level of interest. Esther Peterson, former advisor on consumer affairs to Presidents Johnson and Carter, started her career as a local union organizer, moved up to state and regional positions, worked on a national level, and at 87 is now the Consumer's Union's international representative to the U.N.

What About the Future?

In a long-lived society, inevitably more people will make career changes during the course of a lifetime, simply because they have more time available in which they can master and grow beyond a given job or career. Of course, not everyone will have multiple careers; some will still stay in the same career all their lives.

A cause for real concern is the paradox that at a time when human beings are living longer than ever—and remaining youthful and in good health—American corporations and businesses are going in the opposite direction. They are downsizing and early-retiring people out of the workforce in their 50's or even their late 40's.

This is a dysfunctional trend in a society where there are so many people who may want to continue working even beyond the conventional retirement age, and who have much skill, experience, and knowledge to contribute.

It also raises the question of how effective a company can be if a large segment of our population is over 50, while the majority of the company's employees are under 50. A workforce that is predominantly younger may not understand or be able to serve effectively the needs of a mature consumer group.

It seems to me that there must be some correction in the negative attitude of corporations towards maturity if companies wish to remain viable. The research of University of Pennsylvania psychologist Frank Landy has shown that mature workers play roles that are different from those of younger workers, and that a workforce with a broad spectrum of ages functions better than a workforce with a narrow age spectrum.

Another related change is the disappearance of the longstanding "psychological contract" of loyalty between the worker and the corporation, which so long was a foundation for American worklife.

For the most part, **the people in the Long Careers Study who were able to continue doing work that they loved at older ages had made themselves independent**. Their identity as workers did not depend on a company but on their own skills and expertise. Frequently they had an individual practice—as a lawyer, artist, doctor, writer, etc.—or they formed their own business.

In a long-lived society, until the prevailing age prejudice has diminished or disappeared, every one of us should have as a goal to achieve the kind of professional, psychological, and financial independence that will enable us to continue working for as long (or short) a time as we choose.

Then perhaps we will be able to say—as Norman Cousins remarked when he was in his early 70's—"I find that now I'm using everything I've ever learned—all of it together at the same time, and more effectively than I could ever have done at any earlier time in my life."

Lydia Bronte, Ph.D., is the author of
*The Longevity Factor: The New Reality of Long Careers
and How They Are Leading to Richer Lives,*
Harper/Collins. This piece originally appeared in
The Five O'Clock News

PART TWO

DECIDING WHAT YOU WANT

START BY UNDERSTANDING YOURSELF

*You are a child of the universe no less than the trees
and the stars; you have a right to be here.
And whether or not it is clear to you, no doubt the
universe is unfolding as it should.*
Desiderata

Change As Opportunity

Don't expect to hold on to the way things have worked for you in the past. Get on with the new way the world is operating. You cannot stop the changes, but you *can* choose the way you will respond. You can see change as a threat to resist—or an opportunity to move forward.

Change represents danger to you when you choose to resist it. While your energy goes into trying to keep your situation the same, you will become more dissatisfied as you see others taking advantage of changes.

You can use change to your advantage if you decide to see it as a source of opportunity. Then, it won't be so threatening. You will reduce your chances of being run over. You will be running your own life.

To look at change as a source of opportunity, become more aware of the changes taking place around you— the events that can affect you and your job. Decide which are best for you and how to take advantage of those that interest you. The pace of change in today's economy can be overwhelming—unless you can assess changes more objectively. In doing so, you will have more control *over the way you respond.*

An Internal Reference Point

How can you make the most of changes? How can you decide which ones bode well for you and which ones bode ill? You need a stable, internal point of reference—a clear picture of what you need to feel satisfied with your job and with your life. You can measure a changing situation against your list of the *elements* you require, to decide if a change is in your favor or not. You can perhaps alter the

situation to suit you, or get out of there at the earliest point.

To feel in control and actually to *be* in control of your life, make choices based on your inner direction. With so many changes swirling around, the only stabilizing point must be inside of you. Nothing outside can be your anchor. This book has exercises to help you determine your inner direction.

A Career Counselor Cannot Decide For You

*We can help one another find out the meaning of life. . . .
But in the last analysis, each is responsible
for "finding himself."*
Thomas Merton
No Man Is an Island

Let's be practical about it: a career counselor cannot possibly know all the options out there for you. There are so many choices and the world is changing so fast, how *could* one person know the answer that is right for you? And when things change again, as they will, will you expect a career counselor to tell you what to do then?

What you do with your life is *your* decision. A counselor cannot decide for you, but can only *help* you decide. Blaming someone else for your lack of progress can be a reflection of your attitude about life. Do you basically feel you control what happens to you? Or do you feel what happens is essentially in the hands of others? When you blame others, you give up your power. You are saying that someone else is deciding what will happen to you. When you do not blame others, you have more power: you are taking control over your own life.

Those who take responsibility for their own lives do better than those who expect others to solve their problems.

Accepting responsibility means, generally, not blaming others for your situation. You accept that your choices have gotten you where you are. You are in control. You can make new choices to head your life where you want.

Why Use a Career Coach?

Nobody owns a job, nobody owns a market,
nobody owns a product. Somebody out there
can always take it away from you.
Ronald E. Compton, president/chairman, Aetna, as
quoted in *The New York Times*, March 1, 1992

In this changing marketplace, increasingly we
all have to be out there selling ourselves. This is
causing people a great deal of understandable
stress. Most of us would rather just do our jobs and
trust that we will be treated fairly. Since we cannot
depend on this, some people have made a career
coach a normal part of their lives—as normal as
having a regular tune-up on your car or an annual
physical. They go to their coach not only when they
are conducting a job search or when they have
problems, but perhaps once or twice a year for a
checkup.

An important component of the career assessment
process is to help clients accept themselves:
their strengths as well as what
does not come naturally to them.
Barry Lustig
Director of The Professional Development Institute,
Federation Employment and Guidance Services, N.Y.

Clients working with a career coach learn what
works for them personally and what does not,
come to better understand the kinds of environ-
ments in which they should be working (bosses,
corporate cultures, pace, and so on), learn how to be
more effective in their work relationships (bosses,
peers, subordinates, clients), learn how to balance
their lives more effectively, and also lay the ground-
work for the next career move they may have to
make. They talk about their long-term career goals
and the steps they need to take to reach them—or
perhaps simply to stay even. They make sure they
are doing what they must to develop their careers
as the economy changes, such as getting specific
experience, taking courses, or joining organizations.

Over time, your coach gets to know you, just as
your family doctor gets to know you, and can warn
you against things that may cause you problems, or
advise you about things you could be doing next.

Just as a family doctor would want to give you a
complete physical if you are to become his patient,
so, too, your coach would want to give you an
assessment to find out as much as possible about
you. I tell clients that if I don't know enough about
them, it is as if they were someone on the street
coming up to me to ask advice. I need to know
something about them so I can be a real coach.

If you decide to use a private coach, use someone who charges by the hour. Do not pay a huge
up-front fee. After you have worked with the
counselor a number of times, assess your relationship with that person. There should be a good
personality fit between you and your counselor. For
example, some counselors are very intense, while
others have a softer approach. If the relationship is
not good, or if the meetings damage your sense of
self-worth, go to someone else.

For your part, make sure you are willing to
make the necessary commitment. If you go only for
one hour to have the counselor handle an emer-
gency you are facing, do not expect that counselor
to come to know very much about you. If you
decide to use a counselor, you are likely to learn
more about the wonderful person you are, so you
can figure out how you fit into this changing world.
You will have increased self-esteem and increased
effectiveness.

One of the most important aptitudes we all
have to offer is our personality.
Barry Lustig

Develop a Vision;
Make a Commitment

The field cannot well be seen from within the field.
Ralph Waldo Emerson

Take a stand. Decide where you want to head,
and go for it. You'll be happier because you'll have
a goal and you'll work toward it. Work will no
longer be "work," but an activity that brings pleasure, pride, and a sense of accomplishment, and
that carries out your vision.

When you know yourself and make a commit-

> *You can never enslave somebody who knows who he is.*
> Alex Haley

ment, things become clearer. You act more decisively, have less stress, and cope better with the progress of your career and the changes around you. Negative things will not bother you as much. The direction will not be coming from someone else, but from inside you.

Without commitment, we are wanderers without roots in a rapidly changing world. We feel a lack of meaning in our lives.

Commitment means accepting that you are responsible for your own career direction. It means *choosing* what you want to do in this changing society without losing your inner bearings.

Looking for Where You Fit In

For I know the plans I have for you, declares the Lord,
plans to prosper you and not to harm you,
plans to give you a hope and a future.
Jeremiah 29:11

We each fit in. What you're looking for is *where* you fit in. As you learn more about what is inside you, as well as what is outside, you will progressively change your situation to suit yourself better, and so you will also fit better into the world.

To grow with the world, know what you want and what you want to offer. Knowing yourself, in the context of career development, means knowing how you prefer to operate, what you like to do, and what you can do well. Knowing what you want to offer means stepping outside yourself to see what the world values. Take what you want to offer and market it.

Don't be *too* specific about what you want. If you are open to new opportunities, surprising things can happen. A large number of jobs are created with a certain person in mind. A job created with you in mind would probably be more satisfying than one in which you would have to mold yourself to fit a rigid job description. You would enjoy your job more and do better because you would be doing what you want.

What are the chances of having a job created to suit you? If you don't know what would suit you, chances are slim. Having definite ideas increases

your chances of finding such a job, or even of changing your present job to better suit your goals. Opportunities come along all the time. You won't recognize them unless you know what you are looking for.

We change the world and the world changes us. As we grow, we are developing ourselves—in relation to the world. We are each trying to know what we want and how to get it, while we are also trying to understand and fit into a changing world. It is a lifelong process, but a happy one. It is a process of seeing change as an opportunity while accepting the limitations of the world.

CASE STUDY: HENRY
Aiming Too Low

Henry, an executive of about forty-five, had just been fired, and I was asked to be his counselor. Henry said he already had a clear idea of what he wanted to do next—something that was quite in demand—loan workouts (when loans go bad, he would try to salvage them). Henry could certainly get a job like that, and quickly, but I felt as though I didn't know him at all, so I asked if we could do a few exercises. If I understood him better, I would be in a better position to coach him.

In his Seven Stories (an exercise you will do in this book), Henry stated that he was proud that he had grown up in a tiny Midwestern town (there were only sixty people in his entire high school), had gotten into Harvard, and graduated very high in his class.

Where was that little boy now? What had caused him to settle for a loan workout position that would have been right for lots of *other* people? I told Henry that I thought he could do better than that. I asked him to aim to find a job that would make him so proud it would wind up on his *future* Seven Stories list.

Within two and a half months, Henry had landed a job that was better than anything he had ever dreamed possible. At an excellent salary, he became a very senior executive in a major corporation. Henry was so proud, he beamed. He's still

It is the first of all problems for a man to find out what kind of work
he is to do in this universe.
Thomas Carlyle, *Sartor Resartus*

there now and doing very well.

You Need Information
—Out in the World

You need information about yourself and about the changing world of work. Find an optimal fit by matching what you learn about yourself against what you learn about the world.

If you're like most people, at least part of your career plan was decided by someone else. If that decision was not best for you, something has to change. You must either change to fit the job, or you must change the job to fit you. If you have often changed yourself to suit the job you were in, you may not know what you want. Soon we will help you figure out what you would enjoy doing in a job.

You cannot find out about yourself in a vacuum. Go out and test your ideas about yourself against what others think of you. That's the only healthy way. With more knowledge about the world, and with a clearer sense of our place in it, options will appear that we never noticed before.

The Steps to Finding Your Place

The basic steps to finding your place are covered in greater detail in the other chapters in this section. Spend as much or as little time as you want on each. The process can go on forever. Do what you want now, and do more later.

Step 1: Determine what you want. Develop a long-term view of yourself—a guiding light that can see you through a number of jobs. In fact, you could develop a view that will see you through your entire life.

Step 2: Decide what you want to offer. Notice that I say what you *want* to offer—not what you *have to* offer. You may be tempted to offer what you have been offering all along. Although a pragmatic choice may see you through a job transition, it is more important to decide what you *want* to offer. If you offer things you do not want to do, you increase your chances of *doing* things you do not want to do.

I looked at a secretary's résumé. It mentioned heavy phone work as one of her duties. When I asked her if she liked phone work, she responded, "I hate phone work." I advised her to remove it from her résumé, or someone would say, "That's just what we need: someone who can do heavy phone work."

Of course, every job has parts you don't like. In fact, you may decide to offer such an aspect as one of your strong skills until you develop yourself in the areas on which you want to focus. That's often a good approach.

I'll use my own life as an example. I started out in computers as a way of working my way through school. After learning so much about them, I have always used computers to my advantage even though working with them was not central on my list of life goals. Sometimes the fact that I knew computers gave me an edge over other job hunters. While I didn't want working with computers to be a central part of my job, the skill has been a handy one to offer.

In this step you will develop a menu of everything you have to offer, and then you can decide to offer what you want.

Step 3: A combination of the results of Steps 1 and 2. You'll do best in a job that relies on some of your strengths and experiences, but also provides you with some growth toward your goals. Bring something to the job. This book will help you select a job target that considers both.

CASE STUDY: AARON
Knowing Where He Wants to End Up

> *Having gifts that differ according to the*
> *grace given to us, let us use them.*
> Romans 12:6

Aaron has been in corporate marketing for eight years. Through the Seven Stories exercise and his Forty-Year Plan (which you will see in the next chapter), he developed a long-term view of himself: the head of a five-hundred-person public-sector-related agency or organization, such as the World Wildlife Fund.

Now that he knows where he wants to end up,

he can work backward to figure out how he could get there. To head up such a large organization, he has two choices: he can start it from scratch, or he can take over an existing organization. Aaron decided that five years from now, he would prefer to become the head of an existing fifty-person organization and expand it to a five-hundred-person organization.

But how can he go from where he is now to becoming the head of a fifty-person organization? What he has to offer is his corporate marketing background. Therefore, his next logical step is to try to get a marketing job in a not-for-profit organization that is similar to the one he would eventually like to head up. That way, his next job will be one that positions him well for the moves after that, and increases his chance of getting where he wants to go.

The Benefits of Knowing What You Want

As I have stressed so far, you are responsible for your own career development. Decide what you want, rather than hoping someone will think about it for you. The next chapter will get you started.

Now, I can look at you, Mr. Loomis, and see you a man who done forgot his song. Forgot how to sing it. A fellow forget that and he forget who he is. Forget how he's supposed to mark down life.
August Wilson
Joe Turner's Come and Gone

America has entered the age of the contingent or temporary worker, of the consultant or subcontractor, of the just-in-time work force—fluid, flexible, disposable. This is the future. Its message is this: You are on your own. For good (sometimes) and ill (often), the workers of the future will constantly have to sell their skills, invent new relationships with employers who must, themselves, change and adapt constantly in order to survive in a ruthless global market.
Lance Morrow, "The Temping of America,"
Time, 1993

God grant me the serenity to accept the things I cannot change, the courage to change the things I can, and the wisdom to know the difference.
"Serenity Prayer"

Alice: *"Will you tell me please, which way I ought to go from here?"*
Cat: *"That depends a good deal on where you want to get to."*
Alice: *"I don't care much where—so long as I get somewhere."*
Cat: *"Oh, you're sure to do that if only you walk long enough."*

Lewis Carroll
Alice in Wonderland

. . . we have to create a new organizational architecture flexible enough to adapt to change. We want an organization that can evolve, that can modify itself as technology, skills, competitors, and the entire business change.
Paul Allaire, CEO, XEROX Corporation

Let me listen to me and not to them.
Gertrude Stein

What seems different in yourself;
that's the rare thing you possess.
The one thing that gives each of us his worth,
and that's just what we try to suppress.
And we claim to love life.
André Gide

Looking Ahead
—A Career Instead of a Job

If you don't decide where you want to go, you may wind up drifting from one company to another whenever you're dissatisfied, with pretty much the same job each time. Even if you decide that you want to continue doing what you're doing right now, that's a goal in itself and may be difficult to achieve.

The first step in career management is goal setting. There are a lot of processes involved in the goal-setting area. But the one considered most central is that by which a person examines his or her past accomplishments, looking at the strongest and most enjoyable skills.

This process is not only the one favored by counselors, it is also the one most often used by successful people. In reading the biographies of such people, I see again and again how they established their goals by identifying those things they enjoy doing and also do well. This process of identifying your "enjoyable accomplishments" is the most important one you can go through.

What Successful People Do

When Steven Jobs, the founder of Apple Computers, was fired by John Sculley, the man he had brought in to run the company, he felt as though he had lost everything. Apple had been his life. Now he had lost not only his job, but his company. People no longer felt the need to return his phone calls. He did what a lot of us would do. He got depressed. But then:

> *Confused about what to do next . . . he [Jobs] put himself through an exercise that management psychologists employ with clients unsure about their life goals. It was a little thing, really. It was just a list. A list of all the things that mattered most to Jobs during his ten years at Apple. "Three things jumped off that piece of paper, three things that were really important to me," says Jobs.*
> Michael Meyer, *The Alexander Complex*

The exercise Steven Jobs went through is essen-

Make no little plans; they have no magic to stir men's blood and probably themselves will not be realized. Make big plans; aim high in hope and work.
Daniel Burnham

tially what you will do in the Seven Stories exercise. The threads that ran through his stories formed the impetus for his next great drive: the formation of NeXT computers. If the Seven Stories exercise is good enough for Steven Jobs, maybe it's good enough for you.

"Successful managers," says Charles Garfield, head of Performance Services, Inc., in Berkeley, California, "go with their preferences." They search for work that is important to them, and when they find it they pursue it with a passion.

Lester Korn, Chairman of Korn, Ferry, notes in his book *The Success Profile*: "Few executives know, or can know, exactly what they aspire to until they have been in the work force for a couple of years. It takes that long to learn enough about yourself to know what you can do well and what will make you happy. The trick is to merge the two into a goal, then set off in pursuit of it."

This book will help you decide what you want to do in your next job as well as in the long run. You will become more clear about the experiences you have enjoyed most and may like to repeat. You will also examine your interests and values, and look at past positions to analyze what satisfied you and what did not. In addition, you will look farther ahead (through your Forty-Year Plan) to see if some driving dream may influence what you will want to do in the short term. I did my Forty-Year Plan about fifteen years ago, and the vision I had of my future still drives me today.

Knowing where you would like to wind up broadens the kinds of jobs you would be interested in today.

Look at it this way:

A B   C

The line represents your life. Right now, you are at A. Your next job is B. If you look only at your past to decide what to do next, your next job is limited by what you have already done. For example, if you have been in finance and accounting for the past fifteen years, and you base your next move on your past, your next job is likely to be in finance or accounting.

If you know that at C you would like to wind up as vice president of finance and administration, new possibilities open up. Think of all the areas you would manage:

Finance	Operations
Administration	Personnel
Accounting	Computers

Experience in any one of these would advance your career in the right direction. For example, you may decide to get some computer experience. Without the benefit of a Forty-Year Plan, a move to computers might look like the start of a career in computers, but *you* know it's just one more assignment that leads to your long-term goal. You'll keep your plan in mind and take jobs and assignments that will continually position you for the long run. For example, in the computer area, you may focus on personnel or administrative systems, two areas that fit your goal. Then your computer job will be more than a job. You will work hard for your employer, but you will also know why you are there—you are using your job as a stepping stone to something bigger and better.

Happy in Your Work

People are happy when they are working toward their goals. When they get diverted—or don't know what their goals are—they are unhappy. Many people are unhappy in their jobs because they don't know where they are going. People without goals are more irked by petty daily problems than are those with goals.

To control your life, know where you are going, and be ready for your next move—in case the ax falls on you. When you take that next job, continue to manage your career. Companies rarely build career paths for their employees any more. Make your own way. There are plenty of jobs for those who are willing to learn and to change with the times.

Deciding What You Want: Selecting Your Job Targets

It may sound surprising when I say, on the basis of my own clinical experience as well as that of my psychological and psychiatric colleagues, "that the chief problem of people in the middle decade of the twentieth century is emptiness." By that I mean not only that many people do not know what they want; they often do not have any clear idea of what they feel.
Rollo May, *Man's Search for Himself*

In the Nazi death camps where Victor Frankl learned the principle of proactivity, he also learned the importance of purpose, of meaning in life. The essence of "logotherapy," the philosophy he later developed and taught, is that many so-called mental and emotional illnesses are really symptoms of an underlying sense of meaninglessness or emptiness. Logotherapy eliminates the emptiness by helping the individual to detect his unique meaning, his mission in life.
Once you have that sense of mission, you have the essence of your own proactivity. You have the vision and the values which direct your life. You have the basic direction from which you set long- and short-term goals.
Stephen R. Covey, *The Seven Habits of Highly Effective People*

To have a great purpose to work for, a purpose larger than ourselves, is one of the secrets of making life significant; for then the meaning and worth of the individual overflow his personal borders, and survive his death.
Will Durant

Studies have shown that up to 85 percent of all American workers are unhappy in their jobs. They feel that they would be happier elsewhere, but they don't know where. After going through an evaluation process (assessment), many decide that their present situation is not so bad after all, and that no change is required. Some may find that a small change is all that is needed. On the other hand, some may want to make a major career change.

The exercises in this book will help you assess your work life so that you can better understand the situations in which you perform your best and are happiest. And, since we will *all* have to change jobs—and probably even careers—more often in the future, we should get to know ourselves better.

Assessment is helpful even if you do not want to change jobs. You will learn more about the way you operate and how to improve the situation where you are currently working.

Getting Started

The following exercises help you identify the aspects of your jobs that have been satisfying and dissatisfying. You will know which parts need to be changed and which parts need to stay the same.

You may do certain exercises and skip others. But don't skip the Seven Stories Exercise, and try to do the Forty-Year Plan. If you have had problems with bosses, you need to discover what those problems were and analyze them. Or perhaps examining your values may be an issue at this time. Your insights about yourself from the Seven Stories Exercise will be the primary source for your accomplishment statements, help you interview better, and serve as a template for selecting the right job.

After you do the exercises, brainstorm a number of possible job targets. Then research each target to find out what the job possibilities are for someone like you.

This workbook will guide you through the entire process.

Consider Your History

If you have enjoyed certain jobs, attempt to understand exactly what about them you enjoyed. This will increase your chances of replicating the

. . . and then I decided that to turn your life around
you had to start from the inside.
Ethan Canin, *Emperor of the Air*

---

enjoyable aspects.

For example, an accounting manager will probably not be happy in just any accounting-management job. If what he really enjoyed was helping the business manager make the business profitable, and if this thread of helping reappears in his enjoyable experiences (Seven Stories Exercise), then he would be unhappy in a job where he was *not* helping.

If, however, his enjoyment repeatedly came from resolving messy situations, then he needs a job that has messes to be resolved and the promise of more messes to come.

Furthermore, if he wants to do again those things he enjoyed, he can state them in the summary on his résumé. For instance:

Accounting Manager
Serve as right-hand to Business Manager, consistently improving company's profitability.
or
Accounting Manager
A troubleshooter and turn-around manager.

The Results of Assessment:
Job Targets—*then* a Résumé

A job target contains three elements:

- industry or company size (small, medium or large company);
- position or function; and
- geographic location.

If a change is required, a change in any one of these may be enough.

Geographic Location

Let's take Joseph, for example. Joseph had been in Trusts and Estates for twenty-five years, and had taken early retirement. He didn't know what he wanted to do next, but he knew that it had to be "completely different."

Joseph did all of the exercises in this section. I also gave him a personality test, and did "confidential phone calls" on his behalf—a process by which I called people who know him well and asked them about him. I assured them that I would compile the results and not tell him who said what.

Based on all of this information, we developed a number of targets for him to investigate. We also developed a résumé that positioned him for these new targets.

Joseph conducted a campaign to get interviews in each of his three target areas. However, once he clearly looked at these new fields, his old field began to look more appealing. (This happened to me years ago when I desperately wanted museum work—until I actually looked into it and found it wasn't for me.)

Joseph decided to stay in his old field—but on the West Coast rather than the East—because he is bothered by the climate in the East and because many of his old friends had moved West. This change in location would get him out of the old rut and give him a new lease on life. But it was a relatively minor change compared with what he originally had in mind.

Industry or Company Size

Many unhappy people may be in essentially the right position but in the wrong industry. A minor adjustment may be all that is needed.

A person could be a lawyer, but it makes a great deal of difference whether that person is a lawyer in a corporation, in a stuffy law firm, or in a not-for-profit organization. A change in industry may end the dissatisfaction.

By the same token, moving from a large company to a small one—or vice versa—could increase your satisfaction.

Position or Function

On the other hand, a new field may be what is called for. My own career is a case in point. I had a successful career in computers, advertising and the financial end of business, with a respectable amount of prestige and money. However, when I did the Seven Stories Exercise (to identify those things I enjoyed doing and also did well), I discovered that only one of my "stories" related to my work life. The message was clear: my true enjoyment was coming from those things I was doing on the outside, such as running The Five O'Clock Club and other entrepreneurial ventures. I had a choice to make:

- I could stay in the lucrative field I was in, and continue to do on the side those things that gave me the most satisfaction; or
- I could move my career in the direction of those things I found most satisfying.

Being risk-averse, I was reluctant to give up the twenty-plus years I had invested in a business career for a profession that might have proved to be financially or otherwise unsatisfying. I decided to hedge my bets. I took a job as the chief financial officer of a major outplacement firm, and *also* headed up one of their career counseling offices. That way, I could slide into the new career, or go back into the old one if I was unhappy.

Many major career changes are made this way. A person *somehow* gets some experience in the new field while holding on to the old one. In general, it is relatively easy to get experience in the new field if you really want it.

Looking Ahead—A Career Instead of a Job

Assessment will help you decide what you want to do in your next job as well as in the long run. You will become clearer about the kind of boss you work best with and about all the other things that are important to you in a job.

Through your Forty-Year Plan, you will have the opportunity to look ahead to see whether there is some hidden dream that may dramatically influence what you will want to do in both the short and long run. I did my own Forty-Year Plan about fifteen years ago, and the vision I had of my future still drives me today, even though that vision was actually rather vague at the time. Knowing where you would like to wind up in ten, twenty, thirty, or forty years can broaden your ideas about the kinds of jobs you would be interested in today.

The Forty-Year Plan is a powerful exercise. It will help you think long-term and put things into perspective.

The Seven Stories Exercise is equally powerful. Without it, many job hunters develop stilted descriptions of what they have accomplished. But the exercise frees you up to brag a little, and express things very differently. The results will add life to your résumé and your interviews, and also dra-

matically increase your self-confidence.

No Easy Way

It would be nice if you could simply take a test that would tell you what you should be. Unfortunately there is no such sure-fire test. But fortunately, in today's rapidly changing world, we are allowed to be many things: we can be a doctor, a lawyer *and* an Indian chief. We have an abundance of choices.

A Clear Direction

People are happy when they are working toward their goals. When they get diverted from their goals, they are unhappy. Businesses are the same. When they get diverted from their goals (for instance, because of a major litigation or a threatened hostile takeover), they too are unhappy. Life has a way of sneaking up and distracting both individuals and businesses. Many people are unhappy in their jobs because they don't know where they are going.

A happy person going toward his or her goal.

An unhappy person being deflected from his or her goal.

People without goals are more irked by petty problems on their jobs. Those with goals are less bothered because they have bigger plans. To control your life, you have to know where you are going, and be ready for your next move—in case the ax falls on you.

Even after you take that next job, continue to manage your career. Companies rarely build career paths for their employees any more. Make your own way.

Your health is bound to be affected if, day after day, you say the opposite of what you feel, if you grovel before what you dislike and rejoice at what brings you nothing but misfortune.   Boris Pasternak, *Dr. Zhivago*

Wherever I went, I couldn't help noticing, the place fell apart. Not that I was ever a big enough wheel in the machine to precipitate its destruction on my own. But that they let me—and other drifters like me— in the door at all was an early warning signal. Alarm bells should have rung.   Michael Lewis, *Liar's Poker*

My illness helped me to see that what was missing in a society is what was missing in me: a little heart, a lot of brotherhood.

The 80's were about acquiring wealth, power, prestige. I acquired more . . . than most. But you can acquire all you want and still feel empty. . . . I don't know who will lead us through the 90's, but they must be made to speak to this spiritual vacuum at the heart of American society, this tumor of the soul.
Lee Atwater, formerly of the Republican National Committee, shortly before he died, *Life* magazine, February, 1991

I've never been poor, only broke.
Being poor is a frame of mind.
Being broke is only a temporary situation.
Mike Todd

Natural talent, intelligence, a wonderful education— none of these guarantees success. Something else is needed: the sensitivity to understand what other people want and the willingness to give it to them. Worldly success depends on pleasing others. No one is going to win fame, recognition, or advancement just because he or she thinks it's deserved.
Someone else has to think so too.
John Luther

Aim so High You'll Never Be Bored

The greatest waste of our natural resources is the number of people who never achieve their potential. Get out of that slow lane. Shift into that fast lane. If you think you can't, you won't. If you think you can, there's a good chance you will. Even making the effort will make you feel like a new person. Reputations are made by searching for things that can't be done and doing them. Aim low: boring. Aim high: soaring.

(c) United Technologies Corporation, June 1981.

Exercises to Analyze Your Past and Present: The Seven Stories Exercise

*The direction of change to seek is not
in our four dimensions: it is
getting deeper into what you are, where you are, like
turning up the volume on the amplifier.*
Thaddeus Golas, *Lazy Man's Guide to Enlightenment*

In this exercise, you will examine your accomplishments, looking at your strongest and most enjoyable skills. The core of most counseling exercises is some version of the Seven Stories exercise. A counselor may give you lots of tests and exercises, but this one requires *work* on your part and will yield the most important results. An interest or personality test is not enough. There is no easy way. Remember, busy executives take the time to complete this exercise—if it's good enough for them, it's good enough for you.

Do not skip the Seven Stories exercise. It will provide you with information for your career direction, your résumé, and your interviews. After you do the exercise, brainstorm about a number of possible job targets. Then research each target to find out what the job possibilities are for someone like you.

If you're like most people, you have never taken the time to sort out the things you're good at and also are motivated to accomplish. As a result, you probably don't use these talents as completely or as effectively as you could. Too often, we do things to please someone else or to survive in a job. Then we get stuck in a rut—that is, we're *always* trying to please someone else or are *always* trying to survive in a job. We lose sight of what could satisfy us, and work becomes drudgery rather than fun. When we become so enmeshed in survival or in trying to please others, it may be difficult to figure out what we would rather be doing.

When you uncover your motivated skills, you'll be better able to identify jobs that allow you to use them, and recognize other jobs that don't quite fit the bill. "Motivated skill"" are patterns that run through our lives. Since they are skills from which we get satisfaction, we'll find ways to do them even if we don't get to do them at work. We still might not know what these skills are—for us, they're just something we do, and we take them for granted.

Tracking down these patterns takes some thought. The payoff is that our motivated skills do not change. They run throughout our lives and indicate what will keep us motivated for the rest of our lives.

*One's prime is elusive. . . . You must be on the alert to recognize your prime
at whatever time of life it may occur.*
Muriel Spark, *The Prime of Miss Jean Brodie*

The Seven Stories Approach: Background

This technique for identifying what people do
well and enjoy doing has its roots in the work of
Bernard Haldane, who, in his job with the U.S.
government forty-five years ago, helped to determine assignments for executives entering the
armed forces. The Seven Stories (or enjoyable
accomplishments) approach, now quite common,
was taught to me by George Hafner, who used to
work for Haldane.

The exercise is this: make a list of all the enjoyable accomplishments of your life, those things you
enjoyed doing *and also* did well. List at least twenty-
five enjoyable accomplishments from all parts of
your life: work, from your early career up to the
present, volunteering, hobbies; your school years. It
doesn't matter how old you were or what other
people thought about these accomplishments, and
it doesn't matter whether you got paid for doing
them.

Examine those episodes that gave you a sense of
accomplishment. Episodes from your childhood
are important, too, because they took place when
you were less influenced by trying to please others.

You are asked to name twenty-five accomplishments so you will not be too judgmental—just list
anything that occurs to you. Expect this exercise to
take you four or five days. Most people carry
around a piece of paper so they can jot down things
as they occur to them. When you have twenty-five,
select the seven that are most important to you by
however you define important. Then rank them: list
the most important first, and so on.

Starting with your first story, write a paragraph
about each accomplishment. Then find out what
your accomplishments have in common. If you are
having trouble doing the exercises, ask a friend to
help you talk them through. Friends tend to be
more objective and will probably point out
strengths you never realized.

You will probably be surprised. For example,
you may be especially good interacting with
people, but it's something you've always done and
therefore take for granted. This may be a thread
that runs through your life and may be one of your
motivated skills. It *may* be that you'll be unhappy in
a job that doesn't allow you to deal with people.

When I did the Seven Stories exercise, one of the
first stories I listed was from when I was ten years
old, when I wrote a play to be put on by the kids in
the neighborhood. I rehearsed everyone, sold
tickets to the adults for two cents apiece, and served
cookies and milk with the proceeds. You might say
that my direction as a "general manager"—running
the whole show, thinking things up, getting everybody working together—was set in the fourth
grade. I saw these traits over and over again in each
of my stories.

After I saw those threads running through my
life, it became easy for me to see what elements a job
must have to satisfy me. When I interview for a job,
I can find out in short order whether it addresses
my motivated skills. If it doesn't, I won't be as
happy as I could be, even though I *may decide to take
the job as an interim step toward a long-term goal.* The
fact is, people won't do as well in the long run in
jobs that don't satisfy their motivated skills.

Sometimes I don't pay attention to my own
motivated skills, and I wind up doing things I
regret. For example, in high school I scored the
highest in the state in math. I was as surprised as
everyone else, but I felt I finally had some direction
in my life. I felt I had to use it to do something
constructive. When I went to college, I majored in
math. I almost flunked because I was bored with it.
The fact is that I didn't enjoy math, I was simply
good at it.

There are lots of things we're good at, but they
may not be the same things we really enjoy. The
trick is to find those things we are good at, enjoy
doing, and feel a sense of accomplishment from
doing.

To sum up: Discovering your motivated skills is
the first step in career planning. I was a general
manager when I was ten, but I didn't realize it. I'm a
general manager now, and I love it. In between, I've
done some things that have helped me toward my
long-range goals, and other things that have not
helped at all.

... be patient toward all that is unsolved in your heart and try to love the questions themselves like locked rooms and like books that are written in a foreign tongue.
Rainer Maria Rilke, *Letters to a Young Poet*

It is important to realize that the Seven Stories exercise will *not* tell you exactly which job you should have, but the *elements* to look for in a job that you will find satisfying. You'll have a range of jobs to consider, and you'll know the elements the jobs must have to keep you happy. Once you've selected a few job categories that might satisfy you, talk to people in those fields to find out if a particular job is really what you want, and the job possibilities for someone with your experience. That's one way to test if your aspirations are realistic.

After you have narrowed your choices down to a few fields with some job possibilities that will satisfy your motivated skills, the next step is to figure out how to get there. That topic will be covered in our book *Job Search Secrets*.

A Demonstration of the Seven Stories Exercise

To get clients started, I sometimes walk them through two or three of their achievement stories, and tell them the patterns I see. They can then go off and think of the seven or eight accomplishments they enjoyed the most and also performed well. This final list is ranked and analyzed in depth to get a more accurate picture of the person's motivated skills. I spend the most time analyzing those accomplishments a client sees as most important. Some accomplishments are more obvious than others. But all stories can be analyzed.

Here is Suzanne, as an example: "When I was nine years old, I was living with my three sisters. There was a fire in our house and our cat had hidden under the bed. We were all outside, but I decided to run back in and save the cat. And I did it."

No matter what the story is, I probe a little by asking these two questions: What gave you the sense of accomplishment? and What about that made you proud? These questions give me a quick fix on the person.

The full exercise is a little more involved than this. Suzanne said at first: "I was proud because I did what I thought was right." I probed a little, and she added: "I had a sense of accomplishment because I was able to make an instant decision under pressure. I was proud because I overcame my fear."

I asked Suzanne for a second story; I wanted to see what patterns might emerge when we put the two together:

"Ten years ago, I was laid off from a large company where I had worked for nine years. I soon got a job as a secretary in a Wall Street company. I loved the excitement and loved that job. Six weeks later, a position opened up on the trading floor, but I didn't get it at first. I eventually was one of three finalists, and they tried to discourage me from taking the job. I wanted to be given a chance. So I sold myself because I was determined to get that job. I went back for three interviews, said all the right things, and eventually got it."

What was the accomplishment? What made her proud?

- "I fought to win."
- "I was able to sell myself. I was able to overcome their objections."
- "I was interviewed by three people at once. I amazed myself by saying, 'I know I can do this job.'"
- "I determined who the real decision-maker was, and said things that would make him want to hire me."
- "I loved that job—loved the energy, the upness, the fun."

Here it was, ten years later, and that job still stood out as a highlight in her life. Since then she'd been miserable and bored, and that's why she came to me.

Normally after a client tells two stories, we can quickly name the patterns we see in both stories. What were Suzanne's patterns?

Suzanne showed that she was good at making decisions in tense situations—both when saving the cat and when interviewing for that job. She showed a good intuitive sense (such as when she determined who the decision-maker was and how to win him over). She's decisive and likes fast-paced, energetic situations. She likes it when she overcomes her own fears as well as the objections of others.

If one advances confidently in the direction of his dreams, and endeavors to live the life which he has imagined, he will meet with success unexpected in common hours.
Henry David Thoreau

We needed more than two stories to see if these patterns ran throughout Suzanne's life and to see what other patterns might emerge. After the full exercise, Suzanne felt for sure that she wanted excitement in her jobs, a sense of urgency—that she wanted to be in a position where she had a chance to be decisive and operate intuitively. Those are the conditions she enjoys and under which she operates the best. Armed with this information, Suzanne can confidently say in an interview that she thrives on excitement, high pressure, and quick decision-making. And, she'll probably make more money than she would in "safe" jobs. She can move her life in a different direction—whenever she is ready.

Pay attention to those stories that were most important to you. The elements in these stories may be worth repeating. If none of your enjoyable accomplishments were work-related, it may take great courage to eventually move into a field where you will be happier. Or you may decide to continue to have your enjoyment outside of work.

People have to be ready to change. Fifteen years ago, when I first examined my own motivated skills, I saw possibilities I was not ready to handle. Although I suffered from extreme shyness, my stories—especially those that occurred when I was young—gave me hope. As I emerged from my shyness, I was eventually able to act on what my stories said was true about me.

People sometimes take immediate steps after learning what their motivated skills are. Or sometimes this new knowledge can work inside them until they are ready to take action—maybe ten years later. All the while internal changes can be happening, and people can eventually blossom.

Motivated Skills—
Your Anchor in a Changing World

Your motivated skills are your anchor in a world of uncertainty. The world will change, but your motivated skills remain constant.

Write them down. Save the list. Over the years, refer to them to make sure you are still on target— doing things that you do well and are motivated to do. As you refer to them, they will influence your life. Five years from now, an opportunity may present itself. In reviewing your list, you will have every confidence that this opportunity is right for you. After all, you have been doing these things since you were a child, you know that you enjoy them, and you do them well!

Knowing our patterns gives us a sense of stability and helps us understand what we have done so far. It also gives us the freedom to try new things regardless of risk or of what others may say, because we can be absolutely sure that this is the way we are. Knowing your patterns gives you both security and flexibility—and you need both to cope in this changing world.

Now think about your own stories. Write down everything that occurs to you.

The Ugly Duckling was so happy and in some way he was glad that he had experienced so much hardship and misery; for now he could fully appreciate his tremendous luck and the great beauty that greeted him.
... And he rustled his feathers, held his long neck high, and with deep emotion he said: "I never dreamt of so much happiness, when I was the Ugly Duckling!"
Hans Christian Anderson, *The Ugly Duckling*

The
Five
O'Clock
Club®

The Seven Stories
Exercise Worksheet

This exercise is an opportunity to examine the most satisfying experiences of your life and to discover those skills you will want to use as you go forward. You will be looking at the times when you feel you did something particularly well that you also enjoyed doing. It doesn't matter what other people thought, whether or not you were paid, or when in your life the experiences took place. **All that matters is that you felt happy about doing whatever it was, thought you did it well, and experienced a sense of accomplishment.** You can even go back to childhood. When I did my own Seven Stories Exercise, I remembered the time when I was ten years old and led a group of kids in the neighborhood, enjoyed it, and did it well.

This exercise usually takes a few days to complete. Many people review different life phases in order to capture the full scope of these experiences. Most carry around a piece of paper to jot down ideas as they think of them.

SECTION I:

Briefly outline below *all* the work/personal/life experiences which meet the above definition. Come up with at least twenty. We ask for twenty stories so you won't be too selective. Just write down anything that occurs to you, no matter how trivial it may seem. Try to **think of concrete examples, situations and tasks, not generalized skills or abilities**. It may be helpful if you say to yourself, "There was the time when I . . . "

RIGHT	WRONG
• Got extensive media coverage for a new product launch.	• Writing press releases.
• Delivered speech to get German business.	• Delivering speeches.
• Coordinated blood drive for division.	• Coordinating.
• Came in third in the Nassau Bike Race.	• Cycling.
• Made a basket in second grade.	• Working on projects alone.

1. _____

2. _____

3. _____

4. _____

5. _____

6. _____

7. _____

8. _____

9. _____

10. _____

11. _____

12. _____

13. _____

14. _____

15. _____

16. _____

17. _____

18. _____

19. _____

20. _____

21. _____

22. _____

23. _____

24. _____

25. _____

SECTION II:

Choose the seven experiences from the above which you enjoyed the most and felt the most sense of accomplishment about. (Be sure to include non-job-related experiences also.) Then **rank them**. Then, for each accomplishment, describe what *you* did. Be specific, listing each step in detail. Notice the role you played and your relationship with others, the subject matter, the skills you used, and so on. Use a separate sheet of paper for each.

If your highest-ranking accomplishments also happen to be work-related, you may want them to appear prominently on your résumé. After all, those were the things that you enjoyed and did well. And those are probably the experiences you will want to repeat again in your new job.

Here's how you might begin:

Experience #1: Planned product launch that resulted in 450 letters of intent from 1500 participants.

a. Worked with president and product managers to discuss product potential and details.

b. Developed promotional plan.

c. Conducted five-week direct-mail campaign prior to the conference to create an aura of excitement about the product.

d. Trained all product demonstrators to make sure they each presented our product in the same way.

e. Had a great product booth built; rented the best suite to entertain prospects; conducted campaign at the conference by having teasers put under everyone's door every day of the conference. Most people wanted to come to our booth.

—and so on—

Now it is time to analyze your stories. You are trying to look for the threads that run through them so that you will know the things you do well that also give you satisfaction. Some of the questions below sound similar. That's okay. They are a catalyst to make you think more deeply about the experience. The questions don't have any hidden psychological significance.

If your accomplishments happen to be mostly work-related, this exercise will form the basis for your "positioning" or summary statement in your résumé, and also for your two-minute pitch.

If these accomplishments are mostly not work-related, they will still give you some idea of how you may want to slant your résumé, and they may give you an idea of how you will want your career to go in the long run.

For now, simply go through each story without trying to force it to come out any particular way. Just think hard about yourself. And be as honest as you can. When you have completed this analysis, the words in the next exercise may help you think of additional things. **Do this page first.**

Story #1.

What was the *main accomplishment* for you? _____

_____

What about it did you *enjoy most*? _____

_____

What did you *do best*? _____

_____

What was your *key motivator*? _____

_____

What *led up to your getting involved*? (e.g., assigned to do it, thought it up myself, etc.) _____

_____

What was your *relationship with others*? (e.g., leader, worked alone, inspired others, team member, etc.) _

_____

Describe the *environment* in which you performed. _____

_____

What was the *subject matter*? (e.g., music, mechanics, trees, budgets, etc.) _____

Story #2.

Main accomplishment? _____
Enjoyed most? _____
Did best? _____
Key motivator? _____
What led up to it? _____
Your role? _____
The environment? _____
The subject matter? _____

We are here to be excited from youth to old age, to have an insatiable curiosity about the world . . . . We are also here to help others by practicing a friendly attitude. And every person is born for a purpose. Everyone has a God-given potential, in essence, built into them. And if we are to live life to its fullest, we must realize that potential.

Norman Vincent Peale

Story #3.
Main accomplishment? _____
Enjoyed most? _____
Did best? _____
Key motivator? _____
What led up to it? _____
Your role? _____
The environment? _____
The subject matter? _____

Story #4.
Main accomplishment? _____
Enjoyed most? _____
Did best? _____
Key motivator? _____
What led up to it? _____
Your role? _____
The environment? _____
The subject matter? _____

Story #5.
Main accomplishment? _____
Enjoyed most? _____
Did best? _____
Key motivator? _____
What led up to it? _____
Your role? _____
The environment? _____
The subject matter? _____

Story #6.
Main accomplishment? _____
Enjoyed most? _____
Did best? _____
Key motivator? _____
What led up to it? _____
Your role? _____
The environment? _____
The subject matter? _____

Story #7.
Main accomplishment? _____
Enjoyed most? _____
Did best? _____
Key motivator? _____
What led up to it? _____
Your role? _____
The environment? _____
The subject matter? _____

Skills From Your Seven Stories

The numbers across the top represent each of your seven stories. Start with story #1 and check off all of your specialized skills that appear in that story. When you've checked off the skills for all seven stories, total them.

Story #	1	2	3	4	5	6	7	Total	Story #	1	2	3	4	5	6	7	Total
Administration									Operations Mgmt.								
Advising/Consulting									Org. Design/Devel.								
Analytical Skills									Ownership								
Artistic Ability									Perceptiveness								
Budgetary Skills									Perseverance								
Client Relations									Persuasiveness								
Communication									Planning								
Community Relations									Policy-Making								
Contract Negotiation									Practicality								
Control									Presentation Skills								
Coordination									Problem-Solving								
Creativity									Procedures Design								
Decisiveness									Production								
Design									Program Concept								
Development									Program Design								
Financial Skills									Project Management								
Foresight									Promotion								
Frugality									Public Relations								
Fund Raising									Public Speaking								
Human Relations									Quality Assessment								
Information Mgmt.									Research								
Imagination									Resourcefulness								
Individualism									Sales Ability								
Initiative									Service								
Inventiveness									Showmanship								
Leadership									Speaking Skills								
Liaison									Staff Dev./Mgmt.								
Logic									Strategic Planning								
Management									Stress Tolerance								
Marketing									Systems								
Mathematical Skills									Teamwork								
Mechanical Skills									Tenacity								
Motivational Skills									Training								
Negotiation									Travel								
Observation									Troubleshooting								
Organization									Writing								
Other Talents:									Other Talents:								

Note: Job hunters enjoy exercises like this because they are simple. But your experiences are more complex than the words on this page. These words alone do not reflect the richness of what you have to offer. So combine these words with the more in-depth answers you came up with on the preceding page, and continue to analyze your stories throughout your life. You will find deeper and deeper answers about yourself.

Top Six or Seven Specialized Skills, according to which had the most check marks:

1. _____
2. _____
3. _____
4. _____
5. _____
6. _____
7. _____

Your Current
Work-Related Values

What is important to you? Your values change as you grow and change, so they need to be reassessed continually. At various stages in your career, you may value money, or leisure time, or independence on the job, or working for something you believe in. See what is important to you *now*. This will help you not to be upset if, for instance, a job provides you with the freedom you wanted, but not the kind of money your friends are making.

Sometimes we are not aware of our own values. It may be that, at this stage of our life, time with our family is most important to us. For some people, money or power is most important, but they may be reluctant to admit it—even to themselves.

Values are the driving force behind what we do. It is important to truthfully understand what we value, and we will increase our chances of getting what we want.

Look at the list of values below . Think of each in terms of your overall career objectives. Rate the degree of importance that you would assign to each for yourself, using this scale:

1—Not at all important in my choice of job	3—Reasonably important
2—Not very but somewhat important	4—Very important

Add other values that don't appear on the list or to substitute wording you are more comfortable with.

___ the chance to advance	___ artistic or other creativity
___ work on frontiers of knowledge	___ learning
___ having authority (responsibility)	___ location of the work place
___ helping society	___ tranquility
___ helping others	___ money earned
___ meeting challenges	___ change and variety
___ working for something I	___ having time for personal life
believe in	___ fast pace
___ public contact	___ power
___ enjoyable colleagues	___ adventure/risk taking
___ competition	___ prestige
___ ease (freedom from worry)	___ moral fulfillment
___ influencing people	___ recognition from superiors,
___ enjoyable work tasks	society, peers
___ working alone	___ security (stability)
___ being an expert	___ physical work environment
___ personal growth and development	___ chance to make an impact
___ independence	___ clear expectations and procedures

Of those you marked "4," circle the 5 **most** important to you today:

- If forced to compromise on any of these, which one would you give up? _____

- Which one would you be most reluctant to give up? _____

Describe in ten or twenty words what you want most in your life and/or career.

Other Exercises:
Interests, Satisfiers, and Bosses

CASE STUDY: LAURA
Using Her Special Interests

For many people, interests should stay as interests—things they do on the side. For others, their interests may be a clue to the kinds of jobs they should do next or in the long run. Laura had food as her special interest. She had spent her life as a marketing manager in cosmetics, but she assured me that food was *very* important to her.

We redid her résumé to downplay the cosmetics background. Next, Laura visited a well-known specialty food store. She spoke to the store manager, a junior person, asked about the way the company was organized, and found that there were three partners, one of whom was the president. Laura said to the store manager, "Please give my résumé to the president, and I will call him in a few days." We prepared for her meeting with the president, in which she would find out the company's long-term plans, and so on. At the meeting, he said he wanted to increase revenues from $4 million to $40 million. Laura and I met again to decide how she could help the business grow through her marketing efforts, and to decide what kind of compensation she would want, including equity in the company. She met with the president again, and got the job!

It was the Interests exercise that prompted her to get into that field. Remember, all you need to do is make a list of your interests. Laura simply wrote "food." Other people list twenty things. Here is the exercise:

Interests Exercise

List all the things you really like to do. List anything that makes you feel good and gives you satisfaction. List those areas where you have developed a relatively in-depth knowledge or expertise. For ideas, think back over your day, your week, the seasons of the year, places, people, work, courses, roles, leisure time, family, etc. These areas need not be work-related. Think of how you spend your discretionary time.

If you cannot think of what your interests may be, think about the books you read, the magazines you subscribe to, the section of the newspaper you turn to first. Think about the knowledge you've built up simply because you're interested in a particular subject. Think about the volunteer work you do—what are the recurring assignments you tend to get and enjoy? Think about your hobbies—are there one or two you have become so involved in that you have built up a lot of expertise/information in those areas? What are the things you find yourself doing—and enjoying—all the time, things you don't *have* to do.

Your interests may be a clue to what you would like in a job. Rob was a partner in a law firm, but loved everything about wine. He left the law firm to become general counsel in a wine company. Most people's interests should stay as interests, but you never know until you think about it.

Satisfiers and Dissatisfiers Exercise

Simply list every job you have ever had. List what was satisfying and dissatisfying about each job. Some people are surprised to find that they were sometimes most satisfied by the vacation, pay, title, and other perks, but were not satisfied with the job itself.

Bosses Exercise

Simply examine those bosses you have had a good relationship with and those you have not, and determine what you need in your future relationship with bosses. If you have had a lot of problems with bosses, discuss this with your counselor.

Your Special Interests

For many people, interests should stay as interests—things they do on the side. For others, their interests may be a clue to the kinds of jobs they should do next or in the long run. Only you can decide whether your interests should become part of your work life.

List all the things you really like to do—anything that makes you feel good and gives you satisfaction. List those areas in which you have developed a relatively in-depth knowledge or expertise. For ideas, think of your day, your week, the seasons of the year, places, people, work, courses, roles, leisure time, friends, family, etc. Think of how you spend your discretionary time.

- Think about the books you read, the magazines you subscribe to, the section of the newspaper you turn to.
- Think about knowledge you've built up simply because you're interested in it.
- Think about the volunteer work you do—what are the recurring assignments you tend to get and enjoy?
- Think about your hobbies—are there one or two you have become so involved in that you have built up a lot of expertise/information in those areas?
- What are the things you find yourself doing all the time and enjoying, even though you don't have to do them?

_____   _____

_____   _____

_____   _____

_____   _____

_____   _____

_____   _____

_____   _____

_____   _____

_____   _____

_____   _____

_____   _____

_____   _____

_____   _____

Satisfiers and Dissatisfiers in Past Jobs

For each job you have held in the past, describe as fully as possible those factors which made that job especially exciting or rewarding (satisfiers) and those which made that job especially boring or frustrating (dissatisfiers). **Be as specific as possible** (See the example below, which shows that sometimes the satisfiers can be the perqs, while the dissatisfiers can be the job itself).

<u>JOB</u>	<u>SATISFIERS</u>	<u>DISSATISFIERS</u>
VP of Mfg., ABC Co.	1. Status—large office, staff of 23, Exec. Dining Room 2. Fringes—4 weeks' vacation, travel allowance time for outside activities.	1. Manager —cold and aloof. Too little structure and feedback; no organizational credibility. 2. Limited promotional opportunities —none laterally, only straight line.
<u>JOB</u>	<u>SATISFIERS</u>	<u>DISSATISFIERS</u>

The
Five
O'Clock
Club®

Your Relationship with Bosses

1. Make a list of all the "bosses" you have ever had in work situations. Use a very broad definition. They don't have to have been "bosses" in the strictest sense of the word. Include bosses from part-time jobs, summer jobs, and even professors with whom you worked closely in your student days.

2. Divide the names from above into three lists: those people with whom you had no problems, those with whom you had some problems, and those with whom you had severe problems.

NO PROBLEMS	SOME PROBLEMS	SEVERE PROBLEMS

3. Look for factors that might help explain why you had some problems or severe problems with some bosses and not with others (or why you have never had problems). For example, consider:

• the type of people involved: age, sex, personality, etc.
• the structure of your relationship with the people: how much and what type of power they had over you.
• the broader contexts: the kind of work involved, the type of organizations involved, etc.

Think about it. Do you see any patterns . . .

. . . regarding the type of people?

. . . regarding the structure of the relationship?

. . . regarding the contexts?

This exercise is based on lectures given by John P. Kotter in his classes in power dynamics at the Harvard Business School.

Getting Feedback From Others

The most important finding my study yielded was:
The men who were introspective, who valued their
logic and intuition, were happier and more self-
confident than their less introspective counterparts
and better able to deal with the stresses of life. How-
ever, those who appeared outwardly successful, but
ignored their inner life, were often confused, empty, or
discontented, which resulted in their feeling
overwhelmed or depressed and caused them to
run from their problems.
Jan Halper, Ph.D.,
Quiet Desperation—The Truth about Successful Men

No, but every time one of the execs rents Boyz-n-the-
Hood, they come to me and ask me to explain it to
them. They think I'm some kind of channel into the
heart of the ghetto. I don't even know what to say to
them—usually I want to smack 'em, but I don't think
that would help my career in Boston banking much.
Bruce Faulk,
You Still Got to Come Home to That

How many folks you seen get shot lately? Don't get
many drive-by's in the board room do you?
Bruce Faulk,
You Still Got to Come Home to That

Did you know that the highest-perform-
ing executives are the most self-aware
and are most aware of the impact they
have on others? Yet 80 percent of all managers
think they are self-aware and think they know
how they come across. Statistically, most of these
managers are wrong. So even if they are promoted, they will probably eventually get derailed.

You cannot expect direct, honest feedback
from your bosses about how you are doing on
the job. It's a fact: "Five out of seven executives
and managers prefer to lie to an employee about
his or her performance rather than to give constructive criticism." (*Quiet Desperation—The Truth
About Successful Men* by Jan Halper, Ph.D.)

Even so, you can make yourself more like the
high-performers by increasing your personal self-
awareness.

One thing you can do immediately is **assess
all of your work-related relationships—loosely
defined as relationships with those who affect
your performance and livelihood**. Make a list of:

•   your bosses—those above you. This
certainly includes your immediate supervisors
and their bosses. But "bosses" could also include
those in other departments, management in other
companies that are customers of your company,
and those more senior to you who can refer
business to you.

•   all your peers. You may have to figure out
who your peers *really* are. They may be in other
geographic areas, other divisions, and even in
other companies. But you work with them on a
peer level.

•   your subordinates—those below you. This
means both direct and indirect reports. The
group can even include the person at the local
copy shop, the secretary of some of your bosses,
receptionists, and others with whom you may (or
may not) interact.

•   your "clients." Again, these may be inside
or outside your company. They are the people
using your service.

Most people wind up with a list of 8 or 10

bosses, 10 to 12 peers, and 4 to many more subordinates. Assess your relationship with *each* of these people. Decide which ones you should do something about immediately. Then develop a long-term plan for assessing and doing something about your relationship with each person.

You may need to develop methods and procedures for keeping your boss(es) better informed, building stronger ties with your peers, keeping your staff more up-to-date, and paying attention to your clients. If you think you can ignore your boss while doing a great job for your clients, you are wrong.

Ask yourself how well aware you are of the way you come across to each of these people. To make yourself more objective, put yourself in your boss's shoes. What would your boss say about your performance and your relationship with *each* of your peers? If you are ignoring certain peers because you think they are stupid, think again. Ignoring them may not be your smartest response. What would your boss rather have you do about your stupid peers? Think about it, and get rid of the ways you may be causing problems for your boss.

Why You Should Pay Attention to Your Work-Related Relationships

1. Getting work done in the new corporate environment now often depends more on influencing others (even your subordinates) than on formally directing them.
2. Corporations are changing so quickly that an exec can be blindsided if he or she is not plugged in to what's happening. The corporation could be heading in a new direction while the exec is following the old one. Often these changes in direction are informal and unannounced—no one will officially say that things have changed. Or it will be said almost in passing. The exec is expected to "catch on" by osmosis. If not, he or she is labeled "out of step."
3. You never know who can do you in—your bosses, peers, subordinates, or "clients."

Increasing Your Self-Knowledge Through Self-Assessment

You have already analyzed yourself through the Seven Stories, the Forty-Year Plan, and other exercises. In a methodical way, you have learned what many already know about themselves but have not learned to articulate. These exercises helped you discover:

• Your skills, as seen through your life experiences; those things you did well and found especially satisfying. This helps increase your knowledge of situations you will be good at, or where there is a skill match or "fit."

- interests/subject-matter knowledge
- job-related values
- job-related satisfiers/dissatisfiers
- relationships with bosses.

If you happen to be attending The Five O'Clock Club or working privately with a career counselor, that experience can also provide you with some valuable feedback. However, you must still increase your level of knowledge and awareness by gathering information directly from bosses, peers, and subordinates. Then you can take corrective action.

Getting Feedback From Others—the Exercise

This outside source of information is critical. The feedback is gathered from people selected by you. When you combine it with your self-assessment results, you wind up with a realistic and thorough picture of your skills, strengths, and style—and areas for improvement.

1. Select five people whom you think know you well in the work situation. These may be either inside or outside the organization. It is best if you select a mix of bosses, peers, and subordinates so you can get feedback on your likely problems and issues.
2. Call each person and say something such as: "I am participating in a career development program, and I would like your feedback. I have selected five people who I think know me well from a work point-of-view, and you are one of

A state without the means of some change is without the means of its conservation.
Edmund Burke, *Reflections on the Revolution in France*, 1790

them. I hope you will be honest, because the information I will be getting will help me in my career planning."

Then say either:

"I will send you a sheet with five questions, which I would appreciate your answering. You will also receive a stamped, self-addressed envelope so you can mail your responses back to me. But the questionnaire will not have your name on it, so I will not be able to tell who said what."

Or, if you are having a career counselor make calls on your behalf, you would say instead: "Please be open with the career counselor who will be calling you."

The counselor will call each participant and ask the same five questions:

1. Could you describe in general what you think of John/Jane from a work point-of-view?

2. What do you see as his/her most important strengths?

3. What do you see as his/her downsides or limitations or things that could hold him/her back, whether or not you think he/she would choose to change them?

4. If you could think of the ideal job for John/Jane, what would it be or what would it be like?

5. If you had one piece of career advice to give John/Jane, what would that be?

To keep the feedback even more confidential, the counselor can combine all the responses before feeding them back to you.

If you decide to do it by sending a questionnaire to each person, simply use the form on the next page, and sign your name. You will notice that there is more room for the person to answer question 3, which solicits opinions about your limitations. Don't be alarmed: Suggestions for improvement usually take longer to describe than simply stating your positives.

Selecting the Participants

You want a balanced assessment of how you come across to people. Therefore, if your present work situation is unhappy, and everyone dislikes

you, and this is unusual for you, do not select those people.

Instead, select five people who you feel know you well from a work point-of-view. This means you have worked closely with each of them over a number of years. Make sure you include in the mix at least one boss, one peer and one subordinate. Then select two others.

The Result of Feedback

After doing this, you will have a good idea of your strengths and weaknesses and a clear picture of how you are viewed by others.

You may uncover problems you need to address. You may do this alone or with the help of a career counselor.

Optional: Working With a Career Counselor

If you decide to work with a career counselor, it may take several months, depending on the issues you want to cover. After you have shown the counselor the feedback you have received, the coaching may include the following:

1. Your regular reporting of what is going on at your job.

2. The development of a strategy for handling whatever problems exist.

3. Role-playing with the counselor to prepare you for discussions you may have with bosses, peers, or subordinates.

4. The development of strategies for how you can better manage your job, work, time, communications—or whatever situations may arise.

5. Intermittent scheduled follow-up sessions to assess your continuing success with incorporating all that you have learned.

Open, honest feedback can help you determine whether or not there is consistency between your perceptions of yourself and the perceptions of others. If there is a gap, you can close it and be more like the high-performing executives. Simply make five copies of the form on the next page. Good luck!

The
Five
O'Clock
Club®

Career Development Program

I appreciate your help in giving me feedback that will help me with my career. I have selected approximately five people who I think know me well from a work point-of-view. I sincerely value your feedback. Please return to me the enclosed stamped, self-addressed envelope. Since this sheet does not have your name on it, your responses will be confidential: I will not be able to tell who said what. To be more sure of confidentiality, you may want to type this on a separate sheet.

Thank you for your time.

_____
(Signed)

1. Describe in general what you think of me from a work point-of-view.

_____

_____

_____

_____

_____

2. What do you see as my most important strengths? _____

_____

3. What do you see as my downsides or limitations or things that could hold me back, whether or not

you think I would choose to change them? _____

_____

_____

_____

_____

_____

_____

4. If you could think of the ideal job for me, what would it be or what would it be like? _____

_____

5. If you had one piece of career advice to give me, what would that be?_____

_____

Looking Into Your Future

A study was made of alumni ten years out of Harvard to find out how many were achieving their goals.
An astounding 83 percent had no goals at all. Fourteen percent had specific goals, but they were not written down. Their average earnings were three times what those in the 83 percent group were earning. However, the 3 percent who had written goals were earning ten times that of the 83 percent group.

Forrest H. Patton, *Force of Persuasion,*
as quoted by Ronald W. Miller,
Planning for Success

Your motivated skills tell you the *elements* you need to make you happy, your Values exercise tells you the values that are important to you right now, and the Interests exercise may give you a clue to other fields or industries to explore. But none of them give you a feel for the *scope* of what may lie ahead.

Dreams and goals can be great driving forces in our lives. We feel satisfied when we are working toward them—even if we never reach them. People who have dreams or goals do better than people who don't.

Setting goals will make a difference in your life, and this makes sense. Every day we make dozens of choices. People with dreams make choices that advance them in the right direction. People without dreams also make choices—but their choices are strictly present-oriented with little thought of the future. When you are aware of your current situation, and you also know where you want to go, a natural tension leads you forward faster.

When you find a believable dream that excites you, don't forget it. In the heat of our day-to-day living, our dreams slip out of our minds. In some respects this is good, because it means we're absorbed by the daily events of our lives. If we focused *only on the future*, we'd all be very upset and worried people. We each should be appropriately challenged and involved in what we're doing in the present, with a reminder every once in a while of where we want to go. Happy people keep an eye on the future as well as the present.

"Freeing-Up" Exercises

This next group of exercises may help you imagine broader dreams for yourself—dreams to inspire you and move you forward, add meaning to your everyday life, and give it some long-term purpose.

It's okay if you never reach your dreams. In fact, it can be better to have some dreams that you will probably never reach, so long as you enjoy the *process* of trying to reach them. For

In my practice as a psychiatrist, I have found that helping people to develop personal goals has proved to be the most effective way to help them cope with problems.
Ari Kiev, M.D., *A Strategy for Daily Living*

example, a real estate developer may dream of owning all the real estate in Phoenix. He may wind up owning much more than if he did not have that dream. If he enjoys the *process* of acquiring real estate, that's all that matters.

Exercise #1—Write Your Obituary

Every now and then I think about my own death, and I think about my own funeral. . . . I ask myself, "What is it that I would want said?"

Say I was a drum major for justice; say that I was a drum major for peace; say that I was a drum major for righteousness. And all of the other shallow things will not matter. I won't have any money to leave behind. I won't have the fine and luxurious things of life to leave behind. But I just want to leave a committed life behind.
Martin Luther King, Jr.

Martin Luther King, Jr., knew how he wanted to be remembered. He had a dream, and it drove his life. Write out what you would want the newspapers to say about you when you die. Alfred Nobel had a chance to *rewrite* his obituary. The story goes that his cousin, who was also named Alfred, died. The newspapers, hearing of the death of Alfred Nobel, printed the prepared obituary—for the wrong man. Alfred read it the day after his cousin's death. He was upset by what the obituary said because it starkly showed him how he would be remembered: as the well-known inventor of a cheap explosive called dynamite.

Alfred resolved to change his life. Today, he's remembered as the Swedish chemist and inventor who provided for the Nobel Prizes.

Write your obituary as you want to be remembered after your death. It should also include parts that are *not* related to your job. If you don't like the way your life seems to be headed, change it—just as Alfred Nobel did. Some people do this exercise every five or ten years. It keeps them on track and moving

forward. Write your own obituary, and *then make a list of the things you need to do to get there.*

Exercise #2—Invent a Job

If you could have any job in the world, what would it be? Don't worry about the possibility of ever finding that job—make it up! Invent it. Write it out. It may spark you to think of how to create that job in real life.

Exercise #3—If You Had a Million

If you had a million dollars (or maybe ten million) but still had to work, what would you do?

When I asked myself this question some time ago, I decided I'd like to continue doing what I was doing at work, but would like to write a book on job hunting because I felt I had something to say. I did write that book—and I've gone on to write others!

People often erroneously see a lack of money as a stumbling block to their goals. Think about it: is there some way you could do what you want without a million dollars? Then do it!

Exercise#4—Your Forty-Year Plan

Take a look at this very important exercise, which starts on the next page.

There are more things in heaven and earth, Horatio, than are dreamt of in your philosophy.
Shakespeare, *Hamlet*

Your Forty-Year Plan ™

HAVE A DREAM.
MAKE A PLAN.
TAKE A STEP.
KEEP ON CLIMBING.

Motto of Workforce America® in Harlem

If you could imagine your life five years from now, what would it be like? How would it be different from the way it is now? If you made new friends during the next five years, what would they be like? Where would you be living? What would your hobbies and interests be? How about ten years from now? Twenty? Thirty? Forty? Think about it!

Some people feel locked in by their present circumstances. Many say it is too late for them. But a lot can happen in five, ten, twenty, thirty or forty years. Martin Luther King, Jr. had a dream. His dream helped all of us, but his dream helped him too. He was living according to a plan (which he thought was God's plan for him). *It gave him a purpose in life.* Bill Clinton had a plan. Most successful people have a plan.

A lot can happen to you over the next few decades—and most of what happens is up to you. If you see the rest of your life as boring, I'm sure you will be right. Pick your own vision of the future, and be as sure as you can be that it is what you really want. If it is what you want, chances are you will find some way to make it happen.

Write down, in the present tense, the way your life is right now, and the way you see yourself at each of the time frames listed above. **This exercise should take no more than one hour**. Allow your unconscious to tell you what you will be doing in the future. Just quickly comment on each of the questions listed below, and then move on to the next. If you kill yourself off too early in the process (say, at age sixty), push it ten more years to see what would have happened if you had lived. Then push it another ten, just for fun.

When you have finished the exercise, ask yourself how you feel about your entire life as you laid it out in your plan. Some people feel depressed when they see on paper how their lives are going, and they cannot think of a way out. But they feel better when a good friend or a counselor helps them think of a better future to work toward. If you don't like your plan, you are allowed to change it—it's your life. Do what you want with it. Pick the kind of life you want.

Start the exercise with the way things are now so you will be realistic about your future. Now, relax and have a good time going through the years. Don't think too hard. Let's see where you wind up. You have plenty of time to get things done.

Your Forty-Year Plan™ Worksheet

1.   The year is **xxxx** (current year).   Year: _____   Your Age _____
      You are _____ years old right now.   _____
➤ Tell me what your life is like right now.   _____
   (Say anything you want about your life as it is now.)   _____
➤ Who are your friends? What do they do for a living?   _____
➤ What is your relationship with your family,   _____
   however you define "family"?   _____
➤ Are you married? Single? Children? (List ages.)   _____
➤ Where are you living? What does it look like?   _____
➤ What are your hobbies and interests?   _____
➤ What do you do for exercise?   _____
➤ How is your health?   _____
➤ How do you take care of your spiritual needs?   _____
➤ What kind of work are you doing?   _____
➤ What else would you like to note about your life   _____
   right now?   _____

Don't worry if you don't like everything about your life right now. Most people do this exercise because they
want to improve themselves. They want to *change* something. What do *you* want to change? **Please continue.**

2.   The year is **xxxx** (current year + 5).   Year: _____   Your Age _____
      You are _____ years old. (Add 5 to present age.)   _____
      Things are going well for you.   _____
➤ What is your life like now at this age?   _____
   (Say anything you want about your life as it is now.)   _____
➤ Who are your friends? What do they do for a living?   _____
➤ What is your relationship with your "family"?   _____
➤ Married? Single? Children? (List their ages now.)   _____
➤ Where are you living? What does it look like?   _____
➤ What are your hobbies and interests?   _____
➤ What do you do for exercise?   _____
➤ How is your health?   _____
➤ How do you take care of your spiritual needs?   _____
➤ What kind of work are you doing?   _____
➤ What else would you like to note about your life   _____
   right now?   _____

3. The year is xxxx (current year + 15).

   You are _____ years old. (Current age plus 15.)

   ➤ What is your life like now at this age?
     (Say anything you want about your life as it is now.)
   ➤ Who are your friends? What do they do for a living?
   ➤ What is your relationship with your "family"?
   ➤ Married? Single? Children? (List their ages now.)
   ➤ Where are you living? What does it look like?
   ➤ What are your hobbies and interests?
   ➤ What do you do for exercise?
   ➤ How is your health?
   ➤ How do you take care of your spiritual needs?
   ➤ What kind of work are you doing?
   ➤ What else would you like to note about your life
     right now?

   Year: _____ Your Age _____

   _____
   _____
   _____
   _____
   _____
   _____
   _____
   _____
   _____
   _____
   _____
   _____

The fifteen-year mark is an especially important one. This age is far enough away from the present that people often loosen up a bit. It's so far away that it's not threatening. Imagine *your* ideal life. What is it like? Why were you put here on this earth? What were you meant to do here? What kind of life were you meant to live? Give it a try and see what you come up with. If you can't think of anything now, try it again in a week or so.

4. The year is xxxx (current year + 25).

   You are _____ years old! (Current age plus 25)

   Year: _____ Your Age _____
   Using a blank piece of paper, answer all of the
   questions for this stage of your life.

5. The year is xxxx (current year + 35).

   You are _____ years old! (Current age plus 35)

   Repeat.

6. The year is xxxx (current year + 45).

   You are _____ years old! (Current age plus 45)

   Repeat.

7. The year is xxxx (current year + 55).

   You are _____ years old! (Current age plus 55)

   Keep going. How do you feel about your life?
   You are allowed to change the parts you don't like.

   (Keep going—don't die until you are past 80!)

You have plenty of time to get done everything you want to do. Imagine wonderful things for yourself. You have plenty of time. Get rid of any "negative programming." For example, if you imagine yourself having poor health because your parents suffered from poor health, see what you can do about that. If you imagine yourself dying early because that runs in your family, see what would have happened had you lived longer. It's your life—your only one. As they say, "This is the real thing. It's not a dress rehearsal."

The Ideal Scene

*Every great personal victory was
preceded by a personal goal or dream.*
Dennis R. Webb

From *The Art of the Long View*
by Peter Schwartz:

---

*In order to make effective decisions, you must
articulate them to begin with. Consider, for example,
the choice of a career in biotechnology.*
*A scenario-planner would tackle the decision
differently. It depends, he or she might argue, on
another set of questions: What is the future of the
biotechnology industry? (That in turn depends on:)*
*What is the path of development in the biotech
industry? (Moreover:) What skills will have enduring
value? (And:) Where will be a good place to begin?*
*The hardest questions will be the most important.
What is it that interests you about biotechnology in
the first place? What sorts of things about yourself
might lead you to make a decision with poor results?
What could lead you to change your mind?*

---

*Scenarious are not predictions. It is simply not
possible to predict the future with certainty.*

---

*For individuals and small businesses, scenarios are a
way to help develop their own gut feeling and assure
that they have been comprehensive, both realistic and
imaginative, in covering all important bases.*

---

*If you look at yourself on the level of historical time, as
a tiny but influential part of a century-long process,
then at least you can begin to know your own address.
You can begin to sense the greater pattern, and feel
where you are within it, and your acts take on meaning.* Michael Ventura, quoted by P. Schwartz

This is another exercise to help you imagine
your future. Relax for a while. Arrange a
time when you will not be distracted. Set
aside about an hour. Sit by yourself, have a cup of
tea, take out a pad of paper, and imagine yourself
five, ten, fifteen, or twenty years from now—at a
phase in your life when all is going well. Just pick
one of these time frames.

Imagine in very general terms the kind of life
you were meant to have. Start writing—it's important to write it down, rather than just thinking
about it.

What is your ideal life like? Describe a typical
day. What do you do when you get up in the morning? Where are you living? Who are your friends?

If you are working, what is it like there? What
kind of people do you work with? How do they
dress? What kind of work are they doing? What is
the atmosphere (relaxed? frantic?)? What is your
role in all of this? Describe it in greater and greater
detail.

In addition to describing your work situation,
think about the other parts of your life. Remember:
we each have twenty-four hours a day. How do
you want to spend your twenty-four hours? Where
are you living? What do you do for exercise? How
is your health? What is your social life like? Your
family life? What are your hobbies and interests?
What do you do for spiritual nourishment? What
are you contributing to the world? Describe all of
these in as much detail as possible. But don't worry
if you are not able to identify seemingly important
things, such as the city in which you are living, and
the field in which you are working.

Keep on writing—include as many details as
you can—and develop a good feel for that life.
Work on your Ideal Scene for a while, take a break,
and then go back and write some more. Change the
parts you don't like, and include all the things you
really enjoy doing or see yourself doing at this
imaginary time frame in the future.

CASE STUDY: MAX
Identifying His Future Career
Max, age forty, is a lawyer. A temporary place-

Difficulty need not foreshadow despair or defeat. Rather achievement can be
all the more satisfying because of obstacles surmounted.
William Hastie, *Grace Under Pressure*

---

ment firm sends him on assignments to various companies. He imagined working in a suburban office of six casually-dressed people who were on the phones all day talking excitedly to people all over the world. He had a partner in this business. His own role was one of making contacts with prospective customers. He also saw himself writing about the topic they were engaged in, and becoming relatively well-known within their small segment of the industry.

Max's Ideal Scene may seem general, but it contains a lot of information. It appears that he would like to be in his own small but hectic business, operating on an international level. It would be a niche business where he could develop an expertise and become known to his small marketplace.

The international element was strong in this exercise. It was also evident in his Seven Stories Exercise and his Forty-Year plan. It was clear that an international focus had to be central in his future.

You Can Develop Multiple Scenarios for Your Future

If you simply do the exercise up to this point, you will have done more than most people. You will have developed one scenario for your future. Some people develop multiple scenarios and think about the various possible futures they could have. Then they decide which they would like best, and which they think is do-able.

It all starts with describing an Ideal Scene, but it takes a lot more than that. Writing down the scene makes it more serious, and is the start of a more concrete plan. The written dream and the plan are a lot of work, so you can see why most people do not develop plans—and therefore may tend to drift. But those who write down their plans usually find that they have a lot of fun doing it, and those who keep going realize that their future is, in large part, up to them.

Some people become less self-conscious and braver when they think not of what *they* would like to do, but what they think God has in mind for them. They try to discern God's plan for them, and it is this that motivates and inspires them. Whatever technique or inspiration you use to make your plan, you will be better off for having done it.

The Next Step: Define It Better and Research It

Some people are more ambitious, and want to go on to the next step: they want to flesh out their vision and then test it against reality. In Max's case, he had to figure out what kind of international business he could go into that would rely on his skills and support his values. He came up with a few ideas that excited him. Now he needs to investigate the potential for the various ideas, come up with a plan, develop new skills in the areas where he may be lacking, and take other steps toward fulfilling that plan.

You too will need to flesh out your bare-bones idea and then check it against reality. But be aware that other people will almost always tells you that it's not do-able. Conduct enough research so that you can decide for yourself.

Then, if you are serious about achieving the kind of life that you have envisioned, think of what you need to do to succeed. Take a few little steps immediately to help you advance towards your goal.

Encountering Roadblocks

Remember that this is not a sprint; it is a long-distance run. Do not become discouraged the first time you venture out. You will come up against lots of roadblocks along the way. That's life. Say to yourself, "Isn't this interesting? Another roadblock. I'll take a short breather (and perhaps even allow myself to feel a tingle of discouragement for a little while) and then I'll think of how I can get around this barrier."

Ask yourself what you have learned from the experience, because these experiences are here to teach us something. "What is the lesson for me in this setback?" And then get moving again.

My Forty-Year Plan

My own Ideal Scene evolved from the Forty-

Year Plan I did twenty years ago. I imagined myself at age eighty in a beautiful living space with a housekeeper. I had a strong visual image of someone from the community coming to the door to ask my advice. What this "vision" meant to me was that I had lived my life in such a way that I had had a great impact on the community—people were asking my advice even when I was old. However, I wasn't poverty-stricken because of my devotion to the community.

In my Forty-Year Plan I hadn't yet thought of The Five O'Clock Club or even considered a life in career counseling. But the image that came to me, and which I later developed, served as a template for my ideas and my research. My Seven Stories Exercise told me I had better be working with groups, and perhaps writing and lecturing. My Forty-Year Plan eliminated other interests of mine which would not have helped the community as much as career counseling.

It took many years to develop the concept and the focus of The Five O'Clock Club. For years, I continually used the Seven Stories Exercise and the Forty-Year Plan as my template. If an idea fit in with my plan and abilities, I considered it. If an idea didn't fit, I rejected it. I spent many long hours doing library and other research to select the field I wanted to be in. All of this finally evolved into the concept of The Five O'Clock Club.

As you can see, the Forty-Year Plan is simply a vision of your future. By studying it, along with the Ideal Scene, you can get at unconscious desires you may have. Making your desires conscious increases your chances of being able to do something about them.

First, write out your Ideal Scene. Then in the next section, follow Howard step by step as he uncovers his dream.

The
Five
O'Clock
Club®

The Ideal Scene Worksheet

Imagine yourself five, ten, fifteen, or twenty years from now—at a phase in your life when all is going well. Just pick one of these time frames. Imagine in very general terms the kind of life you were meant to have. Start writing—it's important to write it down, rather than just thinking about it.

What is your ideal life like? Describe a typical day. _____

_____

_____

_____

_____

_____

What do you do when you get up in the morning? Where are you living? _____

_____

_____

_____

Who are your friends? _____

_____

_____

If you are working, what is it like there? _____

_____

_____

What kind of people do you work with? How do they dress? _____

_____

What kind of work are they doing? _____

_____

What is the atmosphere (relaxed or frantic)? _____

_____

What is your role in all of this? _____

_____

_____

Use another sheet of paper to describe it in greater and greater detail.

I mean if you're gonna do it—go and do it. You can't let anything stop you.
But he gave up and lived that "What if. . . . " life.
Bruce Faulk, *You Still Got to Come Home to That*

In addition to describing your work situation, think about the other parts of your life. How do you want to spend your twenty-four hours?

Where are you living? _____

What do you do for exercise? _____

How is your health? _____

What is your social life like? _____

Your family life? _____

What are your hobbies and interests? _____

What do you do for spiritual nourishment? _____

What are you contributing to the world? _____

Describe all of these in as much detail as possible. But don't worry if you are not able to identify seemingly important things, such as the city in which you are living, and the field in which you are working.

Keep on writing—include as many details as you can—and develop a good feel for that life. Work on your Ideal Scene for a while, take a break, and then go back and write some more. Change the parts you don't like, and include all the things you really enjoy doing or see yourself doing at this imaginary time frame in the future. _____

_____

_____

_____

_____

_____

_____

Howard:
Developing a Plan

*In the thick of active life, there is more need to
stimulate fancy than to control it.*
George Santayana, *The Life of Reason*

*We live in an age when art and the things of the spirit
come last. The truth still holds, however, that through
dedication and devotion one achieves another kind of
victory. I mean the ability to overcome one's problems
and meet them head on.*

*"Serve life and you will be sustained." That is a truth
which reveals itself at every turn in the road.*

*I speak with inner conviction because I have been
through the struggle. What I am trying to emphasize is
that, whatever the nature of the problem, it can only be
tackled creatively. There is no book of "openings," as in
chess lore, to be studied. To find an opening one has to
make a breach in the wall—and the wall is almost always
in one's own mind. If you have the vision and the urge to
undertake great tasks, then you will discover in yourself
the virtues and the capabilities required for their accomplishment. When everything fails, pray! Perhaps only
when you have come to the end of your resources will the
light dawn. It is only when we admit our limitations that
we find there are no limitations.*

Henry Miller, *Big Sur and the Oranges of
Hieronymous Bosch*

HAPPY: *All I can do now is wait for the merchandise
manager to die. And suppose I get to be merchandise
manager? He's a good friend of mine, and he just
build a terrific estate on Long Island. And he lived
there about two months and sold it, and now he's
building another one. He can't enjoy it once it's
finished. And I know that's just what I would do. I
don't know what the hell I'm workin' for.*

Arthur Miller, *Death of a Salesman*

Howard came to one of the Affiliates of The
Five O'Clock Club that specializes in
helping people who are not yet in profes-
sional-level jobs. He had done the Seven Stories
and other exercises, and had tried to do the Forty-
Year Plan. Like most people, he had left out important parts, such as what he would be doing for a
living. That's okay. I asked him if he would mind
doing it in the small-discussion group.

At the time, Howard was thirty-five years old
and worked in a lower-level job in the advertising
industry. He wanted to advance in his career by
getting another job in advertising. Based on our
research into the jobs of the future, which showed
that his current industry was a shaky choice, we
asked him to postpone selecting an industry while
we helped him complete his Forty-Year Plan.

Filling in His Forty-Year Plan

Kate: "Howard, you're thirty-five years old right
now. Tell me: who are your friends and what
do they do for a living?"

Howard: "John is a messenger; Keith minds the
kids while his wife works; and Greg delivers
food."

Kate: "What do you do for a living?"

Howard: "I work in the media department of an
advertising agency."

Kate: "Okay. Now, let's go out a few years. You're
forty years old, and you've made a number of
new friends in the past five years. Who are
these people? What are they doing for a living?"

Howard: "One friend is a medical doctor; another
works in finance or for the stock exchange; and
a third is in a management position in the
advertising industry."

Kate: "That's fine. Now, let's go out further. You're
fifty years old, and you have made a lot of new
friends. What are they doing for a living?"

Howard: "One is an executive managing one to
two hundred people in a corporation and is
very well respected; a second one is in education—he's the principal or the administrator of
an experimental high school and gets written
up in the newspapers all the time; a third is a

A human being certainly would not grow to be seventy or eighty years old
if his longevity had no meaning for the species.
C. G. Jung

vice president in finance or banking."

Kate: "Those are important-sounding friends you have, Howard. But who are you and what are you doing that these people are associating with you?"

Howard: "I'm not sure."

Kate: "Well, how much money are you making at age fifty in today's dollars?"

Howard: "I'm making $150,000 a year."

Kate: "I'm impressed. What are you doing to earn that kind of money, Howard? What kind of place are you working in? Remember, you don't *have* to be specific about the industry or field you're in. For example, how do you dress for work?"

Howard: "I wear a suit and tie every day. I have a staff of sixty people working for me: six departments, with ten people in each department."

Kate: "And what are those people doing all day?"

Howard: "They're doing paperwork, or computer work."

Kate: "That's great, Howard. We now have a pretty good idea of what you'll be doing in the future. We just need to fill in some details."

I said to the group: "Perhaps Howard won't be making $150,000, but he'll certainly be making a lot by his own standards. And maybe it won't be sixty people, but it will certainly be a good-sized staff. What Howard is talking about here is a concept. The details may be wrong, but the concept is correct."

Howard said: "But I'm not sure if that's what I really want to do."

Kate: "It may not be exactly what you want to do, Howard, but it's in the right direction and contains the elements you really want. What you just said fits in with your Seven Stories Exercise (one story was about your work with computers; another was about an administrative accomplishment). Think about it for next week, but I'll tell you this: You won't decide you want to be a dress designer, like Roxanne here. Nor will you say you want to sell insurance, like Barry. What you will do will be very close to

what you just described.

"If you come back next week and say that you've decided to sell ice cream, for example, I'll tell you that you simply became afraid. Fear often keeps people from pursuing their dreams. Over the week, read about the jobs of the future [which is included in this book] and let me know the industries you may want to investigate for your future career. It's usually better to pick growth industries rather than declining ones. You stand a better chance of rising with the tide."

The Next Week

When it was Howard's turn in the group the next week, he announced that he had selected health care as the industry he wanted to investigate. That sounded good because it is a growth field and because there will be plenty of need for someone to manage a group of people working on computers.

We brainstormed the areas within health care that Howard could research. He could work in a hospital, an HMO, a health-care association, and so on. He could learn about the field by reading the trade magazines having to do with health-care administration, and he could start networking by meeting with someone else in the group who had already worked in a hospital.

Week #3

Howard met with the other person in the group and got a feel for what it was like to work in a hospital. He also got a few names of people he could talk to—people at his level who could give him basic information. He had spent some time in a library reading trade magazines having to do with health-care administration.

Howard needed to do a lot more research before he would be ready to meet with higher-level people—those in a position to hire him.

Week #4

Howard announced to the group that he had done more research, which helped him figure out that he should start in the purchasing area of a hospital, as opposed to the financial area, for example. In previous jobs, he had worked both as a buyer and as a salesman, so he knew both sides of the picture. He would spend some time researching the purchasing aspect of health care. That could be his entry point, and he could make other moves after he got into the field.

Week #5

Today Howard is ready to meet with higher-level people in the health-care field. As he networks around, he will learn even more about the field, and select the job and the organization that will position him best for the long run—the situation that fits in best with his Forty-Year Plan.

After Howard gets his next job, he will occasionally come to the group to ask the others to help him think about his career and make moves within the organization. He will be successful in living his plan if he continues to do what needs to be done, never taking his eye off the ball.

If Howard sticks with his vision, he will make good money, and live in the kind of place in which he wants to live. Like many people who develop written plans, Howard has the opportunity to have his dream come true.

You Can Do It Too

The group that Howard attended was Workforce America®, our program in Harlem. In Harlem, there is a large professional and executive population, but Workforce America works mostly with adults who are not yet in the professional or managerial ranks, and helps them get into professional-track jobs. For example:

Emlyn, a thirty-five-year-old former baby-sitter, embarked on and completed a program to become a nurse's aide. This is her first step toward becoming an R.N., her ultimate career goal.

Calvin, who suffers from severe rheumatoid arthritis, hadn't worked in ten years. Within five weeks of starting at Workforce America, he got a job as a consumer advocate with a center for the disabled, and has a full caseload. Workforce America is continuing to work with him.

These ambitious, hard-working people did it, and so can you. It's not easy, but what else are you doing with your twenty-four hours a day? Follow the motto of Workforce America: "Have a dream. Make a plan. Take a step. Keep on climbing."

You can complain that you haven't gotten lucky breaks, but Howard, Emlyn, and Calvin didn't either. They made their own breaks, attended an Affiliate of The Five O'Clock Club, and kept plugging ahead despite difficulties. If they can do it, you can do it too.

You can either say the universe is totally random and it's just molecules colliding all the time and it's totally chaos and our job is to make sense of that chaos, or you can say sometimes things happen for a reason and your job is to discover the reason.
But either way, I do see it meaning an opportunity and that has made all the difference.
Christopher Reeve, former star of *Superman*,
in an interview with Barbara Walters.
Reeve became a quadriplegic
after a horseback-riding accident.

This is a real test of the wedding vows. He's my partner. He's my other half, literally. It's not within the realm of my imagination to do anything less than what I'm doing.
Mrs. Christopher Reeve (Dana),
in that same interview

The
Five
O'Clock
Club

Self-Assessment Summary

Summarize the results of all of the exercises. This information will help define the kind of environment that suits you best, and will also help you brainstorm some possible job targets. Finally, it can be used as a checklist against job possibilities. When you are about to receive a job offer, use this list to help you analyze it objectively.

1. What I need in my relationship with bosses:

_____

2. Job satisfiers/dissatisfiers:
    Satisfiers: _____
    Dissatisfiers: _____

3. Most important work-related values:

_____

4. Special interests:

_____

5. The threads running through the Seven Stories analysis:
    Main accomplishments:_____
    Key motivators: _____
    Enjoyed most; Did best:_____
    My role: _____
    The environment: _____
    The subject matter: _____

6. The top six or seven specialized skills:
    _____
    _____
    _____
    _____
    _____
    _____
    _____

7. From the Forty-Year Plan:
    Where I see myself in the long run:

_____

    What I need to get there:

_____

8. My basic personality and the kinds of work cultures it will fit:

_____

For deep in our hearts
We do believe
That we shall overcome someday.
"We Shall Overcome"
African-American freedom song

Resolve to be thyself and know that
he who finds himself loses his misery.
Matthew Arnold

To repeat part of a quote we included earlier:

OPTIMISM EMERGES AS BEST PREDICTOR
TO SUCCESS IN LIFE

Hope has proven a powerful predictor of outcome in
every study we've done so far," said Dr. Charles R.
Snyder, a psychologist at the University of Kansas.
Having hope means believing you have both the will
and the way to accomplish your goals, whatever they
may be. . . . It's not enough to just have the wish for
something. You need the means, too. On the other
hand, all the skills to solve a problem won't help if you
don't have the willpower to do it.
Daniel Goleman,*The New York Times*,
December 24, 1991

How many cares one loses when one decides not to be
something but to be someone.
Coco Chanel

You move from obsessing about why me and
it's not fair and when will I move again and all of those
things into well, what is the potential?
And now, four months down the line, I see potential I
wasn't capable of seeing. . . So I really sense
being on a journey that's very interesting.
Christopher Reeve, former star of *Superman*,
in an interview with Barbara Walters.
Reeve became a quadriplegic
after a horseback-riding accident.

Sometimes we get so caught up in the path we are on that we think we have no choice. We forget what we would rather be doing. It is easy to lose sight of what would make us happy. We forget we have made choices that have brought us to where we are.

Approach career planning and job hunting with an open mind—be open to the possibilities available to you. It is only by going out into the world and testing your ideas that the possibilities present themselves. Explore. Don't rush to take a job just because it is something well-known to you.

The purpose of knowledge, and especially historical
knowledge, is understanding rather than certainty.
John Lukacs, A History of the Cold War

Although your motivated skills do not change, keep reexamining them so you can see how they fit into various situations in your changing world. You will always fit in because your motivated skills adapt themselves to new situations and new possibilities.

Expect to be surprised. And think of surprise as a pleasant thing, because it adds interest to your life. Every move you make will open a new range of possibilities.

The step you are now taking is one that can alter the direction of your life. If you are aware, it can have as much or as little effect as you want it to have. If it turns out to be a mistake, you can move on.

This is not the last step: it is a transition. The next step is a preparation for the one after that. In the future, it will rarely be possible to say, in concrete terms, "I want to be this for the rest of my life." The past is over and is subject to a new interpretation depending on the situation you are now in and where you want to go from here. It's your story, and it is a story you make up as you go along. You don't know how the story will end, and the ending really doesn't matter. What matters is that you are living your life, enjoying the process of living. It's a journey, not a battle.

The Five O'Clock Club

PART THREE

HOW TO SELECT YOUR JOB TARGETS

BRAINSTORMING POSSIBLE JOBS

But when the family continued to struggle, and when Steve Ross was a teenager, he was summoned to his father's deathbed to learn that his sole inheritance consisted of this advice: There are those who work all day, those who dream all day, and those who spend an hour dreaming before setting to work to fulfill those dreams.

"Go into the third category," his father said, "because there's virtually no competition."

Obituary of Steven J. Ross, creator of Time Warner, *The New York Times*, December 21, 1992

The very core of what I believe is this concept of individual worth, which I think flows from all of us being creatures of God and being imbued with a spirit.
Hilary Clinton

I've got peace like a river ina my soul.
African-American spiritual

It is never too late to be what you might have been.
George Eliot

CHARLEY: *Yeah. He was a happy man with a batch of cement.*
LINDA: *He was so wonderful with his hands.*
BIFF: *He had the wrong dreams. All, all, wrong.*
HAPPY, almost ready to fight Biff: *Don't say that!*
BIFF: *He never knew who he was.*
Arthur Miller, *Death of a Salesman*

U se the worksheet on the next page to help you brainstorm possible jobs that you can then explore.

1. **Across the top of the page**, list the following elements as they apply to you. Use as many columns as you need for each category.
- Your Basic Personality
- Interests
- Values
- Specialized Skills
- From the Seven Stories Exercise:
  - the role you played
  - the environment in which you worked
  - the various subject matters in your stories
- Long-range Goals
- Education
- Work Experience
- Areas of Expertise.

Here is one person's list of column headings across the top:
- Personality: <u>outgoing</u>;
- Interests: <u>environment</u>, <u>computers</u>, <u>world travel</u> (three different interests—takes three columns);
- Values: <u>a decent wage</u> so I can support a family;
- Specialized Skills: <u>use of PC</u>;
- From the Seven Stories Exercise:
  - being <u>part of a research group</u>;
  - enjoy <u>Third-World countries</u> (takes two columns);
- Goals from the Forty-Year Plan: <u>head up not-for-profit organization</u>;
- Education: <u>Master's in Public Policy</u>;
- Work Experience: <u>seven years' marketing experience</u>.

This takes a total of eleven columns across the top.

2. **Down the side of the page, list possible jobs, fields, or functions** that rely on one or more of these elements. For example, combine marketing

You must have long-range goals to keep you from being frustrated
by short-range failures.
Charles C. Noble, Major general

with environment, or computers with research and Third-World countries.

At this point, do not eliminate anything. Write down whatever ideas occur to you. Ask your friends and family. Do library research and talk to lots of people. Open your eyes and your mind when you read or walk down the street. Be observant and generate lots of ideas. Write down whatever anyone suggests. A particular suggestion may not be exactly right for you, but may help you think of other things that *are* right.

3. **Analyze each job possibility**. Check off across the page the elements that apply to the first job. For example, if the job fits your basic personality, put a checkmark in that column. If it uses your education or relies on your work experience, put checkmarks in those columns. If it fits in with your long-range goals, put a checkmark there.

Do the same for every job listed in the left column.

4. **Add up the checkmarks for each job, and write the total in the right-hand column**. Any job that relies on only one or two elements is probably not appropriate for you. Pay attention to ones with the most checkmarks. Certain elements are more important to you than others, so you must weight those more heavily. In fact, there are probably some elements that *must* be present so you will be satisfied, such as a job that meshes with your values.

Those jobs which seem to satisfy your most important elements are the ones you will list as some of the targets to explore on the Preliminary Target Investigation worksheet (two pages ahead). Also list positions that would be logical next steps for you in light of your background.

CASE STUDY: AGNES
Broadening Her Targets

Agnes has been a marketing/merchandising/promotion executive in the fashion, retail, and banking industries. Her only love was retail, and her dream job was working for one specific, famous fashion house. Perhaps she could actually get a job with that fashion house, but what kind of job could she go for after that? The retail and fashion industries were both retrenching at the time of her search, although she could probably get a job in one of them. She needed more targets, and preferably some targets in growing industries so she would have a more reasonable career path.

In addition to the retail and fashion industries, what other industries could Agnes consider? In the banking industry, where she had been for only three years, some of the products she promoted had been computerized. In combining "computers" with "retail" we came up with "computerized shopping," a new field that was threatening the retail industry. Computerized shopping and related areas were good fields for Agnes to investigate. What about something having to do with debit cards and credit cards or Prodigy—all computer-based systems aimed at retail? Or what about selling herself to banks that were handling the bankrupt retail companies that she was so familiar with? We came up with twenty areas to explore. Agnes's next step is to conduct a Preliminary Target Investigation (which you will read about soon) to determine which fields may be worth pursuing in that they hold some interest for her and there is some possibility of finding a job in them. At this point she has an exciting search lined up—one with lots of fields to explore and one that offers her a future instead of just a job.

The
Five
O'Clock
Club

Brainstorming Possible Jobs Worksheet

Assessment Results →																				Total check-marks across
Possible Jobs																				

Chiron:
Finding a Future

*Growing up means eliminating
what doesn't work for you.*
Jan Halper, Ph.D., *Quiet Desperation—
The Truth about Successful Men*

Chiron is worn out. He is forty-five years old, and has had lots of different jobs in his life. Getting jobs has never been a problem. He has just gotten another one, and is afraid that it too will go nowhere. His wife is in her early thirties, and they would like to have children, but feel they cannot afford them on Chiron's income, which is approximately $60,000 a year.

In addition to his day job, where he works thirty hours a week, Chiron still has the small business he started on the side—keeping the books for a small company—just in case. He earns very little at this business, which is why he answered the ad for the job he just landed: director of development for a small not-for-profit in the medical field.

My Role As a Counselor

Chiron came to see me because his career path had caused him so much stress. He couldn't take the instability. My job is to help him uncover the central things that may be holding him back in his career—the things that may cause him not to live up to his abilities.

To save him money and time in the career-counseling session, I asked Chiron to complete the exercises in this book before we met. I told him that if he could not complete all of them, he should at least complete the Seven Stories.

Chiron was very serious when he came for his session. He hoped he could turn his life around. I will give you some highlights from our sessions.

Every client is different, and every counselor is different. But most counselors have similar goals. The purpose of the exercises is to get a sense of the person's career-related issues in an organized, methodical way. The exercises simply help a person talk about those issues. In addition, I try to teach the client the process we are going through so that he or she can think more deeply about the issues and do more self-analysis when I am not around.

Our Initial Session

We reviewed Chiron's Seven Stories Exercise. I will show you how the discussion went. First, I asked him to rank his seven stories so that we could work first on the one he ranked number-one.

The First Story

Kate: "Chiron, tell me your first accomplishment."

Chiron: "I planned and organized a free folk concert."

Kate: "When did this happen, or how old were you?"

Chiron: "It happened in 1972. I was twenty-three or twenty-four."

Kate: "Tell me about it."

Chiron: "I came up with the idea and organized the event. This was back when people were still upset about the war in Vietnam, and there had been a lot of protests. I wanted to turn that discontent into something good."

Kate: "So exactly what did you do? What was involved?"

Chiron: "I coordinated with various government offices to get permission for the concert. The government folks liked the idea because it was peaceful. It wasn't a political protest. Everything was donated, and everyone performed for free."

Kate: "How successful was it? For example, how many people attended?"

Chiron: "Twenty to thirty thousand people attended."

Kate: "Good grief! That's a lot of people! What prompted you to do this event? What led up to it?"

Chiron: "I wanted to make a difference. I wanted to do the community a favor."

Kate: "This was your number-one accomplishment. What about it made it number-one for you?"

Chiron: "I picked this experience as number-one because I was doing good and also having fun."

Kate: "What kind of time frame was involved? How long did the whole project take?"

Chiron: "Two months from start to finish."

Kate: "Even if you've already told me, what about it was most enjoyable for you? What was the most fun?"

Chiron: "Coordinating the folk groups and the other performers and all of the government offices. I also loved working with the press."

Kate: "What about it gave you a sense of accomplishment?"

Chiron: "Creating something out of nothing and having it be a success."

The Second Story

Kate: "That was great. Let's look at your next accomplishment. What was it?"

Chiron: "I taught myself journalism and got hired as a reporter."

Kate: "When did this happen and how old were you?"

Chiron: "Around 1978. I was twenty-nine."

Kate: "So tell me about it."

Chiron: "I went after a job creatively. I targeted one newspaper where I knew there was a job opening. The other people going after the job were all journalism majors. But I figured out how to write a story by studying books on my own. Then I covered some news events as if I were actually writing for the newspaper. I sent the editor the stories and said, 'This is how I would have covered the story if I had been writing for you.' I did this with a few stories, and actually had a lot of fun doing it. After each one, I would call him. I got the job and beat out all those people who had better qualifications."

Kate: "That's a great accomplishment. What led up to your doing it?"

Chiron: "I had spent two sessions working with the Connecticut legislature, and that's what got me interested in being a journalist."

Kate: "You mentioned as your success the fact that you got hired; what about the job itself? You didn't mention that as a success."

Chiron: "I loved the job."

Kate: "What about it did you love?"

Chiron: "I covered a diverse range of subjects: kids and skateboards; arson. Each time, I had to teach myself the subject area."

Kate: "What did you enjoy the most?"

Chiron: "Teaching myself and getting hired and covering a wide range of subjects. I enjoyed doing the research required."

Kate: "Is there anything else you'd like to tell me about this experience?"

Chiron: "Yes. I loved meeting new people."

Kate: "How long did you have this job?"

Chiron: "Only two months. My wife got transferred to a new job in another city. We weighed it and decided to move."

Analysis of the First Two Stories

After I have heard two stories, I give the client some feedback so he or she will see the process I use. Later, the client should be able to do a better job analyzing the stories than I could. After all, he or she was there; I wasn't.

In this case, I gave Chiron my initial impressions, based solely on what he had told me:

"Chiron, it may be that your other stories show things very differently from these first two, but I'll tell you what I've noticed so far, for what it's worth.

"Both of these happened a long time ago—fifteen to twenty years ago. Part of our quest in going through the assessment process is to come up with goals for you so that your *next* experience has a better chance of winding up as one of your top seven stories.

"A second thing I noticed is that they were both of short duration. In addition, a lot of the jobs on your résumé were also of relatively short duration.

"This is not necessarily bad. A person can choose to work on short-term things forever, such as people who get involved in fads—like the 'pet rocks' people. They don't expect these fads to last. They expect them to be short-lived. Then they move on to the next thing. Planning fads is their focus, and they become expert at it.

"Other examples are people who run events, or head up special projects. Some people can be very successful working on short-term projects—but they tend to have a specific area of expertise and they tend to *intend* to have project-oriented work.

"On the other hand, a person can decide to hunker down and remain in something more long-term so that he or she can become somewhat expert at it. That's another way to go.

The traditional admonition of one generation to the next, "Get a job," has been replaced with the more complex and bewildering mandate, "Go out and create a job for yourself."
George Gendron, editor, *Inc.*

"So, a person can choose to have a short-term project orientation, or a longer-term orientation. One is not better than the other. The important point is *planning*. An opportunistic approach of doing whatever happens to present itself rarely works. It's gets very tiring to constantly learn new things and not to build on your previous experiences.

"Other threads that appear in both stories are:

"You came up with an idea and did it. You had to be convincing. There was a lot of creativity and coordination. You showed initiative in both stories.

"I'm struggling to find a subject matter that appears in both. This may have no significance at all, but politics appears in both. In one story, you had to deal with the government, and in the other, you watched the state legislature for two sessions.

"Another possible thread having to do with subject matter is 'the press.' In the first story, you dealt with the press. In the second story, you *were* the press."

As I show Chiron my thought patterns, he can decide whether or not what I am saying has any significance. He can think more about his own experiences. Then he can decide what's important about them and come up with conclusions of his own.

The Third Story

Kate: "Tell me your third accomplishment."

Chiron: "Last year, I started my own bookkeeping business for a grocery store."

Kate: "Tell me about this one."

Chiron: "I needed something to do. I had lost my job. Friends and I brainstormed ideas. I liked the idea of performing a service that people would appreciate. I also like food, and I have an M.B.A., so doing bookkeeping for a food business seemed logical."

Kate: "What for you was the real accomplishment?"

Chiron: "I started the business from nothing. I built it myself. And now it's successful. When I collect the money every week, it tells me that I made this thing work."

Kate: "Even if you've already told me, what about this did you enjoy the most?"

Chiron: "It was 'my thing,' and I made money from it."

Other Accomplishments

Chiron then went on to tell four additional stories. For example, the fourth was when he ran a successful political campaign for someone who was running for city council. At this time, Chiron was only about twenty-six years old.

After we reviewed all seven stories, I told Chiron that I noticed that three had the government or politics or power in them. They all showed his ability to convince, required creativity, organization, and initiative.

In the bookkeeping business, he did *not* mention any interaction with the people—the people he did the bookkeeping for or even the bookkeepers he had hired to help him. In all of the other stories, he had mentioned enjoying the people: meeting new people through journalism, working with the legislature and the folk groups, or recruiting and organizing volunteers in the political campaign. This "people orientation" was an important element missing in the bookkeeping business. My impression was that he did not like the business. What he liked was the idea that he had started it and made it work well enough.

Other strong threads appeared to be:

- running a campaign
- being a natural leader
- being a major influencer
- developing strategies
- doing his own thing.

What did Chiron have to say about this? He was solemn and intense: "Yes. I see myself as the General. In the army, there's a platoon leader who deals with day-to-day tactics. I'm the General who sees the overall picture. I'm making only $60,000 a year, but I really feel that I should be making double this."

I replied, "Based on what you've told me, I too see you as the General. You seem to be the type of person who *has* to lead, to develop strategies, to influence people. It may be that the subject matter doesn't matter much—as long as you feel you're

When all is said and done, you have just one irreplaceable resource: this particular, unique, unrepeatable lifetime of yours. What were you meant to do with it?
William Bridges, *JobShift: How to Prosper in a Workplace Without Jobs*

---

contributing to the public good—providing a service."

That's it for his Seven Stories Exercise. The other assessment results were also important, although I won't go into them here. I did find it significant that he has an M.B.A.

As I review the results, I look to make sure all of the results are in agreement. For example, if a person says he or she does not value money, but imagines living in a palatial house, I would want to know how he or she planned to afford such a place. Most often, people's results are in sync. That is, there is usually some correlation between the various exercises.

Unresolved conflicts can hold a person back. In Chiron's case, there were a number of conflicts. The most important showed up in his Values exercise. Chiron places a very high value on his lifestyle. In fact, he and his wife go away just about every weekend to the cabin they have in the woods. They are able to do this because it doesn't cost much, and Chiron essentially works only 36 hours a week in both of his jobs combined. He leaves work early every Friday so they can go to the country. In addition, he takes French horn lessons and goes to the gym once a week. Traveling is another interest of his. At present, his lifestyle is important, and he is not willing to give it up. Yet he also wants to make $120,000 a year.

That's a lot of money. People who make that much—even far less than that—work very hard and tend to work long hours. Chiron would have to resolve this conflict of wanting to maintain his lifestyle, work a 36-hour week, and yet make a large amount of money. This rarely happens unless a person develops some highly valued expertise.

It Is Not Easy to Find Out
What Is Holding a Person Back

Chiron's conflict may seem obvious to you: How could he not see the problem? You can see Chiron's problem because I'm spelling it out for you. However, I may be wrong. It may be that the real problem is not apparent to me. Chiron is the only one who can know for sure why he is not reaching the level to which he aspires.

Perhaps you too have something that is holding you back. It may not be obvious to you or to anyone else. Our conflicts and beliefs are subtle and often rigid. Most people do not recognize their own conflicts. Even when a conflict is pointed out to them, it is difficult to take the steps necessary to correct it. People usually continue to do what they have been doing. Changing one's beliefs takes a great deal of insight and courage.

It would take some time for Chiron to resolve this conflict in his values. So we moved on to the next part of the process. We worked on Chiron's Forty-Year Plan. He came up with a number of possibilities. It's best if you too come up with a number of scenarios for yourself. Then you can match them against your requirements. To be thorough, Chiron also filled out the "Brainstorming Possible Jobs Worksheet." Across the top of the worksheet, I noted his assessment results: his Seven Stories, his interests, values, education, and so on. That worksheet is shown on the next page.

Down the left-hand side of the worksheet, Chiron brainstormed possible jobs, and also asked his friends to think of job possibilities for him. Those suggestions helped him to think of still others. Then he put check marks wherever a job possibility fit in with a characteristic. This helped him to get rid of possibilities that would not fit most of his requirements.

The Three Scenarios

After all of this, Chiron came up with three possibilities that he thought he would find satisfying. He also thought that all three of these could happen within the next five years—when he would be fifty years old. The three possibilities were:
- be president of my own company
- be political director of a large national organization
- be COO of the medical not-for-profit for which he now worked.

We examined each of these so he could realistically see what would be involved—at least at the start. Then he could research each further, and think more about the direction he really wanted his life to take.

106

Brainstorming Possible Jobs Worksheet

Assessment Results → / Possible Jobs	Driving force: idealism	Service-orientation	Artistic	Enterprising	Writer/journalist	Sales/influencing	Leader/the "General"	Strategist	Meet with leaders	"Business owner"	Advisor	Politics/government	Food/health	Non-bureaucratic	M.B.A.	Earn $100,000/yr.	Make large impact	Complex problems			Total check-marks across
Lobbyist	✔				✔	✔		✔	✔		✔	✔									7
Bookkeeping business		✔		✔						✔	✔										4
Political campaign mgr.	✔	✔		✔	✔	✔		✔	✔		✔	✔									9
Executive, present co.	✔	✔	✔	✔	✔	✔	✔	✔	✔	✔	✔	✔			✔	?	✔	✔			15
Development director	✔	✔		✔	✔	✔		✔	✔		✔						✔				9
Journalist	✔				✔	✔		✔	✔			✔									6
Political activist	✔	✔			✔	✔	✔	✔	✔		✔	✔									9
Union organizer	✔	✔			✔	✔	✔	✔	✔		✔	✔									9
Arts organization	✔	✔	✔		✔	✔	✔	✔	✔		✔	✔									10
Fund-raiser: music	✔	✔			✔	✔		✔	✔		✔	✔									9
Pres. of my own co.	✔	✔		✔	✔	✔	✔	✔	✔	✔			✔	✔	✔	?	✔				14
State senator	✔	✔			✔	✔	✔	✔	✔		✔	✔									9
Pol. director, large org.	✔	✔		✔	✔	✔	✔	✔	✔		✔	✔				?	✔				11
. . . and so on																					

> *Not everything that is faced can be changed;*
> *But nothing can be changed until it is faced.*
> James Baldwin

Analyzing the Possibilities

Let's take a look at each possibility. Chiron and I had a preliminary discussion so he could get a feel for how long it would take for him to move to the level he described in each of the three scenarios. In real life, a person has to do a "Preliminary Target Investigation" by talking to people in those fields and assessing the likelihood of being able to make such a transition.

Scenario 1: "Be president of my own company"

I asked Chiron what kind of company he could see himself heading up. He thought a publishing company sounded good. What size staff would he have? He thought ten to twenty people. What kind of publishing company? He thought a magazine, such as in the health, cooking, or travel area. He imagined it as being a few monthly publications, subscription only (as opposed to street sales).

It takes most people about two years from the time they decide to start their own small business until the time they actually start it. They have a lot of research and planning to do: Who else is in that market? How are they doing? What are they doing? How much will it cost? Where will I get the money? Even if a person works 15 hours a week on the new business while working full-time doing something else, it still takes two years.

Therefore, by the time Chiron is forty-seven, he will be able to start the business—probably on the side while continuing to work at his day job. He could run it for a few years part-time until it is far enough along that he could tackle it full-time. Then he would be forty-nine or so. It is unlikely that he would have a staff of ten to twenty at that time. It is more likely that it would be five or so employees—if he is lucky.

Even if Chiron opted to raise the money instead of trying to finance the enterprise himself, that still takes lots of time.

The question is whether Chiron has the discipline to investigate this idea objectively, plan it, and carry it out. If not, he should not go impulsively into this business just because it sounds like a fine idea to him. He will only repeat past mistakes where he tackled something without being properly prepared.

Scenario 2: "Be political director of a large national organization"

Chiron imagined himself in an organization that has a corporate staff of 12 or so. He would be the chief lobbyist with a staff of four to six. I asked him to pick an organization—any organization—just to make this example more real. He selected the National Association of Manufacturers, which is headquartered in Washington, D.C. Let's brainstorm this scenario.

Of course, Chiron would have to be willing to live in Washington, D.C., at some point. After resolving that barrier in his own mind, one scenario for moving ahead with this plan would be to get a job as a junior lobbyist *in an area that would eventually be of interest to the organization he targeted.* It would not be good enough to get lobbying experience, for example, in the utilities or tobacco field. He would need relevant experience because his future employers would want to capitalize on the contacts he had made. Then he could become a more powerful lobbyist, and he would be desirable to organizations such as the one he mentioned.

Chiron would have no trouble getting his first lobbying job. After all, it would not be that high-level, and Chiron is very convincing in interviews. But since it would require a geographic move, that step could take a year. Then he would have to do extremely well in that field so he would have a few things to brag about. That would take two or three years, for sure. Then he would have to get into the right organization, and move up within it. That would be a few more years. I guessed that Chiron would be in his ideal job, making the kind of money he wanted in nine years, at age fifty-four.

I think it's do-able, and he has plenty of time, since most of us are living longer. The question, again, is one of commitment.

The third scenario will take the same length of time to achieve and require the same commitment. Life takes time. Making good money takes most people a lot of time and commitment. Chiron needed to decide what his priorities were. That also would take time.

Chiron had always prided himself on his ability to learn things quickly. However, at a certain age, those areas that were our greatest strengths can become our greatest weaknesses if we don't watch out. Chiron tends to not learn any area in depth, keeping him stuck at $60,000 or so a year.

There is no end to this story yet. We will all have to wait and see what Chiron decides to do with his life.

Chiron's Options

Lucky Chiron has many options. Many people would envy the life he and his wife have created for themselves. Chiron and his wife do not work long hours, earn decent money, go to the country every weekend, and have time to pursue other interests. Sometimes people are unhappy with their lives until they complete the assessment and discover they don't have it so bad after all. In Chiron's case, he and his wife can keep their lives—and their income—essentially as is. To gain the career stability Chiron wants, all he needs to do is stick with something long enough to become expert. Then he will have the kind of life many Americans want.

On the other hand, he could join the rat race with the rest of us. He may choose to do that because, for example, he thinks he needs the money to have and raise children (although people do raise children on what Chiron makes, and most wives work today).

If he wants to make a good deal more than he does now, he will have to work a good deal harder. Those who have spent years becoming expert in a marketable area can work less hard. But Chiron still has to develop marketable skills to command more money. Within that, he has many choices.

He has energy and brains and talent. He needs direction and hard work. That's not so bad.

For each of the three scenarios he targeted, he could develop a plan similar to the one Deborah did in "Developing a Detailed Plan," a few chapters back. That would help him to chart a course that he could then stick to if he is committed enough. The sooner he makes a commitment to a clear direction,

the more likely he is to achieve that direction. If he keeps on hedging, his energies will continue to be dispersed. In his present job, he could develop a skill that he feels sure would also help him later.

If the direction he selects later proves to be wrong, Chiron will still be better off for having chosen something and for developing a marketable skill. Then he can build on his new marketable experience.

As far as the bookkeeping business is concerned, I think Chiron should keep at it until he has made a commitment to a new path. Otherwise, he may continue his pattern of jumping from one thing to another without properly researching it. Although the bookkeeping business is not the right career path for him, the more important lesson he needs to learn is commitment. Then the future will look bright for Chiron.

You too have many options. And you too have plenty of time in which to achieve them. But you too must investigate them, and make a commitment. And give yourself a break. Remember that life takes time.

You do not sing because you are happy;
you are happy because you sing.
William James

In a fight between you and the world,
bet on the world.
Franz Kafka

Some luck lies in not getting what you thought you
wanted but in getting what you have, which once you
have got it you may be smart enough to see is what
you would have wanted had you known.
Garrison Keillor

I arise in the morning torn between
the desire to improve the world and
a desire to enjoy the world.
This makes it hard to plan the day.
E. B. White

Life Takes Time

Great ideas come into the world as gently as doves.
Perhaps then, if we listen attentively, we shall hear,
amid the uproar of empires and nations,
a faint flutter of wings,
the gentle stirrings of life and hope.
Albert Camus

To sum up, here is the process:
Step 1: Understand yourself: your values, interests, skills, and so on. The better you understand yourself, and the more honest you are about it, the better you will be able to assess the opportunities that will come your way.

Step 2: Figure out what you want. What on this earth would you be best served doing? What should your future be like?

Step 3: Figure out how to get there. Later on, we will show you how to develop a Career Plan for yourself.

Step 4: Figure out what within yourself might stand in your way. Chiron had a conflict in values, and also a tendency to lack commitment to a specific path. If he can resolve these issues, nothing can stand in his way.

Internal Issues

Here are some common examples of internal issues that hold people back:
- a conflict in values. "I want to earn $300,000 a year as an exporter in Montana (where there are few export jobs), work a two-day week, and spend three years with Mother Teresa."
- a lack of self-esteem. People rise to their level of self-esteem. If you have low self-esteem, stop thinking about yourself, and instead think of what you were put on this planet to do. Do what you were meant to do. God did not mean for you to bury your talents, but to use them and make them multiply.
- an inability to imagine a more fulfilling future; depression. Get some help with your Forty-Year Plan. Start writing. Get career-counseling help if you need it.

- a lack of focus. Some people see too many possibilities and cannot decide what to do. They flit from one thing to another and do not become expert at anything.
- a lack of possibilities. Other people imagine doing the same thing for thirty years. They need to explore more and see what's out there.
- Too many skills; master of none.
- Too few skills; need to get into the nineties.
- Too tense; don't have enough fun.
- Too much fun; don't buckle under and work.

Add your own thoughts to this list. There are plenty of things that hold people back.

"External" Issues

In addition, most job hunters have something that they think will keep them from getting their next job. It could be that they feel they are too young or too old, have too little education or too much, are of the wrong race, creed, nationality, sex or sexual orientation, weight or height, or are very aware that they have a physical disability.

While it is true that there is prejudice out there, job hunters who are too self-conscious about their perceived handicaps will hold themselves back. In addition, they may inadvertently draw attention to their "problem" during the interview. Your attitude must be: "What problem? There is no problem. Let me tell you about the things I've done."

Now let's move on to look at some of the things *you've* done.

A competitive world has two possibilities for you.
You can lose. Or, if you want to win, you can change.
Lester C. Thurow, Dean,
Sloan School of Management, M.I.T.

Monitor how you're thinking and behaving, and try to
stop negative thoughts and behaviors in their tracks.
Ask yourself: Why am I thinking or behaving this
way? What's the positive alternative? What might
make it easier for me—now and in the future—to
think or act positively in this type of situation?
Jack Maguire, *Care and Feeding of the Brain*

How to Decide What You Want to Offer

*The fastest way to succeed is to
look as if you're playing by other people's rules,
while quietly playing by your own.*
Michael Korda

Your motivated skills and your dreams help you set your long-term direction. In order to go somewhere, you must know where you are right now. In this chapter, you will look down and see where your feet are. You will become more pragmatic. What have you done so far in your life? What do you have to offer the world?

What Do You Have to Offer?

In deciding what you *want* to offer, first list all you *have* to offer—a menu to choose from. When you go after a certain kind of position, emphasize those parts that support your case. If you decide, for example, to continue your career in the same direction, you will probably focus on your most recent position and others that support that direction.

If most of your adult satisfactions have occurred outside your job, you may want to change something about your work life. If you decide to change careers, activities outside your regular job may help you make that change.

Twelve years ago, when I was interested in changing from computers to advertising, I offered as proof of my ability the three years I had spent at night promoting nonprofit organizations. My portfolio of press coverage for those organizations was my proof. Later, when I wanted to work as a career counselor, my proof was my many years' experience in running The Five O'Clock Club at night, the seminars I had given on job hunting and career development, and so on. When I wanted to continue working in business management, I simply offered my on-the-job experience in making companies profitable.

If you have available the entire list of what you have to offer, you can be more flexible about the direction in which you want to go.

How to State Your Accomplishments

Present what you have to offer in terms of accomplishments. Tell your "story" in a way that will provoke interest in you and let the "reader" know what you are really like. Accomplishment statements are short, measurable, and results-oriented. We each handle the situations in our work lives in different ways. What problems have you faced at work? How did you handle them? What was the effect on the organization?

Some of us are project-oriented and others are process-oriented. If you are project-oriented, you will tend to take whatever is assigned to you, break it into "projects" in your mind, and then get those projects done. You like to solve problems, and you get bored when there are none. Your accomplishments will state the problems you faced, how you solved them, and the impact you had on the organization.

On the other hand, if you are process-oriented, you like to run the day-to-day shop. You can be trusted to keep an existing situation running smoothly, and your accomplishments will reflect that. You like stable situations and systems that work. You will state that you ran a department of so many people for so many years.

Work on this exercise now. Start with any of your Seven Stories that are work-related. Note the way you wrote about each accomplishment when you were telling your "story." Chances are, it was a more exciting way to describe that accomplishment than the way you would normally write about it on a résumé or talk about it in an interview. Use those stories as your starting point, and be sure to include details so the reader will be able to see what you actually did. After all, they were important enough for you to include in your Seven Stories. Don't ignore them now.

Next, write down your current or most recent position. State your title, your company name, and list your accomplishments in that position.

Do not worry right now if you do not like your job title, or don't even like your job. In our résumé book we will change your title to make it reflect what you were actually doing, and we can emphasize or deemphasize jobs and responsibilities as you see fit. Right now, get down on paper all of your accomplishments. Then we will have something to work with.

A project-oriented accomplishment could look like this:

• Designed and directed a comprehensive and cost-effective advertising and sales promotion program that established the company as a major competitor in the market.

A process-oriented accomplishment could look like this:
• Reviewed ongoing market performance of investor-owned utility securities. Used multiple equity valuation techniques. Recommended redirection of portfolio mix to more profitable and higher-quality securities.

After you have completed your accomplishment statements for your present or most recent position, examine the job before that one. State your title, your company name, and list your accomplishments.

Work on as many accomplishments as make sense to you. Some people cover in depth the past ten years. If you can, cover your entire career, because you never know what may occur to you, and you never know what may help you later. In doing this exercise, you may remember jobs you had completely forgotten about—and pleasant and satisfying accomplishments. Ask yourself what it was about that job that was so satisfying. Perhaps it is another clue about what you might do in the future.

Do not wish to go back to your youth. What was challenging then will probably not satisfy you today. Look for the *elements* of those early jobs that satisfied you. These elements should be compared with your list of motivated skills to determine lifelong interests.

You will feel better after you have completed this exercise. You will see on paper all that you have to offer. And your accomplishments will be stated in a way that will make you proud.

Discipline yourself to do this exercise now, and you will not have to do it again.

After you have listed your work experiences, list accomplishments outside work. These, too, should be short, measurable, and results-oriented. These outside experiences can help you move into a new field. In fact, that's how I and many others have made career transitions. By volunteering to do advertising and public relations work at night, I developed a list of accomplishments that helped me move from computers to advertising. In those days, my outside experience went like this:

• Walnut Street Theatre Gallery
Planned, organized, and promoted month-long holography exhibition. Attendance increased from less than one hundred visitors per month to over three thousand visitors during the month of this exhibition.

• YMCA
Handled all publicity for fund-raising campaign. Consulted with fund-raising committee on best techniques for them to use. Received plaque in recognition.

• United Way
Received four United Way awards for editorial work in 1979; two awards the prior year. Spoke at the United Way's Editors' Conference.

• Network for Women in Computer Technology
Chair of the Program Committee.

Later, career counseling became my volunteer work, and that eventually helped me move into the field I am now in. In the early days, my outside experience was stated like this:

• Organized and ran The Five O'Clock Club. Conducted weekly groups as well as individual counseling. Trained people in career decisions,

Where I was born and where and how I have lived is unimportant.
It is what I have done with where I have been that should be of interest.
Georgia O'Keefe

marketing techniques, and practice interviewing. Brought in outside lecturers.

I also listed the organizations for which I had done job-hunting seminars, and stated my relevant work experience—such as when I was a training manager.

List all of your accomplishment statements. Depending on the positions you are going after, these accomplishments may be included or not. They may, for example, be unimportant for ten years, and later on become important again, depending on your job target.

Your volunteer work may be important, just as mine was. Summer jobs can count, too.

To get better at stating your accomplishments—no matter what your level or experience—read The Five O'Clock Club's book on résumés.

This is *your* chance to brag—everyone else does. You will rework the wording of your accomplishment statements, and make them sound great, as well as truthful. When you have done this, you will feel terrific because you will be represented well on paper.

For now, think about what you've really done. For most people, the problem is not that they stretch the truth on their résumés; the problem is that they don't say what they've *really* done.

Figuring out what you've really done is much more difficult than simply reciting your job description. That's the importance of doing the Seven Stories exercise. It helps you step back from a résumé frame of mind so you can concentrate on the most important accomplishments of your life (in terms of what you really enjoyed doing and know you also did well). Then the exercise helps you think about each accomplishment in terms of what you *really* did: what led up to the accomplishment, what your role was, what gave you satisfaction, what your motivation was, and so on.

If You Think You Haven't Done a Thing With Your Life

Many people are intimidated when they see other people's accomplishments. They think they have none of their own. Chances are, you aren't thinking hard enough about what you have done. If you think you haven't done much, think again. If you are reading this book, we already know that you are competent, ambitious, and intelligent. Even people in the lowest-level jobs have accomplishments they are proud of. At all levels in an organization, people can be presented with problems and figure out how to handle them.

Don't compare yourself with others, and don't worry about what your boss or peers thought of what you have done: maybe they did not appreciate your talents. Brag about what you have done anyway—even though your boss may have taken credit for the work, and even though you may have accomplished it with the help of others. Think of problems you have faced in your company. What did you do to handle them? What was the result for your company? Think of an accomplishment. Write it down. Then pare it down until you can show the reader what you handled and the impact it made.

Finally, don't say anything negative about yourself. Don't lie, but don't hurt yourself either.

In this chapter, you were to write down everything you've done so that it will serve as a menu you can draw on, depending on the kinds of jobs you are going after. In our résumé book, you will see how people struggle to develop well-written accomplishment statements. In the next chapter, we will become more focused: your goal during your search process is to start out thinking broadly, and then focus.

The next thing most like living one's life over again
seems to be a recollection of that life,
and to make that recollection as durable as
possible by putting it down in writing.
Benjamin Franklin

Jobs/Industries Worth Exploring:
Preliminary Target Investigation

Facts are friendly. Facts that tend to reinforce what you are doing and give you a warm glow are nice, because they help in terms of psychic reward. Facts that raise alarms are equally friendly, because they give you clues about how to respond, how to change, where to spend the resources.
Irwin Miller, Former CEO,
Cummins Engine Co., *The Renewal Factor*

Although it takes up only a few paragraphs in this book, Preliminary Target Investigation is essential.

You met Agnes earlier. Her Preliminary Target Investigation will probably take only a few weeks because she is high in energy and can devote full time to it. She has to test her ideas for targets in the marketplace to see which ones are worth pursuing. As she researches at the library, and by meeting with people in her fields of choice, she will refine those targets and perhaps develop other ones. Then she will know where to focus her job search, and the search will be completed much more quickly than if she had skipped this important step.

People who conduct a Preliminary Target Investigation while employed sometimes take a year to explore various fields while they continue in their old jobs. If you are not at all familiar with some of the job targets you have selected, do some Preliminary Target Investigation *now* through library research (be sure to read this section) and networking. You will find that some targets are not right for you. Eliminate them and conduct a full campaign in those areas that seem right for you and which offer some reasonable hope of success.

Whether you are employed or between jobs, Preliminary Target Investigation is well worth your time and a lot of fun. It is the difference between blindly continuing in your old career path because it is the only thing you know, and finding out what is really happening in the world so you can latch on to a field that may carry you forward for many, many years. This is a wonderful time to explore—to find out what the world offers. Most job hunters narrow their targets down too quickly, and wind up later with not much to go after. It is better for you emotionally as well as practically to develop *now* more targets than you need so you will have them when you are actively campaigning. If, on the other hand, you do not have the inclination or time to explore, you can move on. *Just remember, you can come back to this point if your search dries up and you need more targets.*

Most job hunters target only one job type or industry, take a very long time to find out that this

114

© 1996, Kate Wendleton and The Five O'Clock Club®

Simon: *We can walk right outta here if you want.*
Eric: *And where we gonna go?*
Simon: *Anywhere man. It's a big world.*
Bruce Faulk, *You Still Got to Come Home to That*

target is not working, get depressed, try to think of other things they can do with their lives, pick themselves up, and start on one more target.

Instead, **brainstorm as many targets as possible** *before* **you begin your real job search**. Then you can overlap your campaigns, going after a number of targets at once. If some targets do not seem to be working as well for you as others, you can drop the targets in which you are no longer interested. And when things don't seem to be going well, you will have other targets to fall back on.

1. **List below all of the jobs/industries from the Brainstorming Possible Jobs Worksheet that interest you at this point.**

2. If you are not at all familiar with some of the targets you have selected, do some Preliminary Target Investigation *now* through library research or networking. You will find that some targets are not right for you. Eliminate them and conduct a full campaign in those areas which do seem right for you and seem to offer you some reasonable hope of success.

As you find out what is happening in the world, new fields will open up for you. Things are changing so fast that if you conduct a serious search without some exploration, you are probably missing the most exciting developments in an area.

Spend some time exploring. Don't narrow your targets down too quickly; you will wind up later with not much to go after. It is better for you emotionally, as well as practically, to develop *now* more targets than you need so you will have them when you are actively campaigning. If, on the other hand, you do not have the time or inclination to explore, you can move on to the next step. **Just remember: you can come back to this point if your search dries up and you need more targets.**

JOBS/INDUSTRIES THAT INTEREST ME AT THIS POINT:
(May do some Preliminary Target Investigation to determine what is really going on in each of them.)

_____

_____

_____

_____

_____

_____

_____

_____

_____

_____

_____

_____

_____

_____

_____

_____

_____

_____

_____

Targeting: The Start of an Organized Search

Silence has many dimensions. It can be a regression and an escape, a loss of self, or it can be a presence, awareness, unification, self-discovery . . . Positive silence pulls us together and makes us realize who we are, who we might be, and the distance between these two. Hence, positive silence implies a disciplined choice and what Paul Tillich called the "courage to be." In the long run, the discipline of creative silence demands a certain kind of faith. For when we come face to face with ourselves in the lonely ground of our own being, we confront many questions about the value of our existence, the reality of our commitments, the authenticity of our everyday lives.

Thomas Merton, *Love and Living*

An Organized Search

To organize your search:

1. Brainstorm as many job targets as possible. You will not conduct a campaign aimed at all of them, but will have backup targets in case certain ones do not work out.

2. Identify three or four targets worthy of preliminary research.

3. Research each one enough to determine whether it is worth a full campaign. You can find this out through basic library research and a few networking interviews. This is your Preliminary Target Investigation.

4. If your research shows that a target now seems inappropriate, cross it off your list, and concentrate on the remaining targets. <u>As you continue to network and research, keep open to other possibilities that may be targets for you. Add those to your list of targets to research.</u>

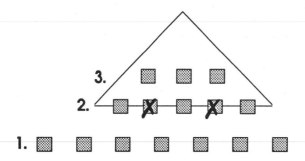

The boxes above represent different job targets. The triangle represents your job search. As you investigate targets, you will eliminate certain ones and spend more time on the remaining targets. You may research your targets by reading or by talking to people. The more you find out, the clearer your direction will become.

During Phase 1 *of your search, you brainstormed lots of possible job targets, not caring whether or not they made sense.*

During Phase 2, *you conducted preliminary research to determine whether or not you should mount a full campaign aimed at these targets.*

During Phase 3 *(covered in* Job Search Secrets)*, you will focus on the targets that warrant a full campaign. This means you will do full research on each target, and consider using all of the techniques for getting interviews: networking, direct contact, search firms, and ads.*

It is not [one] who prays most or fasts most; it is not [one] who gives most alms, or is most eminent for temperance, chastity, or justice; but it is [one] who is always thankful to God, who receives everything as an instance of God's goodness and has a heart always ready to praise God for it.
William Law

As you add new targets, reprioritize your list so you are concentrating first on the targets that should be explored first. Do *not* haphazardly go after everything that comes your way.

5. If you decide the target is worth pursuing, conduct a full campaign to get interviews in that area:

• Develop your pitch.

• Develop your résumé.

• Develop a list of all the companies in the target area and the name of the person you want to contact in each company.

6. Then contact each company through networking, direct contact, ads, or search firms.

Serendipitous Leads

Make a methodical approach the basis of your search, but also keep yourself open to those serendipitous "lucky leads" outside of your target areas that may come your way. In general, it is a waste of your energy to go after single serendipitous leads. It is better to ask yourself if this lead warrants a new target. If it does, then decide where it should be ranked in your list of targets, and research it as you would any serious target.

This process is covered in great detail in our book *Job-Search Secrets*.

I'm talkin' about what I do! You're runnin' around the world makin' deals, but your old friend Eric— your stay at home do nothin' friend, what's he doin'? . . . I want to go places too!
Bruce Faulk,
You Still Got to Come Home to That

The Five O'Clock Club®

How to Target the Job You Want

I always wanted to be somebody,
but I should have been more specific.
Lily Tomlin

You are on your way to finding your place in the world. Using the Seven Stories and other exercises, you made a list of your motivated skills and what you want in a job, and then you brainstormed a number of possible job targets that might fit in with your enjoyable accomplishments and/or your vision of your future. Some of these targets may be very long-term. Then you thought about what you would be willing to offer. (You took it an extra step by stating this as accomplishments.)

Now we will work on firming up your job targets. You will do some preliminary research on each target through the library and by talking to people to see if these areas still interest you and are practical. Then you will *focus* by selecting two, three, or four areas on which to concentrate, based on what appeals to you and what you think you have that is marketable. Then you will conduct a thorough campaign aimed at each area. Because each campaign takes a lot of work, it is best if we spend some time refining your targets.

Selecting Job Targets
—Your Key to Job-Hunting Success

As we have seen, selecting a job target means selecting a specific geographic area, a specific industry or company size, and a specific position within that industry. A job target must have all three.

Select your targets. Using our book, *Job-Search Secrets*, conduct a campaign aimed at each. Concentrate your energies, and you increase your chances for success.

Approach each target with an open mind. Commit to a target, but only as long as it makes sense. You can change your mind after you find out more about it. It makes no sense to strive to be a ballerina after you find you have absolutely no ability as a dancer. Commitment to a target lets you

discover your real possibilities and increases your chances of landing a job of your choice. The unsuccessful ballet student may have something else of great value to offer the world of dance—such as the ability to raise funds or run a ballet company.

The Results of Commitment

Commitment increases the chance that you will come across clearly and enthusiastically about the industry and the position you seek; it will help you do a thorough job of networking the chosen area, of investigating and being knowledgeable about the area, of conducting a thorough search, and of being successful in that search.

If the result of your initial commitment is that you realize a job target is not what you thought it would be, you have resolved the issue and can move on.

Jim, a marketing manager, had targeted four industries: environmental, noise abatement, shipping, and corporate America, a backup target in case the other three did not work. He conducted an excellent search aimed at the environmental target, an area he had always wanted to explore. It was only after a brief but committed job search that he found the environmental area was not for him: the people in it were different from what he had expected. He would not be able to do the things he had imagined he would do there. That target no longer interested him. The noise abatement and shipping industries, however, were very exciting to him, and he found a good match for himself. Later, his exploration of the environmental area paid off. He was employed by a shipping company in the containment of oil spills.

Commitment to a target means you'll give that target your best shot —and results in a better job hunt than if you had no target at all.

Target a Geographic Area

Targeting a geographic area is usually the easiest part of the targeting process. Some people decide that they want to work near their present homes, while others decide that they would be willing to move where the jobs are. Are you willing to move anywhere? Are a small town and a big city

118

---

the same to you? Would you move to the coast? To Arizona? Would you rather be near your family? If you want to stay where you are now, target that area as your first selection—and you'll have a better chance of getting offers there. If you really care about where you live, *target it*.

Think about where you stand on this. You will be assigning yourself an impossible task if, for example, you want to be an export manager but want to work only in a geographic area where there are no export-management positions. If you must live in a particular area, be realistic about the kinds of jobs open to you there.

Resolve this issue. Then you will know if you'd be willing to change your target industry so you can live where you want, or change your geographic area so you can work in the industry or function that interests you.

Target an Industry and a Function in That Industry

Many people say they don't care what industry they work in. When pressed, they usually have stronger opinions than they thought.

If you think *any* industry would be okay for you, let's find out. Would you work in the not-for-profit sector? If so, where? In education? A hospital? How about government? A community organization? Does it matter to you?

Would you work for a magazine? A chemical company? The garment industry? How about a company that makes cardboard boxes? Or cheese? Does it matter to you?

Does it matter if the company has forty employees? What about forty thousand? Four hundred thousand? Does it matter to you?

You've Selected a Target If . . .

. . . you can clearly state the industry or company size in which you'd be interested, your position within each industry, and some guidelines regarding geographic location.

For example, if you're a junior accountant, you may already know that you want to advance in the

accounting field. You may know that you want to work for a small service company as an assistant controller in the geographic area where you are now living.

If you have clearly selected your targets, then you can get on with finding interviews in your target area. To do that, you would conduct a campaign in your target area. (Job-hunting campaigns are covered in *Job-Search Secrets*)

Here is one person's target list:
By geographic area:

- Washington, D.C.
- New York City

By industry:

- Book publishing
- Magazine publishing
- Advertising
- College administration (weak interest)
- Administration of professional firms (weak interest)
- Nonprofit associations
- Direct-marketing companies.

By function:

- Business manager/General manager-publishing
- International controller
- Corporate-level financial planning analysis
- General V.P. finance/General manager— nonprofit organizations.

Other Issues You May Want to Consider Even If You Have a Target

Does the style of the company matter to you? Would you rather be in a fast-paced, dynamic company with lots of headaches or one that's more stable, slow paced, with routine work as the norm? Which would you prefer?

What kind of people do you want to work with? Friendly people? Sharp, challenging people? People interested in making a fast buck? People who want to make the world a better place? Think

It is therefore vital that each of us examine the values by which he lives, to decide what is truly important and what will ultimately give him feelings of fulfillment and well-being.
Michael Lynberg, *The Path With Heart*

about it. You may have said before that you just want a job—any job—but is anything still okay with you?

If you want to be in sales, for example, would it matter if you were selling lingerie or used cars or computers or large office building space? What if you were selling cats? Rugs? Butter? Saying you want to be in "sales" is not enough.

Let's take it a step further. If what appeals to you about being a salesman is that you like to convince people, why not be a politician? Or a clergyman? Or a doctor? Or if what appeals to you is money, why not become a trader? Or a partner in a law firm? Remind yourself where your heart lies.

CASE STUDY: WILLIAM
Finally—An Organized Search

William wanted a job—just about any job he saw in the want ads. He spent months answering those ads. He thought he was job hunting, but he wasn't. He was simply answering ads for positions for which he was unqualified. William didn't stand a chance.

After a long time, William gave up and agreed to follow The Five O'Clock Club system. At first he resisted because, like so many job hunters, he did not want to "restrict" himself. William thought that focusing on only two or three job targets would limit his opportunities and lengthen his search. He wanted to be open to whatever job came his way.

Many job hunters, like William, simply want a job. But William needed to put himself in the position of the hiring manager: Why would he want to hire William? In his cover letters, William took the "trust me" approach. He did nothing to prove his interest in the industry, the company, or even the position for which he was applying. His credentials matched the ad requirements only by the greatest stretch of the imagination.

A shotgun approach like William's may lead to a job offer, but it may also lead your career in a direction that is not what you would have preferred. Later, you may find yourself back in the same boat again—wondering what to do with your life, wanting to do almost anything but what you are doing, hoping your next job will miraculously be in a field that will satisfy you.

William's basic problem was not that he wanted to change careers, but that he didn't know what he wanted to do. He was willing to do anything—anything except focus on a specific area and go after it.

William eventually narrowed himself to two targets in which he was truly interested. Then he worked to find out his chances for getting jobs in those fields. William did the exercises in this book, and came up with this list to focus his search:

What I want in a job:

- A challenge in meeting new situations/variety.
- A complex situation I can structure.
- Something I believe in.
- A chance to express my creativity through my communication skills.
- A highly visible position.
- An opportunity to develop my leadership and motivational skills.
- Sole responsibility for something.

What I have to offer (that I also want to offer):

- Enthusiasm for the company's basic mission/purpose.
- Penetrating analysis that finds the "answer."
- The ability to synthesize diverse parts into a unified whole.
- An ability and desire to be in new/untested situations.
- Effective in dealing with many kinds of people.
- Strong oral and written communication skills.

Goal: A small- or medium-sized organization where I can feel my impact:

- Service
- Health care
- Human care
- Science
- Academia and learning

Let not my thinking become confused by listening to too many opinions, but let me consider each one individually, to see if it can be of help to me.

To make good choices, I must develop a mature and prudent understanding of myself that will reveal to me my real motives and intentions.
Paraphrased from Thomas Merton, *No Man Is An Island*

- Human understanding.

Description of targeted areas:

- Targeted geographic areas:
  - Major East Coast cities or locales:
    - New York
    - Philadelphia
    - Boston
    - Baltimore
    - Washington.

- Targeted industries:
  - First priority is health care:
    - Pharmaceuticals companies
    - Biotechnology companies
    - Hospitals
    - Maybe research labs
  - Second priority is not-for-profit community organizations.

- Targeted positions:
  - marketing/competitive analysis
  - organizational positioning
  - operations planning.

William's first campaign was aimed at pharmaceuticals companies. He discovered what they looked for in new hires, and how he could get a position. In addition, he pursued his second objective: not-for-profit community organizations.

The result: As usual, a career transition takes time. William discovered he could make a transition into the pharmaceuticals industry, but decided not to take the backward step that would require. He learned of a job being created in a not-for-profit organization. Although he was not qualified for this position, he knew he could handle it, and it matched the list of what he wanted.

William went through the steps described in the chapter "How to Change Careers," to convince his prospective employer he could indeed handle the job and was eager to have the chance to do it. This was difficult because the other candidates were better qualified than William—they had been in this kind of job before. For William, it was a career change.

William decided to write a number of proposals. To write them, he first needed to do research, which would not be easy. After some library research, he called the heads of development at six major not-for-profits. He told them he was hoping to get a position at a certain organization, and wanted some ideas of how he could write a proposal of what he would do if he were hired.

Amazingly, his sincerity won the day. All six gave him information over the phone. Because he had done library research, William was able to ask intelligent questions. He wrote a proposal, stating in his cover letter that he had spoken with the heads of development at major not-for-profits, and asked for another interview. It would be nice if that were all it took: William got another interview, but was rejected a *number* of times. Yet he continued to do research, and eventually showed enough fortitude and learned enough that he was hired.

The position was just what he wanted: a brand-new marketing research position at a major not-for-profit organization. He would head his career in a different direction and satisfy his motivated skills. His career was back on track, under his own control. And he's still with the organization today.

Select *Your* Targets

The only difference between caprice and a lifelong passion is that the caprice lasts a little longer.
Oscar Wilde

List your targets in the order in which you will conduct your search. List first the one you will focus on in your first campaign. If you are currently employed and have time to explore, you may want to select as your first target the most unlikely one. (Job hunters sometimes want to target areas they had only dreamed about before.) Concentrate on it and find out for sure whether you are truly interested and what your prospects are. If it doesn't work, you can become more realistic.

On the other hand, if you must find a job

Our doubts are traitors,
And make us lose the good we oft might win
By fearing to attempt.
William Shakespeare, *Measure for Measure*

quickly, concentrate first on the area where you stand the best chance of getting a job—perhaps the field you are now in. After you are settled in your new job, you can develop yourself in the area that interests you in the long run. Remember, it's okay to take something less than your ideal job; just keep working toward your dreams.

Someone who made this work is Nat, who wanted to work for a Japanese company. He thought the Japanese culture suited his temperament. Yet Nat was forced to take a job at another company because the Japanese process was slow (approval had to come from Tokyo). Still, Nat kept pursuing the position with the Japanese firm.

Eventually, his dream job came through—at much more money than he had been making. The Japanese company realized that Nat's personal style, uncommon in America, meshed with Japanese management methods. His maturity—he was fifty-five years old—was also a plus. Nat, his new job, and his new employer were a good fit. Despite many obstacles, Nat pursued his dream and got it. And it was worth it in job satisfaction and in having some say over what happened in his own life.

If you are targeting a geographic area different from where you are now, be sure to conduct a serious, complete campaign aimed at that target. For example, you will want to contact search firms in that area, do library research, perhaps conduct a direct-mail campaign, and network. For in-depth information on all of these topics, please consult our book *Job-Search Secrets*. Use the work sheets on the following pages to plan your targets.

Measuring Your Targets

You've selected three to five targets on which to focus. Will they be enough to get you an appropriate job?

Let's say, for example, that your first target aims at a small industry (ten companies) having only a few positions that would be appropriate for you. Chances are, those jobs are filled right now. In fact, chances are there may be no opening for a year or two. The numbers are working against you. But if you have targeted *twenty* small industries, each of

which has ten companies with a few positions appropriate for you, the numbers are more in your favor. On the other hand, if one of your targets is large and has a lot of positions that may be right for you, the numbers are again on your side.

A Rule of Thumb

A target list of two hundred positions results in seven interviews which result in one job offer. Therefore, if there are less than two hundred potential positions in your targets, develop additional targets or expand the ones you already have. Remember that when aiming at a target of less than two hundred, concentrated effort will be required.

Sometimes, however, one company by itself may be enough. What if a very qualified secretary wanted to work for a regional telephone company? What are the chances she would find a job there? A regional telephone company may have *thousands* of secretaries, and a qualified person would certainly be able to find a job there within a reasonable time frame.

In a tight job market, however, you will probably need to *expand your job-hunting targets*. If you are searching only in Chicago, or only in the immediate area where you live, think of other geographic areas. If you are looking only in large public corporations, consider small or private companies, or the not-for-profit area. If you are looking for a certain kind of position, what other kinds of work can you do? Think of additional targets for your search, and focus on each target in depth.

In *Job-Search Secrets*, you will learn how to position yourself for each of these targets. That way, when you go after a target, you will have a better chance of looking appropriate to the people in each target area.

Live all you can; it's a mistake not to.
It doesn't so much matter what you do in particular,
so long as you have had your life.
If you haven't had that, what have you had?
What one loses one loses; make no mistake about that.
Henry James, *The Ambassadors*

The
Five
O'Clock
Club®

Target Selection

After you have done some preliminary research, select the targets that you think deserve a full campaign. List first the one you will focus on in your first campaign. If you are currently employed and have time to explore, you may want to select as your first target the most unlikely one, but the one that is the job of your dreams. Then you can concentrate on it and find out for sure whether you are still interested and what your prospects are.

On the other hand, if you must find a job quickly, you will first want to concentrate on the area where you stand the best chance of getting a job—probably the area where you are now working. After you get that job, you can explore your other targets. (To expand your targets quickly, consider broadening your search geographically.)

If you are targeting a geographic area different from where you are now, be sure to conduct a serious, complete campaign aimed at that target. For example, you will want to contact search firms in that area, do library research, perhaps conduct a direct-mail campaign, and network.

Target 1:

    Industry or company size: _____

    Position/Function: _____

    Geographic area: _____

Target 2:

    Industry or company size: _____

    Position/Function: _____

    Geographic area: _____

Target 3:

    Industry or company size: _____

    Position/Function: _____

    Geographic area: _____

Target 4:

    Industry or company size: _____

    Position/Function: _____

    Geographic area: _____

Target 5:

    Industry or company size: _____

    Position/Function: _____

    Geographic area: _____

Measuring Your Targets

You've selected three to five (or more) targets on which to focus. Will this be enough to get you an appropriate job?

Let's say, for example, that your first target aims at a small industry (ten companies) having only a few positions that would be appropriate for you.

Chances are, those jobs are filled right now. In fact, chances are there may be no opening for a year or two. The numbers are working against you. Now, if you have targeted twenty small industries, each of which has ten companies with a few posi-tions appropriate for you, the numbers are more in your favor.

On the other hand, if one of your targets is large and has a lot of positions that may be right for you, the numbers are again on your side.

Let's analyze your search and see whether the numbers are working for you or against you.

Fill out the following on your own target markets. You will probably have to make an educated guess about the number. A ball-park figure is all you need to get a feel for where you stand.

For Target 1:

Industry or company size: _____
Position/Function: _____
Geographic area: _____

How big is the market for your "product" in this target?
  A. Number of companies in this target market:
  B. Number of probable positions suitable for me in the average company in this target: _____
  A x B = Total number of probable positions appropriate for me in this target market: _____

For Target 2:

Industry or company size: _____
Position/Function: _____
Geographic area: _____

How big is the market for your "product" in this target?
  A. Number of companies in this target market:
  B. Number of probable positions suitable for me in the average company in this target: _____
  A x B = Total number of probable positions appropriate for me in this target market: _____

For Target 3:

Industry or company size: _____
Position/Function: _____
Geographic area: _____

How big is the market for your "product" in this target?
  A. Number of companies in this target market:
  B. Number of probable positions suitable for me in the average company in this target: _____
  A x B = Total number of probable positions appropriate for me in this target market: _____

Rule of thumb:

A target list of 200 positions in a healthy market results in seven interviews that result in one job offer. Therefore, if there are fewer than 200 potential positions in your targets, develop additional targets or expand the ones you already have. Remember that when aiming at a target of less than 200, a more concentrated effort will be required.

A Job Well Done

*Out of every crisis comes the
chance to be reborn . . .*
Nena O'Neill

---

*This is the true joy in life, the being used for a purpose
recognized by yourself as a mighty one, the being
thoroughly worn out before you are thrown on the
scrap heap; the being a force of nature instead of a
feverish selfish little clod of ailments and grievances
complaining that the world will not devote itself to
making you happy.*
George Bernard Shaw

---

*True commitment transforms you. You really know
where you stand. You have a base on which to build your
life. You're not in shifting sand anymore.*
Christopher Reeve, former star of *Superman*,
in an interview with Barbara Walters.
Reeve became a quadriplegic
after a horseback-riding accident.

---

*We will make the best possible life out of this life that we
now have and there's no question that he will continue to
be a leader and continue to be a strong person and a
funny person and a lively person.*
Mrs. Christopher Reeve (Dana),
in that same interview

---

*We must not be afraid of the future. We must not be
afraid of man. It is no accident that we are here. Each and
every human person has been created in the "image and
likeness" of the One who is the origin of all that is.
We have within us the capacities for wisdom and virtue.
With these gifts, and with the help of God's grace, we can
build in the next century and the next millennium a
civilization worthy of the human person, a true
culture of freedom. We can and must see that the tears
of this century have prepared the ground for a new
springtime of the human spirit.*
Pope John Paul II, speech to the United Nations
General Assembly, October 5, 1995

By selecting and ranking your targets, you have completed a very important task. If your targets are wrong, the campaigns you aim at those targets are wrong. Maintain an exploratory mindset—assessing the targets you are pursuing, and being open to others.

Make an organized search the basis for your campaign. Some lucky job hunters know lots of important people and just happen on to their next jobs. Sometimes those jobs are even satisfying. If that has happened to you in the past, count your blessings, but do not rely on that approach to work for you in the future. The world has changed, and organizations are more serious about whom they hire.

You are now ready to begin an intensive campaign to get lots of interviews in each of the targets you have selected. The campaigns will overlap so you will be able to compare the performance of each and gain perspective. You can begin your campaign right now, by reading the next few chapters—about developing a résumé and conducting research—and then using *Building a Great Résumé* and *Job-Search Secrets*.

On the other hand, you may be ready to read about some advanced career-planning methods. If so, skip to Part Four: Advanced Career Planning.

Elizabeth Ghaffari:
A Résumé Case Study

*Concentrate your strength against your
competitor's relative weakness.*
Bruce Henderson,
Henderson on Corporate Strategy

E very résumé has a pitch—although it may
not be what the job hunter wants it to be. In
scanning Elizabeth's "before" résumé, we
can easily see that she has had communications and
advertising positions in a number of computer
companies. That's the total extent of her pitch.
When she went on interviews, managers commented: "You sure have worked for a lot of computer companies." Her résumé read like a job
description: she wrote press releases, product
brochures, employee newsletters, and so on.

Thousands of people can write press releases, so
citing those skills will not separate Elizabeth from
her competition. But we can get to know her better
is if she tells us about specific accomplishments.

Elizabeth agreed to do the Seven Stories Exercise. She didn't feel like writing down "the things
she enjoyed doing and also did well" because she
felt as though she kept doing the same things again
and again in every company she worked for, and
she enjoyed them all. Still, I urged her to be specific—details can make a résumé more interesting.
And working on the stories exercise is a sure way to
develop a strong overall message.

She started with an experience on a job early in
her career. She had thought of a terrific idea: her
company's product could be sold through the same
computer systems that were used to sell airline
tickets and car and hotel reservations. She convinced the company to let her go ahead with the
idea, promoted it to travel agents across the country, and also to the salespeople in her own company. It was so successful, it became the standard
way to sell foreign currencies when people were
going on a trip.

Most job hunters tend to ignore accomplishments that took place when they were young. But if
you had accomplishments early in your career, they
may be worth relating because they let the reader
know that you have always been a winner.

I said, "That sounds great. Where is it on your
résumé?" Elizabeth said: "Well, it's not said exactly
that way..." Many times job hunters are con-
stricted when they write their résumés, but the
Seven Stories Exercise can free them up to express
things differently. So we restated that accomplishment.

Elizabeth then worked on another story. She
had participated in a conference that had "generated 450 letters of intent."

I said: "It's nice the conference generated 450
letters of intent. But from what you said, I can't tell
that you had anything to do with those results, and
I don't know if 450 is good or not. Tell me more
about it."

Elizabeth said: "There were only 1500 participants in the conference, and 450 letters of intent is a
lot because it's a very expensive product. I had a lot
to do with those results because I developed an
aura of excitement about the product by putting
teasers under everyone's hotel door every morning.

"And before the conference, I had sent five
weekly teasers to everyone who planned to attend.
For example, one week, I sent each person a bottle
of champagne. This direct-mail campaign had
everyone talking about us before the convention
started. People were asking one another whether or
not they had gotten our mailers. When they got to
the convention and found teasers under their
doors, they were eager to come to our booth.

"I also trained the teams of employees who
were demonstrating the product at the convention.
I made sure that each demonstrator delivered the
same message."

Now I understood how Elizabeth had played a
major part in generating those letters of intent.

Next we needed to think of the message behind
this accomplishment. Was her message that she
could stick mailers under doors? Or send out
bottles of champagne? No, her message was that
she knew how to launch a product, and that's what
we put on her résumé as the main point for that
accomplishment.

The successful person has the habit of doing things failures don't like to do.
They don't like doing them either necessarily. But their
disliking is subordinated to the strength of their purpose.
E.M. Gray, *The Common Denominator of Success*

In her "before" résumé, Elizabeth said that she wrote press releases and did direct-mail campaigns. Her "after" résumé gives us some examples of what she accomplished with those efforts, and gives us a feel for her ingenuity and hard work.

The Summary

After we reviewed all of her accomplishments, we tackled the summary. What was the most important point Elizabeth wanted to get across? It wasn't just that she could write press releases and speeches, or do direct-mail campaigns.

She had to think hard about this. The most important thing was that Elizabeth was a key member of the management team. She sat in on meetings when the company was discussing bringing out a new product, or planning how to handle a possible crisis. Elizabeth would not be happy—or effective—in a job where she simply wrote press releases. She needed to be part of the strategy sessions.

What you put on your résumé can both include you and exclude you. A company that does not want the communications person included in those meetings would not be interested in Elizabeth—but then, she wouldn't be interested in them either.

In her summary, instead of highlighting the companies she had worked for, Elizabeth highlighted the industries represented by those companies. She listed Information Services and High-Tech first, because they represented areas of greater growth than Financial Services did.

Elizabeth was—and wanted to be again—a corporate strategist, a crisis manager, and a spokesperson for the corporation. That's how we positioned her.

In every summary in this book (and in *Through the Brick Wall*), the reader can tell something about the writer's personality. It is not enough that someone knows what you have done, they also need to know your style in doing it. For example, a person who had run a department and doubled productivity could have done it in a nasty, threatening way, or could have motivated people to do more, instituted training programs, and encouraged workers

to come up with suggestions for improving productivity. Your style matters.

Look at this case study and then do the Seven Stories Exercise. Come up with accomplishments that will interest your reader. Let him or her know what to expect from you if you are hired.

In Elizabeth's case, we hope the hiring manager will look at her résumé and say: "That's exactly what I need: a corporate strategist who knows how to handle crises, and can also serve as a spokesperson for us."

This is the response you want the reader to have: "That's exactly the person I need!" Look at your résumé. What words pop out? Is this how you want to be seen? If not, let's get going.

After you have worked hard on your résumé, use your summary to develop your brief verbal pitch to be used in interviews and the summary statement in your cover letters. You will see lots of examples of these in *Building a Great Résumé* as well as *Job Search Secrets*.

Great minds have purposes, others have wishes.
Little minds are tamed and subdued by misfortune;
but great minds rise above it.
Washington Irving,
Elbert Hubbard's Scrap Book

ELIZABETH GHAFFARI

207 Dobbs Ferry   Home: (609) 555-6666
Phoenix, AZ 44444

EXPERIENCE

ORANGE COMPUTER SYSTEMS   1988 - Present
Director Corporate Communications

Plan and supervise all corporate communications staff and activities for diversified financial information services company on a global basis.

- Develop, direct and implement global media, public relations, and internal-communications programs in support of corporate and sales objectives, working closely with executive management team.

- Direct all media-relations activities related to new product introductions and product enhancements; initiate media contacts; respond to press inquiries; coordinate and conduct interviews; and develop all press materials.

- Develop and direct advertising and promotional literature activities, overseeing all corporate publications, including corporate and product brochures, sales materials, and customer and employee newsletters.

ELECTRONIC DATA SYSTEMS   1986 - 1988
Manager, Advertising and Promotion

Developed and implemented marketing and promotion strategies for Reuters and its North American subsidiaries.

- Worked with market and product managers to identify opportunities for product and sales promotions and new product development for multiple market segments. Conducted market research, developed marketing strategies and implemented tactical plans (e.g. direct response marketing and sales incentive programs).

- Responsible for planning biannual securities analyst meetings and communication product information to investors and industry analysts.

- Orchestrated six product introductions during three-month period, including public-relations activities, promotional literature and training materials.

- Responsible for forecasting and maintaining $4.0 million budget.

- Managed corporate and product advertising programs, hiring and working with various agencies.

CREDIT LYONNAIS   1984 - 1986
Corporate Investment Officer and Product Manager

Planned and directed the sales and promotion efforts for the bank's corporate and correspondent sales staff for a variety of products including foreign exchange and precious metals.

- Developed active and profitable business relationships with correspondent banks for sale of precious metals and foreign exchange products.

- Established and developed new account relationships. Brought in eleven new corporate accounts which produced significant business in precious metals and foreign exchange trading areas.

- Managed market study to identify size, segments and opportunities of various markets. Prepared analysis and recommendations for new product development and trading vehicles.

WASSERELLA & BECKTON   1979 - 1984
Director of Marketing

Managed all activities of the Marketing Department, including product development, sales promotion, advertising and public relations activities for diversified financial services company.

- Conceptualized and developed national marketing strategy for foreign exchange services offered to travel industry professionals via automated airline reservation systems.

- Developed and implemented business plans for a variety of products, including responsibility for product positioning, pricing, contracts, advertising and promotional materials.

- Promoted from Foreign Exchange Trader to Marketing Representative to Director of Marketing in three years.

EDUCATION

B.A., Psychology, University of Phoenix   1979

ELIZABETH GHAFFARI

207 Dobbs Ferry
Phoenix, AZ 44444

Residence: (609) 555-6666
Work: (493) 345-7777

CORPORATE COMMUNICATIONS EXECUTIVE
with 14 years' experience in

- High-Tech
- Information Services
- Financial Services

Experience includes:

- Global Media and Investor Relations
- Customer Videos and Newsletters
- Advertising/Promotional Literature
- Employee Newsletters
- Employee Roundtables/Awards Programs
- Speech-Writing/Papers/Public Speaking

- **A corporate strategist and key member of the management team** with extensive knowledge of financial markets.

- **A crisis manager:** bringing common sense, organizational skills, and a logical decision-making process to solving sensitive, time-critical problems.

- **A spokesperson for the corporation**: developing and communicating key corporate messages accurately and convincingly, under deadline pressure, to multiple audiences including employees, the media, customers and investors.

**Proven team leader and problem solver with highly developed
analytical, organizational, communications, and strategic planning skills.**

ORANGE COMPUTER SYSTEMS

1988 - Present

Director, Corporate Communications

- Gained extensive positive media coverage in conjunction with launch of company's first product for new market segment.
    - Planned and conducted **media events in 8 countries**.
    - Resulted in **positive stories in 30 major publications** and trade press: *The Wall Street Journal, The New York Times, Barron's, The Financial Times, Forbes*, and various foreign publications.
    - A first for the company, **positive TV coverage in the United States**: CNN, CNBC, **and Europe**: Sky Financial Television, Business Daily, The City Programme.

- Successfully **avoided communications crisis**, gained positive press coverage and customer support when company sold a major division. Within a 60-day period:

    - Planned and managed all aspects of a **13-city, interactive teleconference**.
    - Developed all written materials including various employee and customer communications, background materials and press releases.
    - Wrote speeches for six executives including both company presidents (present and acquiring companies).
    - Wrote and produced an extensive question-and-answer document covering **union, compensation and benefits issues and business rational.**
    - Selected and trained staff representatives for each of 13 cities.

ORANGE COMPUTER SYSTEMS, contd.

Director, Corporate Communications, contd.

- Developed and implemented **company's first employee awards program** for service excellence.
    - Honored employees who participated in planning sessions.
    - **Led to changes in key areas** including improvements in software manufacturing efficiencies, shortening of the product development cycle, and improved employee morale.

- **Introduced desk-top publishing** program for in-house production of all promotional materials and various customer and employee newsletters.
    - **Reduced outside services expense by 75%.**
    - Created new **corporate standards manual** and reorganized promotional literature system to replace inconsistent product literature.

- Conducted group and individual **employee meetings** to gain and disseminate critical information in identifying and resolving employee-relations problems.

- Prepared quarterly management reports and written/oral presentations to top management and employees to describe corporate accomplishments compared to goals.

- Managed all customer/media/employee communications for sale of three business units.

ELECTRONIC DATA SYSTEMS   1986 - 1988

Manager, Advertising and Promotion

- Prepared written and oral **presentations to boards of directors** and senior managers on various services, concepts and results.

- Planned **product launch** and company participation in global foreign exchange conference. Successful product launch resulted in **generating 450 letters of intent from 1500 participants**. Assured successful product introduction:
    - Developed 5-week **direct-mail campaign** to stimulate interest and create an aura of excitement around product prior to conference. Campaign continued at conference with daily newsletter and door stuffer.
    - Maximized impact of **product demonstrations** through use of compelling visual presentation and environment.
    - **Trained teams** of product demonstrators to assure that information regarding benefits and features would be delivered in consistent way.

- Strengthened company relationships with **industry analysts and investors** by arranging product demonstrations in conjunction with bi-annual industry analyst meetings. Demonstrations stimulated interest and **gained support for strategic direction from investor community** by communicating important strategic and product information.
    - Selected products to be demonstrated, developed promotional materials, organized display area, selected and trained product demonstrators to assure delivery of consistent corporate message.

CREDIT LYONNAIS   1984 - 1986
<u>Product Manager</u>

- Established and developed new account relationships.
    - Brought in <u>**11 new corporate accounts during 10-month period**</u> producing significant business in precious metals and foreign exchange trading areas.

WASSERELLA & BECKTON   1979 - 1984
<u>Director of Marketing</u>

- <u>**Developed breakthrough idea to sell**</u> foreign exchange services (currency and travelers' checks) through travel agents the same way hotel space and airline tickets are sold
    — <u>**via automated airline reservation systems**</u>.
    - Sold concept to senior management and <u>**negotiated contracts with three major airlines**</u>.
    - Developed sales and operational procedures. <u>**Hired and trained 10-person sales and operations staff.**</u>
    - <u>**Promoted concept to travel agents**</u> across the country through industry trade shows and sales program.

EDUCATION

B.A., Psychology, University of Phoenix, 1979

Researching Your Job Targets

There are going to be no survivors.
Only big winners and the dead.
No one is going to just squeak by.
Ronald Compton, CEO,
Aetna Insurance Company

Few executives yet know how to ask:
What information do I need to do my job?
When do I need it?
And from whom should I be getting it?
Peter F. Drucker,
"Be Data Literate—Know What to Know,"
The Wall Street Journal, December 1, 1992

Natural talent, intelligence, a wonderful education—
none of these guarantees success. Something else is
needed: the sensitivity to understand what other
people want and the willingness to give it to them.
Worldly success depends on pleasing others.
No one is going to win fame, recognition, or
advancement just because he or she thinks it's
deserved. Someone else has to think so too.
John Luther

Why Is Research Important?

Research can help you decide which field to go into and is a solid way to develop a list of your target companies. Then you can decide how to contact them and can measure your progress against this list. Research will improve your networking and interviewing skills, and increase your confidence during interviews. You will create a good impression, and look like an insider rather than like someone who is trying to break in. Research will give you an edge over your competition and help you decide which company to join.

Library Research

Find a university or big-city library that's conveniently located and has an extensive business collection. You will not be completely on your own: librarians are often expert at helping job hunters, so plan to spend some time with the business reference librarian. Be specific. Tell the librarian what you want to accomplish. I always say, "The librarian is your friend." I personally love libraries. I was a librarian in both high school and college. Get comfortable with the environment. Spend time using the reference books. Photocopy articles you can read at home.

Be prepared for the probability that the library will not look as it used to: many card catalogues have been replaced by computer terminals. If electronic information is a new technology for you, do not be intimidated. Ask for assistance. Computer-aided research will make your work immeasurably faster, easier, and more accurate. Let it work for you.

How I Research

For most of my job hunts, I have **set aside at least two full days strictly for library research**. If I'm not sure of the industry I want to pursue, I may spend two days just researching industries (or professions). One of my favorite sources is the *Encyclopedia of Business Information Sources*. It lists topics, such as "oil" or "clubs" or "finance" or "real estate." Under each topic, it lists the most important sources of information on that topic: periodicals, books, and associations. Using this tool, I can quickly research any field in depth. I also may read the U.S. Department of Labor's reports on various industries or professions.

Once I have selected tentative industries, I may want to network to find out the buzzwords, and to refine my pitch. In addition, networking at this point may uncover other tentative targets, which I may simply add to my list of targets, or I may research at this time.

While networking, I may find someone who will give me a list of people in that field—perhaps an association membership list. Or perhaps someone will invite me to an association meeting and I can get a list there. Otherwise, I could buy the subscriber list from a trade magazine. Or I may need to spend time in the library to gather the list of companies. I may use an industry directory or the local business publication which provides listings of companies.

I have had a lot of success using directories on CD-ROM databases. It cuts my library time in half. By the way, don't let the term "database" intimidate or confuse you. Any collection of information with an organized arrangement can be called a database. Even your phone book could be considered a database, for that matter.

Taking Notes

I use standard letter-size sheets to copy down the company name, address, phone number, size (number of employees and sales), and other relevant information (such as business type if I am not familiar with the company). Then I list the names and titles of all the people I think I may want to contact.

I make note of three to five people in larger organizations who are two levels higher than I am, and perhaps the names of one or two in smaller organizations. *Many* people in one organization may be in a position to hire or recommend you. In larger companies, often the manager of one group has no idea that another manager may consider developing a new posi-

tion or replacing someone.

If I am uncomfortable writing to all three to five people at once, I write to one or two, wait for rejection letters, and then write to a few more. People listed in general directories have a lot of people writing to them because their names are so readily available. Therefore, I often use a targeted mailing, which takes more research per company but increases the number of meetings I get.

In a smaller organization, such as a company of two hundred people or less, the company head is likely to know of all potential openings. Who is in charge of the job openings? The president? Perhaps the general manager? I note both names so I can write to both at once, or one first and the other later. Although names in smaller companies are tougher to come by, these people don't get as many letters as people in larger companies.

If I feel I am able to work in many industries, I get a sense of those that are growing and also fit my needs. I make a long list of the companies that interest me. I call each one for an annual report or company literature (I can easily call thirty companies in half an hour or so). Then I find articles on each industry or company.

My effort is only as good as my list. (One job hunter had a list of sixty companies. But most were out of state and he had no intention of relocating. Only eight were within his geographic target.)

I make sure my list contains companies I am are at least somewhat interested in. Then I'll know I am contacting eight good names—not sixty that aren't worth my time. If I know the real size of my target—and it is small—I may decide to contact them with a different technique, such as a targeted mailing with a follow-up phone call.

What I Do with My Lists

Armed with my list of companies, I have lots of choices. If my target market is large, I may conduct a direct-mail campaign. Or I may divide up my list, do a direct mailing to sixty companies, and a targeted mailing to twenty companies (with follow-up phone calls), and network into a few companies. Or I could network around and ask for specific advice about the companies on my list: which are the good ones, which ones seem right for me, could they recommend others, do they know the names of the people I should contact at these companies, and may I use their name?

I also get the names of companies through magazine articles that cover certain industries, or through networking interviews with people who know that industry. I've also done "research" by going to meetings where the speaker or the attendees were people who should know people in my targeted area.

However I get the names of the people or companies, I use a computer to access a few CD-ROM databases to obtain some more in-depth information. This makes my letters and/or networking meetings much more compelling. Which databases I use depends on the information I am seeking. In the next chapter you will find information on the most well-known, as well as many obscure, automated, electronic tomes.

Where Else Can You Find Information?

* Personal observations. When you go for an interview, observe everything around you. What are the people like? What are they wearing? How well do they seem to get along?

Ask people: How do you like it here? How long have you worked here? Get there early. Ask everyone you see--the receptionist, people in the bathroom, the person who gets you coffee. This will give you a real feel for what it's like to work there, and will also let you know what the turnover rate is. If everyone says they've been there three or four months, you can be sure you'll be there only three or four months. Don't depend on the interviewer as your sole source of information about the company.

* Associations. Associations are an important source of information. If you don't know anything at all about an industry or field, associations are

often the place to start. They tend to be very helpful, and will assist you in getting the jargon down so you can use the language of the trade. *The Encyclopedia of Associations* lists a group for whatever you are interested in. If you are interested in the rug business, there's a related association.

Call them. If they have lots of local chapters, chances are there's one near you, and it will be a great place to network. Call the headquarters, and ask them to send you information and tell you the name of the person to contact in your area. Then call that person, and say you are interested in the association and would like to attend its next meeting. If there is no local chapter in your area, associations can still send you information.

Associations usually have membership directories, which they will sell you. They often publish trade magazines and newspapers that can update you on the business, for instance by noting the important issues facing the industry and telling who's been hired and who's moving. (Perhaps you should try to talk to the people you read about). They may even have a library or research department, or a PR person you can talk to. Often they sell books related to the field.

An association's annual convention is a very quick way to become educated in a field. These conventions are not cheap (they run from hundreds to thousands), but you will hear speakers on the urgent topics in the field, pick up literature, and meet lots of people.

Join an organization related to the field that interests you. Networking is expected. When you meet someone you think may help you, ask if you can meet on a more formal basis for about half an hour.

You can write to members, or network at meetings. If you want to contact them all, you can either continue to network or conduct a direct-mail campaign.

Associations are such an important source of information—especially about the jobs of the future—that they are covered in even greater detail in the next chapter.

- <u>The press</u>. Read newspapers with your target in mind, and you will see all kinds of things you would not otherwise have seen. Contact the author of an article in a trade magazine. Tell him or her how much you enjoyed the article and what you are trying to do, and ask to get together just to chat. I've made many friends this way.

- <u>Mailing lists</u> are not that expensive. You will pay perhaps $100 for several thousand names—selected by certain criteria, such as job title, level, industry, size of company, and so on. You can rent lists from direct-mail houses or magazines. For example, one job hunter contacted a computer magazine and got the names and addresses by selected zip codes of companies that owned a specific kind of computer. It was then easy for him to contact all of the companies in his geographic area that could possibly use his skills.

- <u>Chambers of Commerce</u>. If you are doing an out-of-town job search, call them for a list of companies in their area.

- <u>Universities</u> have libraries or research centers on fields of interest. A professor may be an expert in a field you are interested in. Contact him or her.

- <u>Networking</u> is a great research tool. At the beginning of your search, network with peers to find out about a field or industry. When you are really ready to get a job, network with people two levels higher than you are.

- <u>The Yellow Pages</u> is a useful source of companies in your local area.

- <u>Databases</u>. A CD-ROM database is an organized arrangement of data that is contained on a compact disk. This is important because:
1. One disk can hold several volumes worth of printed material. For example, the Encyclopedia of Associations is comprised of thirteen volumes. That would fill a couple of bookshelves.

However, all thirteen of these volumes are contained on *one* CD!

2. Information can be updated much more frequently on a CD. Publishers can and do release current information on a quarterly basis that is simply "down-loaded" onto a disk. Contrast this with print volumes that have to be reprinted and republished, which can take years. By the time that happens, the new information is often already out of date.

3. You can access and retrieve desired information in a fraction of a second when using CD technology. You simply type into the computer terminal the "key-word" you want to look up. Any information that contains that key-word is presented to you almost instantly. On the other hand, when you use printed works, the job of searching for specific pieces of related information can be very time-consuming.

Get Sophisticated About Using Reference Materials

In the next chapter, Wendy Alfus Rothman, a top career counselor, provides an in-depth examination of how to use specific research resources in all phases of your job search. Her actual case studies show how creative use of the dazzling array of reference works available today has helped real people make great career moves.

The choice of a career, a spouse, a place to live; we make them casually, at times, because we do not know how to articulate the choices. . .
I believe that people often persuade themselves that their decisions do not matter, because they feel powerless to make the <u>best</u> decision.
Some of us feel that, no matter what we do, our decisions won't matter much
. . . But I believe that we know at heart that decisions do matter.
Peter Schwartz, *The Art of the Long View*

The
Five
O'Clock
Club®

List of Companies
to Contact

For Target _____:
Geographic area: _____
Industry or company size: _____
Position/Function: _____

Company Name, Address, Phone	Contacts and Titles	Date & Method	Inter-view Date	Follow-up Dates

Contact Method: N = Networking;   D = Direct Mail;   S = Search firm;   A = Advertisement;
       O = Other;   Also show "R" if résumé given.   Make multiple copies of this page for your search.

Research Resources for an Effective Job Search

by Wendy Alfus Rothman

Wisdom is the principal thing; therefore get wisdom: and with all thy getting get understanding. Exalt her, and she shall promote thee: she shall bring thee to honour, when thou dost embrace her.
Proverbs 4: 7-8

And no grown-up will ever understand that this is a matter of so much importance!
Antoine de Saint-Exupéry,
The Little Prince

Research is to see what everybody has seen and to think what nobody else has thought.
Albert Szent-Gyorgyi,
American biochemist

Research is the process of going up alleys to see if they are blind.
Marston Bates
American Zoologist

If you are like most job hunters, you may have gotten stuck in one or more parts of your job search. You are probably wishing for some magic potion to get you moving again, and in a more productive way.

Research can be the answer. Try to set aside the common notion that research sounds tedious and boring. This is why most people skip it. But they are missing out. You will be at a great advantage if you learn to use this most valuable tool.

Maybe you need help in targeting the right field or industry: you already know what you do well, but you can't turn that information into targets.

Or maybe you need help setting up informational meetings: you just don't know what to say to people that doesn't sound like "job begging." (You know what job begging is: it's when you call your contacts intending to sound intelligent, low-key, and professional, and you end up saying, "So do you know of *any* job openings that might be good for me?")

Or perhaps you wish you were better prepared for an interview so that you could feel confident in your ability to differentiate yourself and rise above your competition. Perhaps you are not sure how to follow up after an interview in order to keep the process moving along.

Whatever phase of the search cycle you are in (phase 1: defining targets and companies within those targets; phase 2: interviewing; or phase 3: negotiating and closing), it's highly likely that you wish you had fresh questions to ask others, and fresh answers to the same old questions others ask you.

That is exactly what research is all about. It is the fastest way to turn a mediocre job search into a powerful, proactive campaign. It gives you the information that drives your search to its destination. It will magnify the results of each step of the job-search process. It is the way to get unstuck from a stalled or stagnating search. (And research can help you keep your job once you have it!)

There are two kinds of research: primary and secondary. Primary research basically means

---

*The will to persevere is often the
difference between failure and success.*
David Sarnoff, *Wisdom of Sarnoff and the World of RCA*

talking to people, while secondary research means reading materials in print. You need to do both kinds. It is usually wise to do some secondary research before you start talking to people so that your questions are more intelligent and focused.

If you take the time to do this, you will feel more confident and empowered, and people will usually respond better. If you are a person who prefers book work to people work, be careful that you do not spend all your time reading. The point is to take the information you learn, and use it in your conversations with people who can move you closer to your goal of obtaining the job that is right for you.

The biggest problem in doing secondary research is that there is so much information available. And there are a multitude of ways to access the information—from the traditional to the futuristic.

There are reference books, directories and guides, trade journals and newspapers, CD-ROM databases, online databases and electronic information transfer. The task can seem overwhelming.

But it doesn't have to be. There is a way to systematically move through the process, beginning with obtaining big-picture industry information, then moving on to company information, then on to job and salary information.

Some of the research tools mentioned in this section will be available to you, others will not. But don't worry. There is so much out there that if one channel is not available to you, another one will be.

Start by identifying what you want to know. Each stage of the job-search process has its own set of questions, and therefore its own corresponding research tools. Let's begin at the beginning.

PHASE 1:
Identifying Targets

In Phase 1 of a job search, you are trying to identify industry targets. First, you do a skills assessment to analyze what you do well and what you like to do. Then the idea is to turn that

knowledge into something that is useful to your search campaign.

Many people get stuck here for a time. Hoping and praying (a popular technique) won't get you unstuck. What *will* get you unstuck is gathering relevant information to help you make a systematic decision.

Here is the information you should be looking for when selecting industry targets:

1) trends and future prospects in a particular industry;

2) areas of growth and decline in that industry;

3) the kinds of challenges the industry faces that could utilize your skills;

4) the "culture" of the industry;

5) the major- medium- andminor- league companies in the industry.

After you get this information, you can begin to determine whether or not you are in sync with a particular industry and whether or not there is a place for you there. It does not require an enormous amount of time and data to begin to address these questions. You really only need a little bit of information, but it has to be the *right* little bit.

One of the first things I suggest to my clients is that they go to the library (almost any library will do for this), and look through **The Encyclopedia of Associations**, published by Gale Research in Detroit, Michigan. This encyclopedia lists a staggering total of 22,000 associations that represent trade and industry groups.

Every industry and almost every niche within that industry is represented here. Thus it is an incredible way to brainstorm possible industry targets. You really begin to get a sense of what you don't know, and what you could find out.

In addition to stimulating fresh ideas, the encyclopedia also provides names of contacts and chief officers, addresses of headquarters, phone numbers, the number of members and chapters, special committees and departments, a description of membership, the aims and activities of the group.

The people who are listed here are people who normally welcome your inquiries—otherwise they wouldn't have their names in the encyclopedia! They are often more than helpful if you phone and ask them to share some information about their industry.

Also listed in the encyclopedia are publications that are a terrific source of information. They can introduce you to industry jargon, issues of importance, authors of significance in the field, and companies that are making news. They also usually have their own section of classified ads that do not typically appear in newspapers.

Another thing that is valuable from this resource is that most associations publish a four-year convention schedule that you can call and request. These schedules include an explanation of panel-discussion groups and conference workshops. They give a sense of what topics have been important in an industry over the past few years.

You can also take note of who led the discussions and workshops, thereby discovering who plays or played a role in shaping the industry. **This resource should not be overlooked!**

There are many other ways to obtain big-picture information, as well. Let's take a look at some examples of real-life situations.

CASE STUDY: THOMAS
Turning an Assessment into a Target

Many people don't even know what they don't know. After seventeen years as a very successful human-resources executive in government administration, Thomas thought he wanted to target the health-care industry, but he didn't really know much about it. He just knew that it was an important growth industry of the nineties. He figured that hospitals were large bureaucracies, similar to government agencies. Therefore he thought he would at least fit into the culture.

After doing an assessment, he realized that, ironically, one of the reasons he wanted to leave his job in the first place was that he actually didn't like working for a large bureaucracy. Now he really didn't know what to do. Rather than

helping him, he felt that his assessment had limited his options.

He had learned that he was happiest when he was helping and directing people. He had also discovered that he wanted to work for a smaller organization, but he had absolutely no idea what to do with this insight.

He decided to do some research. He went to a reference book called **The Encyclopedia of Medical Organizations and Agencies.** This directory lists more than 12,200 organizations and agencies and has 69 subject chapters.

Glancing through the Table of Contents, Thomas realized that health care didn't mean just big hospitals. It could also mean HMO administration, biotechnology, environmental medicine, reproductive medicine, elder care, substance abuse and corporate employee- assistance programs, sports medicine, or many other areas.

By realizing what he hadn't known, he was able to begin to more clearly define his target. And this was just from reading a Table of Contents!

Next, Thomas discovered CD-ROM (Compact Disk Read-Only-Memory) databases. These disks contain highly topical and specialized information that one can access in a fraction of the time it would take to access the same material in its printed form.

The one Thomas chose was **CD Plus/Health.** It is an index to the nonclinical aspects of health-care delivery. These include administration and planning of health-care facilities, health insurance, personnel, HMO's, and related topics. Data are supplied from the National Library of Medicine, the American Hospital Association, and the printed Hospital Literature Index.

As Thomas learned more about the industry, he realized that Employee Assistance Programs (EAP's) are often set up as a business service to corporations through insurance companies. They operate as small business units, while being part of a larger organization—exactly the environment he had been looking for.

Thomas' human-resources and administrative skills would be transferable to these programs, and EAP's would definitely allow him to make a difference in people's lives.

Thomas had found a viable industry target that had both appeal and promise for his personality and background.

CASE STUDY: JOAN
Clarifying Her Career Direction

Joan was six years into her career as an attorney, fulfilling her parents' dream and what she had once thought was her dream as well. However, the twelve-hour days and six- to seven-day work weeks were taking their toll. She decided she wanted a change. Like many people, all Joan knew was what she *didn't* want to do. She did some research to alleviate her confusion.

First she browsed through the **U.S. Industrial Outlook.** This is a U.S. Department of Commerce publication that analyzes recent trends and forecasts for over 350 manufacturing and service industries. It is available in both printed and CD-ROM form.

It offers concise industry overviews, assesses international competitiveness, ranks the ten fastest- and ten slowest-growing manufacturing industries, lists trends in selected service industries, and projects the growth rates for 156 manufacturing industries and groups.

Joan also browsed through **Standard and Poor's Industry Surveys.** This reference book is updated quarterly. It consists of two volumes of up-to-date data for all major domestic industries. Prospects for a particular industry are followed by a historical presentation of trends and problems for that industry. Tables and charts accompany the text. Sales, earnings, and market data for the leading companies in an industry are provided.

As Joan researched, she read more and more about the high-technology industry. She began to see how much she had already known about this industry but had always taken for granted. And she realized how much she liked it. She had used many computer systems throughout her education, and continued to use them for her legal

research and preparation of briefs.

She continued her secondary research, using the **ICP Software Directory** on CD-ROM. It is a directory with descriptions of more than 15,000 publicly available business-applications software from over 5,000 vendors for microcomputers, minicomputers, and mainframes. It also includes proprietary software products and vendor-contact information.

It became clear to Joan that the software industry was consolidating, with a great deal of acquisition activity. Her legal experience had been in the area of corporate acquisitions.

Research had helped Joan see a great opportunity to use this legal background as a launching pad to enter the arena of high-technology.

Expanding Your Targets and Identifying Companies

Once you select an industry, you need to make sure that there are enough companies within that industry to warrant the efforts of an entire campaign. For example, if you find that there are only five small companies in your area, you will know before you begin that the odds are not in favor of your success.

Too many people get frustrated during their job search, thinking that they are doing something wrong, when the simple fact is that they do not have enough companies in their target.

If you see that your target is limited, you can make sure that your expectations are realistic. Instead of being depressed that your campaign isn't producing results, expand your target.

Expanding your target usually means identifying more than just the big companies that everyone else is targeting. It means identifying the mid-size and smaller ones—in fact, they are the ones that usually do most of the hiring.

This does more than expand your search; it also helps you understand each company's competitive position. Often this is actually more than the people working in the companies know. Sometimes they are so busy doing their jobs that they don't have time to stay current in their own industries!

After doing this kind of research, you become a person with valuable information to share, rather than just another person looking for a job (remember job begging?). Here are some questions appropriate at this point in your research with regard to each company on your list:

1) How large is this company?

2) Who owns it?

3) How long has it been in business?

4) What are its major products or services?

5) How many employees work there?

6) What are the revenues of the company?

7) How many branches does it have, and where are they located?

8) How many divisions are there, and which are the most profitable?

9) What are the names of the people that would be in a position to hire me?

Once you can answer these questions, you can prioritize the companies in your target as: most likely, possible, or long shots.

You can begin to strategize how to approach them for interviews: some through networking, some through direct contact and letter campaigns, some through search firms and headhunters, maybe some by answering ads.

You can see that without an extensive list of companies in your target industry, it would be extremely difficult to have six to ten things in the works. With the list, your problem may well be which six to ten things to pick first.

CASE STUDY: SARAH
Better Networking Through Research

Sarah worked for a major cosmetics firm. She loved her job and the industry, but due to some internal politics, she decided she needed to change companies. She knew lots of people to call for networking.

When she called them, she would ask them if they knew of any job openings. They invariably told her no. Sarah grew more and more uncomfortable at the prospect of picking up the phone.

Instead, she went to **Ward's Business Direc-**tory of U.S. Private and Public Companies. It profiles 100,000 companies and details their vital statistics. A special feature of Ward's Directory is that it includes companies with relatively small sales volumes.

The directory has information on private as well as public companies. It offers a ranking of companies, small to large, by sales volume within an industry.

All this gave Sarah a quick way to find a company's competitive place among its peers, and to target even further.

As she researched, Sarah realized how little she knew about other firms in her own industry—especially smaller ones. Using Ward's Directory, she was able to construct a list of ten mid-size cosmetics and health/beauty product firms that she felt were poised for growth.

Now when she called her network contacts, she asked their opinions about the viability of those firms. In addition to being impressed that she had done her homework, her friends knew something about the companies she had identified. They had opinions about which ones would fly and which ones would not. These friends were even able to introduce her to some people in several of the companies she had highlighted.

She learned what she needed to know. She never once had to ask about a specific job opening. Thus she eliminated the embarrassment that she used to feel in her networking.

Research was an empowering experience for Sarah. It enabled her to jump-start a stalled campaign.

PHASE 2:
Preparing for the Interview

One of the biggest errors job seekers make is not properly preparing for the interview. They read the books that give you "answers to difficult interview questions." But the problem is that everyone else has read those same books— including the people interviewing you!

It's pretty simple—the more you know about

a company's issues and objectives prior to interviewing with them, the better prepared you will be and the better able to answer any question.

Most job seekers are busy worrying about their own issues and objectives. Be smart: focus on the problems of this particular company. After all, the reason a manager hires someone is that he or she believes that that person can help the firm in some specific way.

The manager is only interested in your issues if they provide evidence of your ability to solve company problems. This is true whether you are a receptionist or a CEO.

CASE STUDY: GARY
Becoming an Insider

Gary was interviewing at a major consumer-products company for a position as an organizational psychologist in the staffing area. This company was embarking on an enormous project to set up assessment centers to identify high-potential employees for succession planning.

Gary knew next to nothing about assessment centers, but he knew he had better change that situation fast. So off he went to the library.

He used a CD-ROM database called **ABI/Inform**. Updated monthly, it indexes and abstracts 800 business and management journals appearing world-wide. These publications cover a wide variety of topics, including management, accounting, finance, economics, advertising, labor relations, and real estate.

Gary keyed in assessment centers. Up came a synopsis of all the articles that have been written about the subject for the past three years. Within thirty minutes, Gary became something of an expert on the history of assessment centers.

He learned about who first used them, their strengths and weaknesses, the "gurus" of the field, and what directions assessment centers will move in over the next few years. He learned the lingo, the history, and the players.

When Gary went back for his third interview, he ended up interviewing with *seventeen* people in that one day. Someone even followed him into the bathroom to keep the interview going! He won them all over with his expertise in the matter of assessment centers. The decision to offer him a job was unanimous.

PHASE 3:
Negotiating and Closing Deals

CASE STUDY: JENNIFER
Finding Out What She's Worth

Jennifer had been a marketing manager for a tobacco company for a few years. When the company restructured, she lost her job. She had spent a lot of personal time doing volunteer work as a lobbyist for an association. This led her to decide that she wanted to become a lobbyist for a corporation as her next career move.

Initially she had no idea how to find out about these positions. She did not even know that corporations call lobbyists "government-relations representatives." She learned it by reading through **The American Lobbyists Directory**. It lists 57,000 lobbyists and 25,000 organizations, complete with contact information and phone numbers.

Through this resource, Jennifer was able to identify companies in her target, and generate interviews with many of them. These interviews went well and her follow-up was great. In fact, she was about to get three offers. However, one major topic had not yet been addressed: salary.

Jennifer had deliberately avoided this issue, waiting until the companies knew they wanted her. Now she was at the point where she couldn't stall them any longer. Her problem was that she had absolutely no idea what market rates were for these positions, and she knew she couldn't negotiate without this critical knowledge.

Immediately Jennifer went to the library and got a copy of the **American Salaries and Wages Survey.** It answers salary questions for more than 4,500 occupational classifications at different experience levels, as well as for different areas of the country. She was able to find out salary

144

ranges for her industry, her position, and her geographic location.

Jennifer wanted still more. She went to the **Encyclopedia of Associations** and got the names of four different associations that deal with government-relations people and lobbyists. She called them and explained what information she was seeking.

The associations were able either to tell her salary standards or put her in touch with people in their local chapters who could.

When Jennifer went in for her salary-negotiation interviews, she knew the market rates, the highs and lows, and what she could reasonably request. With this information, she was able to negotiate the most attractive package.

Using Research Throughout the Campaign Process

Your research techniques may change as your campaign evolves. It is possible that you will only need to do a little bit of investigative work before you land a new position. On the other hand, you may find yourself returning again and again to resources that enrich all the stages of your job search.

CASE STUDY: SHELLEY
Uncovering Options for a Career Change

Shelley had spent eight years as a financial analyst in a major brokerage firm on Wall Street. He liked financial analysis, but didn't really like the options for career growth within the brokerage industry.

After doing an assessment, he decided that he wanted to position himself for growth within a mid-size corporation, with the goal of becoming CFO. Shelley thought he would try to target something within the environmental area. However, he didn't know very much about it and was pretty sure that he wouldn't have enough qualifications to break in. So he stayed where he was, feeling trapped in his career.

After some counseling, Shelley realized that he needed to do research to learn more about his target industry. He consulted two reference books.

The first was **The U.S. Industrial Outlook**, also available in a CD-ROM version. It has reports and prospects for over 350 manufacturing and service industries, and is put out by the U.S. Department of Commerce on an annual basis. It analyzes trends and presents forecasts for hundreds of industries. Data are given in both narrative and tabular form. A list of additional references is included at the end of each chapter.

The second reference book was **The Environmental Industries Marketplace**, also published by Gale Research. It gives detailed information on companies in the industry. Together, these books helped to break down this $100-billion market into its component parts.

Shelley quickly realized that his target was too big. He would have to pick from among the many areas these two books identified. Before, he had thought, "The environment is for me." Now he learned that much of the industry wasn't for him.

For example, he discovered that his skills might not be transferable to areas dealing with controlling abuses, such as air and noise pollution or hazardous waste. He could more clearly see opportunity for himself working with companies that provide services to the environmental industry, such as consulting, research or financial services. They related to his experience in financial research and analysis from his days on Wall Street.

Now Shelley had identified a target and specific companies within that target. He knew what he wanted, but he also knew that he would be perceived as an outsider by those in a position to hire him.

Using **The Encyclopedia of Associations,** he was able to contact two industry groups that sent him their newsletters. Reading through these, he learned the jargon, the hot issues and the major trends.

Shelley began to network. As he did, people referred him to companies that might actually

*The greatest obstacle to discovery is not ignorance
—it is the illusion of knowledge.*
Edward Bond, *Washington Post*, January 29, 1984

hire him. It was time to prepare for interviews.

He wished he could just wave a magic wand and know everything that had been written about the companies he was interested in, over the past few years. He wished he could just browse through their annual reports, but that would take so long, and his first interview was in just two days . . .

Off to the library! Shelley used **ABI/Inform,** mentioned before, and **Business Periodicals On Disc.** BPOD combines the ABI/Inform database of article references and abstracts of more than 800 business and management periodicals with the ability to view or print the complete text from many of the periodicals. It is updated monthly, and covers from 1987 up to the present.

He also used the **National Newspaper Index.** It offers combined in-depth indexing of five major newspapers: *The New York Times, The Wall Street Journal, The Christian Science Monitor, The Washington Post,* and *The Los Angeles Times.* It covers the most recent four years, and is updated monthly.

After only about thirty minutes, he had practically the next-best thing to that magic wand: a powerful synopsis of the past three years' worth of press about the companies he would be interviewing with.

As far as the annual report and financial information were concerned, he just had to plug into **Corporate Text.** It provides copies of annual reports for companies traded on the NYSE, AMEX, NASDAQ, and OTC, and is updated monthly.

He also used **LaserDisclosure.** It is a full text database of exact reproductions of original SEC filings, including graphs and photographs, from more than 6,000 companies traded on the NASDAQ, OTC, AMEX, and NYSE. It is updated weekly.

So throughout the job-search phases, Shelley used research tools to keep moving forward. He armed himself with enough information to be sincere, informed, and competitive in the growth industry of his choice.

CASE STUDY: JONATHAN
Searching for the Small Private Company

Jonathan was a human-resources manager who specialized in staffing and succession planning at a major bank. After twenty years there, he accepted an early-retirement package, but was not yet ready to leave the workforce.

After analyzing his options, he decided he wanted to be in a much smaller company. He investigated the future of human-resources and staffing issues and concluded that temporary services/interim staffing was a good target.

He knew lots of people in the industry—they had been his vendors at the bank! He thought he wouldn't have any problems networking around to find a great job with a small growth firm.

After five or six calls, he realized that he wasn't getting anywhere talking to the people he knew. Without realizing it, he sounded arrogant and inappropriate. He would ask, "Don't you think I would be a great addition to your industry, with all my connections and knowledge?" Although he didn't know why, he did notice that his contacts were not particularly impressed.

Jonathan needed to do some research. First he went to **The Encyclopedia of Business Information Sources.** It is a bibliographic guide to more than 21,000 citations, covering over 1,000 subjects of interest to business personnel.

This resource includes: abstracting and indexing services, almanacs and yearbooks, bibliographies, biographical sources, directories, encyclopedias and dictionaries, financial ratios, handbooks and manuals, online databases, periodicals and newsletters, price sources, research centers and institutes, statistics sources, trade associations and professional societies. It too is published by Gale Research, Inc.

In it, Jonathan found that a firm called Kennedy Publications in New Hampshire publishes a list of temporary-service companies and their areas of specialization. He sent away for it.

He became knowledgeable about the differences between international, national, regional, and independent firms. He also learned the differences between managed services, outsourcing, payrolling, and employee leasing.

He decided that a regional service would probably be the most likely to need someone at his level. He only found five in that category, and that was not enough.

To see if he could expand his target, he went through **Dun & Bradstreet's Million Dollar Directory.** It has information on some 160,000 U.S. businesses that have indicated net worth of more than $500,000.

Still, he was only able to get another five names. He thought perhaps the companies he was interested in were too small and/or private and therefore not in these reference materials. So he tried the **MacMillan Directory of Leading Private Companies**. It has information on over 12,500 companies and wholly owned subsidiaries with sales of $10,000,000.

He also looked through the **Over the Counter 1,000 Yellow Book.** It has the leading growth companies quoted on NASDAQ. It is a comprehensive directory introducing leading, younger growth companies in the U.S.A. It provides the addresses, phone numbers, and titles of 20,000 executives who manage these smaller companies on the cutting edge of innovation.

He also used the **Small Business Sourcebook.** It is a guide to sources of information furnished by associations, consultants, educational programs, government agencies, franchisers, trade shows and venture-capital firms for 100 types of small businesses.

After all that research, he decided that he should include some national firms as well, in order to expand his target. If he included firms that franchised and firms that were international, but not yet operating on American soil, that brought his total number to 55.

Jonathan next used **Gale Globalaccess: Associations.** It provides information on non-profit membership organizations of international, U.S., regional, state, or local interest.

This resource includes professional societies, labor unions, and cultural and religious organizations. From it, Jonathan got the names of four

associations and five trade journals. He spoke to people who belonged to NATS (National Association of Temporary Services) and he read appropriate literature.

Now that he understood the issues more clearly, he felt confident enough to try networking once again. Instead of bragging about his connections, he was able to talk about industry problems and how he would tackle them.

He impressed his contacts with his preparation and insight. It even appeared that he knew plenty of competitive information and trends that these same people wanted to hear about.

Because of the relationships that he developed at this stage of his job search, he eventually was introduced to the company he would end up working for.

CASE STUDY: MARRISSA
Researching the International Market

Marrissa had just returned from overseas, where she had been living and working as a personal assistant to the U.S. ambassador in an Eastern European country. She came back to the States for personal reasons, and needed to find a job. She was fluent in several languages and knowledgeable about diverse cultures.

She wanted to remain a personal assistant to a high-level executive. However, she didn't know where to start investigating corporate opportunities that would value her cross-cultural background without requiring a tremendous amount of travel.

Marrissa began with the **Directory of Foreign Manufacturers in the United States, Fourth Edition**, published by Georgia State University Business Press, 1990. It lists approximately 6,000 foreign-owned manufacturers with operations in the United States. There is indexing by state location, parent company location, and by product.

Next she went to the **Worldwide Branch Locations of Multinational Companies**. Arranged by country, this volume lists contact and descriptive information for about 500 parent companies and their key branch locations. She also used the **European Consultants Directory.** It contains more than 5,000 European consultants and their fields of endeavor.

She went on to consult a reference book called **Principal International Businesses**, published by Dun's Marketing Services. It provides annual information on approximately 55,000 leading companies in 140 countries throughout the world.

Last she used the **International Directory of Corporate Affiliations,** published by the National Register Publishing Company. It is an annual directory of information for over 1,600 foreign parent companies with listings of their divisions, subsidiaries, and affiliates. Also included are 1,500 U.S. companies with foreign holdings.

Marrissa obtained so much information that she designed an entire direct-contact campaign, demonstrating her ability to create executive correspondence. She was able to interview with several firms, turning down several offers before she secured an appropriate position.

You Can't Always Get What You Want, But If You Work At It, You'll Get What You Need

You've now read several case studies demonstrating the power of research. Sometimes it's difficult to see how these techniques will help you personally. Often the information you get doesn't look as you had hoped. You need to be creative.

Let me say something about being "creative." People frequently give that advice, without explaining.

Doing research does not mean simply collecting data. What you do with the information is critical to your success. Being creative means recognizing the relevance of seemingly irrelevant information. That is what will differentiate you from others.

For example, two clients of mine sold communications equipment in the high-technology industry. Both clients were interviewing at the same company. Both used the same research tools and both were able to learn the same two things: that the company in question had recently been denied FCC approval of a new product and that their third-quarter earnings were significantly lower than anticipated.

My first client, Peter, had been hoping to find specific sales figures, information about the company's top customers, and about their primary competitors. He was greatly disappointed in his meager findings.

Alvin was my second client. Like Peter, he had been hoping for similar sales-oriented information. However, instead of being disappointed, he was creative.

During his interview, he referred to the FCC problem to ask pertinent and thoughtful questions. He asked how one product could so greatly affect the firm's profit picture. He asked about the positioning of *other* products, about the R&D cycle, about how government regulations affect the overall marketing strategy of the firm. In other words, he used the same limited research information to demonstrate his awareness of the company's problems and his concern with something bigger than his own job: the viability of the corporation and its longer-term goals.

Alvin was perceived as an experienced salesperson, able to produce quickly, with an understanding of how sales are linked to the company mission. Peter was perceived as a salesman. Period. Who do *you* think got the offer?

There are many stories like this one. If you find yourself doing research and wondering, "How on earth will this help me?" remember Peter and Alvin. Turn your bewilderment into the question: "How does *this* piece of information impact my particular area of expertise?"

If the answers were easy, everyone would have them. Taking the time and effort to go that extra mile is what makes you stand apart from your competition.

The information is out there. An extensive Bibliography is at the back of this workbook to serve as your guide.

PART FOUR

ADVANCED CAREER PLANNING

HOW TO MANAGE YOUR FUTURE

The
Five
O'Clock
Club

Having a Balanced Life

Let our advance worrying become advance thinking and planning.
Winston Churchill

The more time we spend planning a project, the less total time is required for it. Don't let today's busy-work crowd planning time out of your schedule.
Edwin C. Bliss, *Getting Things Done*

BIFF: And suddenly I stopped, you hear me? And in the middle of that office building, do you hear this? I stopped in the mddle of that building and I saw—the sky. I saw the things that I love in this world. The work and the food and time to sit and smoke. And I looked at the pen and said to myself, what the hell am I grabbing this for? Why am I trying to become what I don't want to be? What am I doing in an office, making a contemptuous, begging fool of myself, when all I want is out there, waiting for me the minute I say I know who I am!
Arthur Miller, *Death of a Salesman*

---

*The most difficult thing—but an essential one
—is to love Life,
to love it even while one suffers,
because Life is all. Life is God,
and to love Life means to love God.*
Leo Tolstoy, *War and Peace*

It is often said that accomplishment makes [dying] easier, that those who have achieved what they set out to do in life die more contentedly than those who have not.
Judith Viorst, *Necessary Losses*

It is very easy to have a life that is out of balance. Some people intentionally have an "out-of-balance" life so they may achieve in a specific area. Or a person's life may become out of balance in one area for a certain length of time so that he or she may "catch up" in that area. However you decide to live your life, it is still good to know what you are missing.

> **Pay attention to all areas.
> For a balanced life, *grow* in all areas:**
>
> - **Spiritual**   • **Recreation**
> - **Financial**   • **Family**
> - **Career**   • **Social**
>   • **Health & Fitness**

People need to pay attention to their careers to meet their basic obligations. But be sure you have a "career" and not just "work." **Career** has a concept of personal development. **Work** has a concept of "I need money to do something else with."

To grow in every area:
1. Have goals in every category.
2. Set priorities.
3. Develop a plan.
4. Live.
5. Review. (Go back to step 1.)

It's a good idea to review annually what you did last year and what you plan for next year. Keep your plans in a folder and review them over the years. Look for growth in each area. Or do it twice a year. You can pick a theme for the year—something that needs extra focus. Some people do a five- or ten-year plan.

Set goals for yourself. The goals you set must be measurable: you must be able to tell when you've accomplished a particular goal.

Set goals that make you stretch. All successful people have failed. It's how you deal with it that's key. If you've never failed, you've never reached.

Life planning is a lot like business planning. A common approach is this one:

1. Get a dream/vision. Formulate a purpose.

---

2. Write it down.
3. Create long-term, measurable goals.
4. Create a series of strategies and action steps to get there.
5. Evaluate these goals and strategies: make sure they represent a "stretch" yet are reasonable.
6. Share these goals with someone.
7. Get some good counsel and advice. (Be prayerful about it.)
8. Act on it.

Criteria for SUCCESS
Someone found this on a plane and passed it on to me:
S - Sense of Purpose —written goals.
E - Excellence — commitment to be the best at whatever you do.
C - Contribution.
R - Responsibility for your actions — You don't work for a company; you work for yourself.
E - Effort.
T - Time Management.
S - Stay with it.

Write down your goals for each area, and your steps for reaching your goals in each area. Some people review their lives once or twice a year. Some families develop a plan together every year. Pay attention to all areas. Feel free to add extra areas that have specific importance to you. For a balanced life, *grow* in all areas:

Area to Plan/Grow	Goals for Each Area	Steps for Getting There
• Spiritual		
• Financial		
• Career		
• Health & Fitness		
• Recreation		
• Family		
• Social		
• Other		

The
Five
O'Clock
Club

Deborah:
Developing a Detailed Plan

Achieve greatness:
Start where you are;
Use what you have;
Do what you can.
Arthur Ashe, tennis champion

There are two kinds of people, those who
finish what they start and so on . . .
Robert Byrne

Barbara Walters: *And you think you will walk again?*
Christopher Reeve: *I think it's very possible I'll walk again.*
Walters: *And if you don't?*
Reeve: *Then I won't walk again.*
Walters: *As simple as that?*
Reeve: *Either you do or you don't. See, it's like a game of cards and if you think the game is worthwhile, then you just play the hand you're dealt. Sometimes you get a lot of face cards, sometimes you don't. But I think the game's worthwhile. I really do.*
Christopher Reeve, former star of *Superman*,
in an interview with Barbara Walters.
Reeve became a quadriplegic
after a horseback-riding accident.

As important as it is to have a vision of your future, it's not enough. You need to test it realistically, and have a plan for getting there.

You may want to hedge your bets and come up with a few scenarios for your future. Then you can explore each one to see which is the most fun for you, as well as the most do-able. For example, you may consider developing a plan for one or two of the following options:

- staying where you are and rising through the ranks to reach a certain position
- having a specific kind of business
- becoming a consultant in your field
- changing careers and becoming an expert in another field
- attaining a certain position in a small company, such as that of controller.

Think as big and as long-term as you can. You may even imagine yourself having "a job and a dream"—a day job to earn money while you pursue your dream on the side.

Whatever your vision, you are more likely to achieve it if it is backed by a plan. Plans, however, are not rigid. As you start to investigate and implement your plan, you will learn things that you could not have known before. Then you will adjust your plan going forward.

If you still don't have a goal—a vision for your future—do the exercises in this book to the extent that you can, and then take the results to a career counselor. Together, you can come up with a vision and a plan for getting there.

Think as big and as
long-term as you can.

CASE STUDY: Deborah
Planned All the Way
Deborah Brown had already completed her Seven Stories Exercise and her Forty-Year Plan, as well as all of the other exercises. She had put off doing the Forty-Year Plan for a long time; it seemed so intimidating. Once she finally put pen to paper, it took her only an hour or so to complete, and she felt relieved. In retrospect, she

wondered why it had taken her so long to start writing it.

Deborah 's vision of herself is to someday be the head of Workforce America®, a community-based, national not-for-profit. I started Workforce America in Harlem in 1991, basing the program on the methodology of The Five O'Clock Club. It serves people who are not yet in the professional or managerial ranks, and helps them to get into professional-track jobs. I asked Deborah —well-educated, dignified, and articulate—to volunteer to help with the Harlem program. I thought she seemed like such a winner; perhaps she could play a major part in running it. She would also serve as a role model for other African-Americans.

Whatever your vision, you will need to learn new things, form relationships that are helpful to you, and start to act in a way that suits the position to which you aspire.

Deborah's Huge Vision

Now Deborah 's vision is to head up the Workforce America program in Harlem, and get it to the point where it runs smoothly. Later, she wants to move the program to other cities, such as Detroit.

Implementing her vision will take a huge effort, and can last her entire lifetime. I know that Deborah can make this vision happen. Now she needs to flesh it out. She needs a very *concrete plan* about how she will get there.

In this section, you will see one planning method. It does not matter what kind of approach you use. If you are comfortable with any other planning tool, use it. If your planning method uses different definitions for words we use here, such as "goals" or "objectives," do not get hung up on our differences. Just use your own definitions and your own method. What is important is that you actually plan, and that you write out your plan.

Think of yourself as a business. Just as any

business needs a plan to get where it wants to go, so do you.

Identifying the Most Important Goals

At a program at The Five O'Clock Club, the group brainstormed the most important goals that Deborah would need to achieve to someday head this not-for-profit on a national level. We came up with the following:

Goal 1. Learn how to run a not-for-profit, especially in the area of fund-raising.

Goal 2. Learn about Harlem, and form strong bonds in the Harlem community. Work closely with other not-for-profits there.

Goal 3. Recruit and retain the best: volunteers, staff, and board.

Goal 4. Create a program that is based on the needs and serves the best interests of the community.

Goal 5. Develop the processes, operations manual, computer systems, and so on that would allow this program to be exported to other geographic areas.

Goal 6. Learn about career development and related areas. This includes the mentoring process, job development, and so on.

Goal 7. Observe the professional behavior of someone who is already the head of a national not-for-profit or similar organization. Emulate that person where appropriate.

The Same Applies to You

Whatever *your* vision, you will need to learn new things, form helpful relationships, and start to act in a way that fits the position to which you aspire.

For example, if you want to rise to a higher level in corporate life, you would need:
- appropriate technical and interpersonal skills
- in-depth knowledge about specific topics
- a network of contacts that you would make and keep
- a certain demeanor, vocabulary, and dress.

The Multiplier Effect:
Select Strategies That Satisfy
More Than One of Your Goals

Next, you need to come up with strategies for reaching each goal. If Deborah needs to learn how not-for-profits work, she could, for example:

- take classes
- talk to people who are already involved in the not-for-profit world
- work for a not-for-profit and get some on-the-job training.

If Deborah actually decides to work for a not-for-profit, she needs to think this through. She could choose to work for a hospital, an association, a university, or the government. But would these be relevant to what she wants to do?

If Deborah could work for a not-for-profit and—at the same time—learn about the Harlem community, or the area of career development,

that's the kind of not-for-profit she should choose. The more goals a strategy supports, the more she will get a multiplier effect.

Her strategy could be refined even more. Deborah needs to be in a position where she will actually learn how to run a not-for-profit herself. Therefore, if she could find a job in a staff function, such as administration or finance, in a not-for-profit that deals with Harlem or with career development, she would achieve a "multiplier effect": one of her strategies would satisfy more than one of her goals.

On her plan, Deborah would write that same strategy—"Work in a staff function in a not-for-profit that deals with Harlem or with career development—under Goals 1, 2 and 6. As she conducts her research, Deborah will decide whether she will get more mileage out of working for an organization that is related to Harlem,

Career Plan

Vision: Head up a national not-for-profit, Workforce America®.

Goal 1: Learn how to run a not-for-profit, especially in the area of fund-raising.

Strategies	Action Steps
1. Take classes.	1. Ask advice: What do I need to learn? 2. Research the organizations that teach what I need. 3. Develop a schedule for taking the classes.
2. Work in a staff function in a not-for-profit that deals with Harlem or with career development.	1. Develop skills in my present job that would make me more marketable elsewhere. 2. I'd like to have strong for-profit experience. Get a job in a for-profit that relates to what I will need later. 3. While in that job, make contacts in the not-for-profit sector. 4. Select exactly the right not-for-profit that will teach me what I need to run Workforce America. I can immediately incorporate those things into Workforce America.
3. Talk to people in the not-for-profit world.	1. Research associations that I can join. 2. Select two and join them, including a fund-raising org. 3. Constantly network and gather information. 4. Keep in touch with the people I meet.

to career development, or to both. Achieving a multiplier effect—even in two goals—will save her years in her effort to reach her vision.

In your career, you will always do better if you can achieve a multiplier effect: *develop strategies that satisfy more than one of your goals.*

It may take you three or four weeks to come up with a plan with multiplier strategies, but that plan that could guide you for the next twenty years or so.

> **In your career, you will always do better when you achieve a multiplier effect:**
> **develop strategies that satisfy more than one of your goals.**

Goals Are Achieved through Strategies; Strategies Are Achieved through Action Plans.

Develop your career plan as if you were planning someone else's business. Don't short-change yourself. Be sure your personal plan is as well thought out as if you were handing in a business plan for a company. If you are serious about reaching your goals, nothing less is good enough. It will affect your whole life.

Even if your goals are not as lofty as Deborah 's, a plan will help you get there. And those who have written plans are more likely to get there than those who don't write down their plans.

So, **for each goal, develop the strategies** you need to get there. See how often you can come up with strategies that serve more than one goal.

Within each strategy, develop action plans. For example, if one strategy for learning about not-for-profits is to take classes, Deborah would need action steps to support that strategy. These could include researching the various organizations that teach what she needs, deciding which classes would be best, and so on.

Review Your Plan and Set Dates

Now step back and take a look at your plan. Set dates for completing those areas where you

have some control. In my own planning, for example, I can very easily set a date by which I should have a book written. Writing a book is completely under my control. There is a good possibility that I will be able to meet that goal if it is what I really want to do.

But if my plan says, for example, "get a book published by a major publishing house by a certain date," that is less under my control. I cannot guess how long the action steps would take—regardless of how long and how hard I work at it. The steps could be: find an agent, write a book proposal, develop a book marketing plan, wait for the agent to sell the book to a publishing house.

I cannot tell how long it would take me to find an agent. And if I put a deadline on it, either I will be inclined to work with an agent who is inappropriate for me, or I will become discouraged that I did not meet that fictitious date. However, I could set dates for writing a book proposal and a book marketing plan, because those two areas are completely under my control.

So if I don't have dates on items which are beyond my control, what can I do to make sure that I do not ignore those uncontrollable areas? How can I make sure I am constantly making progress on my plan?

One technique is to devote a certain amount of *time* to achieving the plan. The second technique is to develop *stages* for the plan.

Spend at Least Fifteen Hours a Week

Make sure you are spending a certain number of hours a week working toward your goals. If you spend no time implementing your plan, or just a few hours, you can see that you would make no progress at all. A rule of thumb is to spend fifteen hours a week—assuming you are working full-time at a job. Then you have to make sure you are doing the right things during those fifteen hours—so you are getting the most from the time you are spending.

Developing the Stages of Your Plan

After you have developed goals, strategies and action steps, the plan usually seems very onerous—even if you are working fifteen hours a

156

week on it. So it's usually helpful to implement your plan in stages. After all, you can only do so much. You may still be working in your present job. You just want to bite off a chunk of this plan, and stay headed in the right direction.

The stages that you lay out for yourself are hypothetical: when you start to implement them, you will change things around. However, looking at the plan in stages helps you to see where you intended to head.

Then, because you are bright and energetic, life will present you with other options that could take you off-track. If you have laid out a plan, you can reject those that do not fit with your plan, and accept those that do fit in with the stage you are at right now.

Stage 1—What can Deborah do right now?

Deborah has to keep her day job. But there are certain things she can do right now to advance toward her long-term goal. She could:

• take on assignments in her day job that would develop skills she will need for the future.
• better develop the plan for Harlem, improve the program somewhat, and think of what she should eventually do to make the program stable and self-supporting.
• think about how she could eventually move into a job that would give her more of a multiplier effect.

For most people, it is advisable to have a day job that somehow supports other career-related goals—rather than one that is completely at odds with their long-term vision.

If your job requires so much energy and brain power that it will take away from your dream, you are unlikely to achieve your dream.

Stage 2 —Free up time to devote to this vision.

We each have the same amount of time. How can we find the time to do what we need to do to reach our goals? No matter how energetic you may be, there is still a limit to your energy. It's better to think through how you want to spend your time and energy.

What are some of the things that Deborah should consider so she is not spending her time and energy on the wrong things?

Certainly she could continue to run the Harlem program. However, she should hold off on growing it. If she increases its size a great deal in Stage 2, she won't have time to learn all the other things that are needed to eventually reach her long-term goal.

To conserve her time and energy, she could spend some of her time gathering information, and other time recruiting people to take over some parts of the program. This would free her up for reaching her long-term goals.

Stage 3—Grow the Harlem program.

Deborah could find out how to raise funds, develop a stronger program, and build the infrastructure that she would need to export the program to other areas, such as the manual for running the operation.

Stage 4—Work on Workforce America full-time.

By this time, the program should be large enough to support Deborah . In addition, it would need its own full-time space for meetings because the program is slated to be a six-day-a-week operation.

Stage 5—Make it into a regional organization.

Deborah could plant the seeds for other Workforce America locations in this region. She could get herself on prestigious boards that would help her even more with fund-raising and with running the organization.

Stage 6—Be a national organization.

Take Workforce America to other geographic areas.

Stage 7—Influence national policy.

Deborah could sit on national boards, and work with those at the highest levels of government. The work that she would be doing affects America and can help to narrow the growing gap between the haves and have-nots. She needs to have some say in national policy.

Deadlines

There are no dates on the "Stages" plan. When Deborah develops a plan for herself (as opposed to the one the group came up with), she will implement it as quickly as she can. In real life, the stages will overlap. That is, an element from Stage 7 may start when she is only in Stage 4. The timing of the plan depends on her dedication—and her ability to plan and keep on moving the plan along despite other demands in her life.

I never put deadlines on my plan stages. I know I would never meet them and that would make me discouraged. Or I would meet them at the expense of quality. The dates are fictitious. I am going as quickly and as sensibly as I can. Putting a date on a stage would not make it happen any sooner in my case. I just keep working toward my plan.

What If I Don't Achieve My Complete Vision?

If your vision is big enough, you may never fully achieve it, but you won't care. You will be doing what you want, your plan will keep you on-track, and you will be having a lot of fun. You will get further with a plan than you ever would have without one.

Some people come up with "plans" that are beyond their abilities. This is less likely when a person actually writes out the details of what it would take to achieve a plan. For example, a person can easily say: "I want to have my own business and earn $100,000 a year. That's my plan."

That's not a plan. That's a dream. When a person actually writes down how he or she will get there, then it becomes more realistic. Either they wind up changing their vision, or develop the steps they need to get there. They stand a better chance of succeeding.

My Own Plan—Dealing With Failure

I wrote my plan for The Five O'Clock Club in 1986. Some of the details turned out differently, but the strategies stayed the same. For example, to get credibility in this field, I had imagined myself teaching at New York University and Columbia. In fact, I wound up at the New School for Social Research, which fit in with my plan very well.

After a stage is completed, I write down the month and year—just for the record. Stage 3 of my plan failed completely. Many years ago, I had been running The Five O'Clock Club in my apartment, and Stage 3 called for me to move it out of my apartment. I took out ads in local magazines, rented a hotel room, and otherwise promoted the program. Only twelve people registered. It wiped me out financially and emotionally.

I thanked God for this clear failure. There was no doubt that this effort had failed. It would have been worse if the results had been ambiguous. Then perhaps I would have kept at it. That would have been worse.

I rewrote Stage 3. I realized that I needed to get more credibility before I "went public" with this program, so I decided to write a book. After the book was written, *then* I moved the program out of my apartment—but more cautiously this time. I moved into a very low-rent location. Everything else in the plan stayed exactly the way it was.

In fact, The Five O'Clock Club failed three times in those early years. Each time, it was a clear failure. Each time, I had to stop the program to recover financially and emotionally. Each time, I thanked God for the clear failure. Each time, I decided that this was still a good vision (to make the highest-quality career-counseling available to people at all levels), and that it was what I wanted to do with my life. To paraphrase the saying, I picked myself up, brushed myself off, and started all over again.

Most successful people fail, I told myself, and in my failures, I collected more quotations that inspired me. And now I pass them on to you.

*Everything depends on execution;
having a vision is no solution.*
Stephen Sondheim

Career Plan Worksheet

Vision:

Goal #___:

Strategies	Action Steps	Due Dates	Measures of Success	Resources Needed
1.				
2.				
3.				
4.				
5.				

The Five O'Clock Club

What You Can Do in Your Present Situation

What has changed most fundamentally is the greater responsibility being given to workers to take charge of ensuring higher quality and to take a proactive role in organizing their own work—responsibilities that in the past management jealously kept for itself.
Hedrick Smith, *Rethinking America*

Language reflects social reality, and the reality of the pre-nineteenth-century world was that people did not "have" jobs in the fixed and unitary sense; they "did" jobs in the form of a constantly changing string of tasks.
William Bridges, *JobShift: How to Prosper in a Workplace Without Jobs*

Now you have a vision of your future, and a plan of what you should do to achieve that vision. You will need new skills and new relationships. To advance, you may feel as though you must get out of the job you are in right now. However, you may be able to add skills, experience and a knowledge base without leaving your current position. Look at the following list of ideas. You may want to add some of these to your Career Plan.

- Talk to colleagues about needs in your present company. Make plans to fill those needs.
- Expand the network of people with whom you interact internally and externally.
- Join an association that fits in with your long-term goals; get on a committee.
- Find out what people in your function do outside of your present company (or the function you are interested in long-term).
- Learn a new technical skill.
- Manage a project.
- Volunteer for a task force.
- Train staff on new software.
- Select/determine software or equipment.
- Write a proposal to fill a need.
- Make a presentation.
- Take some classroom training.
- Substitute for your manager in a meeting.
- Run a meeting.
- Assist with the budgeting process.
- Organize a community activity or do volunteer work to gain a new marketable skill.
- Train a new person.
- Research and write a report.
- Write and implement a "what if" suggestion.
- Observe the demeanor of someone in a high-level position (even if only via video).
- Continue to develop your plan.
- Think of what may stop you from reaching your goals, and overcome those barriers.

The first five items are generally considered to be the most important. These are action steps that will usually help you to do better in your career—no matter what your career goals are. Consider adding them to your list if they are not already on it.

160

The Eight-Word Message

Your security will come first and foremost from being an attractive prospect to employers, and that attractiveness involves having the abilities and attitudes that an employer needs at the moment.
William Bridges, *JobShift: How to Prosper in a Workplace Without Jobs*

You can use an Eight-Word Message to make sure that those more senior than you know what you want them to know about you. It will help you keep your career on track, and improve your chances of getting ahead. Here are a few examples.

CASE STUDY: JUDY
Not Getting Credit

Judy, Jim and Helen had worked seventy hours a week for the last three weeks to complete the Airbag Project. Judy was proud and relieved when it was done on time. Then she found out that Jim and Helen were getting all the credit. In fact, it seemed that no one even knew that Judy had worked on the project. There had been a pattern for her of not getting recognition for her work. Once more, she was being overlooked. She thought about looking for a job and working for a company that would be more fair—someplace that would appreciate her hard work. Or she could go in to her boss and complain about not getting credit. Instead, she decided to start using an Eight-Word Message whenever she wanted people—especially those higher up—to know something about her. And right now she had a strong message to get across. The message was "I worked on the Airbag Project."

Most people miss everyday opportunities to get out information about themselves. For example, when Mr. Coyle, her boss's boss, is in the same elevator with Judy, he always greets her with his predictable "Good morning, Judy. How are you?" Judy, just as predictably, politely responds, "Fine, and how are you, Mr. Coyle?"

This time, however, Judy decided to say, "Great—now that we've completed the Airbag Project." He almost had to ask, "Oh, were you involved with that?" This gave her the opening she wanted. "Yes. Three of us worked seventy hours a week for the last three weeks. I was in charge of all the marketing literature. I think it's an award-winning package."

As she came into contact with other people whom she wanted to know about her work, Judy gave them the same message. Gradually people were showing their appreciation. Her self-esteem went way up. If she continues to do good work, and makes sure the right people know about it, Judy's career will be much different in the future.

Selecting the Targets for Your Message

It's not enough to do a good job. People—especially those more senior than you—have to know that you've done a good job. Managing the message they get about you is even more critical in these turbulent times when those over you come and go, and you don't know who your immediate boss may be tomorrow. In the old days, you established long-term relationships and a long-term reputation. The management ranks changed more slowly. Now you have to make sure from time to time that people know your worth.

CASE STUDY: RALPH
Overcoming Career Stereotypes

Ralph used to be the head of a marketing department before he joined Lavaloc. Now he is in charge of all advertising—a smaller position—and doing a good job. The management here forgets that he used to have a much broader background and could contribute more than he currently is doing. For example, he could be on a task force to market a new Lavaloc product, or have another area reporting to him, such as the direct-marketing department.

Over time, Ralph became so frustrated that he was thinking of writing a memo to personnel to let them know that he had come from a bigger job. Or he thought about asking for a formal meeting with his boss and his boss's boss. Memos and formal meetings are often good techniques for getting ahead. This approach is discussed in another chapter. But an Eight-Word Message is usually a lot less risky. Ralph decided to try it. His message was "I used to be head of marketing."

When Ms. Dolan, the division head, was in that proverbial elevator, she predictably said,

"Hello, Ralph, how are you?" Ralph responded, "The energy in this place is just terrific. It reminds me of the energy at Galomar." She inevitably had to comment, "I forgot you had worked at Galomar." This gave him the opportunity to say, "Yes. I was the head of marketing there." If appropriate, he could have elaborated.

Ralph's goal, at this point, is simply to remind people that he has a broad background. Later, he can change the message. And, at some point, he may even formally approach someone about being on a task force—once he has established a different image of himself.

Giving These Messages to Bosses

Part of the trick of managing your message is figuring out who your "bosses" are. You probably know who your immediate supervisor is (although, in some companies, it may be hard to tell), but who are the other people—senior to you—who can influence your career? Most people come up with a list of six to ten people who are senior to them. The list could include your boss's boss, some of your boss's peers, or your boss's boss's peers. It could also include a few people outside your organization, such as the head of an important industry association, your boss's peer in another company, or someone considered a guru in your field. These are the people you want to consider when you have an important message to get across.

You can't constantly send out messages every time you run into someone, and you'd look like an idiot if you kept saying the same thing. You may, for example, want to send a message that supports your boss or your group, such as "I think we have the best audit team in the industry."

Decide what message you want to send, and to whom you want to send it. *Make sure your message is appropriate.* In the course of promoting yourself, make sure you do not undermine your boss or say anything negative about others. You are simply trying to manage your own career.

Running a company is easy when you don't know how,
but very difficult when you do.
Price Pritchett

Managing Relationships at Work: Bosses

Most people do not lose their jobs because of incompetence, but because of poor relationships at work. By definition, work relationships can be divided into those with people who are at a higher level than you (bosses), at your level (peers), or at a lower level (subordinates). Of course, one must also have good relationships with clients, but we will not be dealing with that here. Your career can be completely derailed by a boss, a peer, or a subordinate—but in very different ways. On the other hand, your career can be greatly enhanced by learning how to communicate well with the people in each of these categories—but, again, in very different ways.

In this chapter, we'll take a look at the instructive examples of two people who totally ignored the importance of having good relationships up the line. And they each suffered the consequences.

CASE STUDY: FRANK
About to Be Fired

Frank's story is a common one: he forgot that it was his job to please his boss. As the person in his company responsible for supporting computer departments all over the world, Frank's work was excellent. He and his boss, Mr. Williams, received many letters of commendation from happy clients who appreciated the work Frank did. However, Frank thought his boss was stupid and nasty, and deserved to be ignored. He would not tell his boss what he was going to say at meetings. What Frank said usually caught his boss by surprise, and that gave Frank pleasure. When Mr. Williams gave him an assignment, Frank was sure his boss was wrong and did it his own way. Sometimes Frank's clients agreed with him and sent more letters praising him. This only reinforced him.

Frank was doing such a great job that he was ready to have his duties expanded. He wanted new assignments and a promotion. In fact, Frank thought he should report directly to his boss's boss. Because Frank served his clients well and

did his job, he thought that was enough. It wasn't. Frank was in trouble. He was about to be fired. Mr. Williams thought Frank was worth saving, and that some executive coaching could help change his attitude and behavior. He was sent to me.

When I discussed the situation with Frank, he was adamant that, as a matter of principle, he would not show respect to his boss. Why should he defer to someone who he thought was inadequate and who treated everyone so horribly? It had become a point of honor with him.

To keep his job, Frank first had to accept the fact that he was in trouble: he had no chance of reporting to his boss's boss; he was not going to get new assignments, given the way he was acting; and I couldn't emphasize enough that he was actually going to lose his job if he didn't change. The turning point came when he saw that it was possible to develop a good relationship with his boss *without* giving up his principles or his rapport with the people in the field.

A subordinate cannot possibly know all the various pressures that affect his or her boss's decisions, and therefore is not the best judge of whether a boss's requests are valid. If your boss says that a certain assignment is the most important thing for you to do, you are in no position to second-guess him or her, in effect saying no. I told Frank that I know from personal experience as a manager that I don't want to always have to explain to my employees why I want them to do something. At some point, I get tired of explaining. Sometimes when I say something is very important, I simply want them to do it.

As we continued our counseling sessions together, Frank came to see that his point of view was not always accurate, and that perhaps it made sense to pay attention to the boss. If Frank didn't learn to deal with this boss, he would probably have the same problem with the next boss—who might be one who would simply fire him, rather than trying to help him as this one was doing.

What could Frank do differently? He could

The pure and simple truth is rarely pure and never simple.
Oscar Wilde

find out his boss's priorities, let his boss know his agenda before he went into meetings, send his boss a copy of all memos (or show him the content of sensitive memos before he sent them). But even if Frank kept making these little changes, how would Mr. Williams be able to tell if Frank was simply trying to placate him, or if he had seen the error of his ways and had had a real change of heart? Over the course of time, Frank's boss would have to watch carefully for signs of Frank's true intentions: was Frank still trying to undermine him or was Frank now supporting him? This situation would create a lot of pressure on both of them.

Making subtle changes at this point would not be enough. Frank's boss was too frustrated. Instead, Frank would have to do something more radical so that his boss could see clearly that his attitude had indeed changed. Frank could make more dramatic and consistent changes in his work, such as overtly deferring to his boss at meetings. An effective alternative would be to actually tell his boss that he had made a conscious decision to change, and that he was determined to become a new person. Then, even if his changes were not dramatic, Frank's boss would recognize the true significance of all of those small changes: Frank is now a different person. Things *will* be better in the future.

To let Mr. Williams know that he had had a change of heart, Frank needed to communicate a very simple message: "I was wrong. I've changed." So Frank said to his boss, "I can see now that I've been wrong. I'm sure that you have plans that I don't know about. I will make sure I do what you want, and also let you know my agenda before we go into meetings." Now Frank was consistently asking his boss for feedback on the things he planned to do, and filling him in before they went into meetings. He developed a good relationship with Mr. Williams. After a few months, Frank got a number of new assignments. After a few more months, he got a promotion. Frank is still working for the same boss, but now he loves it, and Mr. Williams is as happy as can be.

CASE STUDY: MELANIE
Getting Un-Fired

Melanie, an advertising manager, had already gotten fired. She came to me because she wanted help looking for a job. Her employer had offered her only a few weeks of severance and no outplacement help, and she had not quite moved out of her old job. Because she would have no income except unemployment compensation, I asked her if she would like to try to stay with her present company. She reminded me that she had already been fired. I explained that it takes a lot more effort to change jobs than to attempt to stay where you are. If we put the new strategy into effect right away, before our next weekly session she would know whether or not it was working. It might not do the trick, but it would take relatively little effort. Would she like to try it? She said she would. After all, what did she have to lose?

I asked her to tell me about the situation in more detail. She was an account manager in an advertising agency. She and the creative director, slightly higher up than she was, disliked each other intensely. She admitted that she had caused him a lot of problems. In fact, she had irritated a number of important people, including her boss and the president. First, Melanie had to make a list of the people to whom she needed to make amends, decide what she should say to each person, and plan the sequence of this campaign to save her job. She also needed an overall theme to her campaign—a brief message that she could fall back on whenever things seemed to be going poorly in her discussions. Her pitch was "I've loved working here. I want to stay." That's all there was to it—only eight words.

You should be able to sum up the main idea you want to convey in about eight to ten words. Naturally, depending on the context and conversational opportunities, the way you express the message will vary, and may call for a few more words. Your message has to be simple. It gets repeated like a mantra during these discussions. When things are going wrong and they are attacking you and saying things you didn't expect to hear, just keep going back to your pitch like a broken record. If you don't have a main message, the conversation can go off in all directions. You can spend a lot of time defending yourself or rehashing old scenarios.

Melanie met with her boss. She said, "I know I've made mistakes and have irritated a lot of people. But I'm a changed person. I've loved working here, and I want to keep my job." Her boss replied by naming lots of things she had done wrong. She agreed with him, said things would be different, and added, "I've loved working here. I want to stay." When she met with the creative director, she said she was sorry for any problems she had caused in the past, but promised that she would support any creative ideas that he had in the future. She said she now realized that that was part of her job. She added, "I've loved working here. I want to stay." She did that with four more people, and within two days they put her on the most important account in the company! She was dumbstruck.

Melanie had bought herself some time until she could decide what to do. She had turned things around so that she actually could stay if she wanted, or she could leave when she was better prepared. She soon found another job, and then she resigned. But she resigned on very good terms with everyone in the company. They were all sorry to see her go.

This technique of telling someone you have changed—if indeed you have—is very powerful. The key to its power is not only in what you do afterwards, but in *saying* that you have changed. But there is no use in saying that you have changed if you haven't. You will not be able to get away with it. They *are* looking for change. And it will only make the situation worse if you try to con them.

Stories about career crises are interesting and dramatic. However, it is better to manage your career to prevent the kind of crises that you may bring on yourself. You don't have to wait until things get critical. You can make corrections at any stage. First, assess your situation. Make a chart of everyone in the organization with whom you have contact. Think through what your relationship is with each person, and what it should be. If you are in danger of losing your job, make a plan. The most effective ways to buy time for yourself are to make a dramatic change which takes the pressure off you, and to deliver a concise and consistent message.

The
Five
O'Clock
Club

Two Simultaneous Careers: An Interim Step

Use Free Time to Develop Skills in an Entirely New Field

by C.B. Bowman, president of Career Strategies, an Affiliate of The Five O'Clock Club

Many professionals are opting to start second careers while continuing in their current positions. This increase in the number of people with "parallel careers" is due to many factors, including the turbulent economy, greater dissatisfaction with current jobs and longer, healthier life spans leading to later retirements.

The primary reason, though, is that as companies continue to cut costs and eliminate jobs, one-track career paths are no longer reliable. Many executives also are burning out or reaching career plateaus.

> As companies continue to cut costs and eliminate jobs, one-track career paths are no longer reliable.

Those in shaky or dissatisfying jobs often feel they can't start over in new professions because of the financial sacrifices they—and their families—may have to make. For them, starting a parallel career is an ideal way to pursue a new profession without losing income. Then, after becoming proficient in the new career, ideally they can switch jobs without sustaining financial hardship.

Michael Fishelberg, vice-president of Enterchange, an Atlanta-based human resources and management consulting firm, says he endorsed the parallel-career concept because "organizations can no longer be counted on to provide career pathing. It's essential that individuals assume the burdens of their own career development and consider dual career paths as a safeguard against functional obsolescence."

Not Moonlighting

Unlike moonlighting—holding a second job during evenings or weekends to earn additional income—parallel career pathing isn't merely a way to earn extra money. Instead, those who are serious about this strategy want to develop a new career without first giving up the benefits of the old one. By taking steps to control their employment future, they may also increase their motivation, confidence, and initiative in their nine-to-five careers.

> Develop a new career without first giving up the benefits of the old one.

When you choose a parallel career, the following three guidelines should apply:
- While your separate careers can build on each other, they should not conflict.
- Although less time can be devoted to the second or parallel career, you should be fully committed to the profession and consider it a definite future choice. If possible, try to get paid from the outset for your services or the products you provide.
- Both careers can be in different stages of development. For instance, you may have ten years of experience and work normal business hours for a traditional company in Career A, while in Career B, you might be self-employed and work weekends or be taking professional courses to gain additional skills.

Moving Ahead

The following ten steps can help you develop a parallel career path:

1. Choose a second profession.

For many people, future career success and happiness may stem from activities that are so vital to their lives that they overlook them. If you're having trouble choosing a second career,

The man without purpose is like a ship without a rudder—a waif, a nothing, a no man. Have a purpose in life, and, having it, throw such strength of mind and muscle into your work as God has given you.
Thomas Carlyle

try brainstorming with friends and family, or meet with a career counselor. Your decision should be based on your lifestyle, values, passions, strengths, skills, experience, and interests. Ideally, your second career should complement your personal history and turn your dreams into a reality, says Dr. Brian Schwartz, an organizational psychologist in Greenwich, Conn. This requires understanding your needs and any barriers to career success, then becoming the owner of your career destiny.

2. Assemble a group of advisors.

Seek advice and counsel from a support group composed of "can-do" people with expertise in a variety of disciplines. For instance, your advisors might include an attorney, accountant, banker, marketing expert, or other professional who can counsel you in critical areas.

A director of a pain clinic wanted to spearhead the clinic's expansion. She also harbored a secret desire to become a professional singer. To find the time and motivation to pursue both careers, she joined a "Wishcraft" support group composed of people trying to make their wishes come true. Her group—which included a financier, marketing specialist, retail merchandiser vice-president, and package designer—encouraged her to achieve her goals. Now, after working at the pain clinic, on some nights she sings jazz at private parties and clubs.

3. Learn as much as you can about your new field.

Become your own research department and scour print publications and databases for information on path B while still in path A.

4. Network actively in the new profession.

Establish relationships with others and become visible by attending conferences, joining professional associations, doing volunteer work, and serving on boards of directors. If you lack the time, consider using vacation days for some of these activities.

As a member of a university board of trustees, one banker helped develop a job-search program for the school's alumni. His volunteer work and advice from a career counselor helped him switch into the nonprofit field as a director of an educational agency. Meanwhile, he's developing a parallel career as a career counselor for recent college graduates.

5. Keep your parallel career private at work.

Your two career paths should be separate. This way, your present managers won't feel they're competing for your loyalty, and unsupportive colleagues can't undermine your activities.

6. Build on your transferable skills.

Know which of your transferable skills apply to your alternative field. If your current employer can provide training, seek out additional responsibilities now. Or, if you need more training, start taking courses. Your employer may pay for them if the courses relate to your current job, creating a win/win scenario.

After being downsized from her job, an equal-opportunity manager with an oil company realized that a two-career strategy was her best defense against future unemployment. By using transferable skills, she secured a day job as a human-resources specialist with a financial company in the Northeast. She then landed an evening and weekend position as a marketing representative with an international security company.

7. Create a plan.

Write out your plan for an alternative career. This should include information describing your potential product or services, your unique selling points, pricing, distribution, and promotional opportunities. The writing process will help you visualize the career-change process and desired results, and take a concrete step toward commitment.

Write out your plan for an alternative career.

---

8. Enlist your family's support.

Seek their assistance with your goals, and spend as much quality time with them as possible. Out of the mouths of babes comes wisdom, so if you have children, don't hesitate to involve them also.

9. Stay on stable financial footing.

Keep your current income-producing position while you gain experience in the parallel career. Fredi Balzano, a counselor with The Five O'Clock Club and a principal with Effective Management Resources, a human-resources consulting firm in New York, reports that one attorney with a major law firm disliked his job and dreamed of working in the entertainment field, possibly as a writer. The attorney began networking to make contacts in the entertainment industry, enrolled in comedy-writing classes and performed at several comedy clubs. He now has a script that's being considered for a half-hour situation comedy. In the meantime, he is continuing in his job at the law firm.

10. Don't postpone your goals.

When you have developed your plan, done sufficient research, talked with others and tested and revised your strategy, take steps to launch your second career.

Finding the Time

How can you develop two careers simultaneously, especially when you're so busy now? It's amazing how much free time you can create. For instance, do you sleep late on weekend mornings? Watch an hour or more of television at night? Use these chunks of time to pursue your goals.

The following are some other methods to carve out extra time to pursue your goals.

- Cut back on the amount of time you spend socializing at work (e.g., take shorter lunch hours or skip coffee breaks). This can help you to be more productive so you needn't work as late.
- Focus on what your main contribution is at your present job. Let co-workers resolve other problems, where possible.
- Concentrate on the big picture, not on the details.

It's never too late to start a parallel career. The sooner you begin, the less anxiety you'll feel about your current job or career options.

- Since worrying saps time, you can't afford the luxury of negative thinking. Develop a "can-do" attitude.
- Try to accept only those responsibilities that benefit both your careers. Learn to delegate and avoid letting people "down-load" additional work onto you.
- Take care of yourself physically, psychologically, and spiritually by eating well, exercising, and meditating.

It's never too late to start a parallel career. The sooner you begin, the less anxiety you'll feel about your current job or career options. In this era of job insecurity, parallel career pathing can help you to take control of your own future.

This article originally appeared in
The Five O'Clock News.

How Companies Are Helping Employees to Manage Their Own Careers

by: Michael Wheeler, Research Associate, Human Resources, Organizational Effectiveness, The Conference Board

Today's employees can no longer rely on job security. To stay employable, they need to market themselves continually—whether inside or outside their present companies. But is it solely the responsibility of individuals to ensure that they remain marketable? Or do America's corporations have a role in this?

At a time when corporations are striving to remain lean, keep costs low, and create flexibility, why should they invest in the development of their employees? Because there are benefits to the companies that do so. They help their employees remain employable by encouraging personal career development plans. This is borne out by corporate practices and numerous studies.

Despite more than a decade of lost jobs and an increasingly turbulent job market, few people seem to have solid career strategies. Similarly, while many companies have career-development initiatives, few are really providing solid programs or guidance for employees. Organizational psychologist and author Lynn Summers confirms: "Everybody talks about individual development planning, but few organizations are really using it.... It's odd that individual development plans should be so hard to find, especially in these times of corporate leanness and meanness. You would think people would be eager to have solid plans for enhancing their value to their organizations."[1] Internal "career development" may seem like an oxymoron in an era of job insecurity, downsized, restructured, and flatter organizations where employee loyalty has been lost. Yet a few visionary companies are choosing to invest in the development of their employees, with the expectation that their investment will ultimately impact the bottom-line of the organization.

Corporate Benefits of Career-Development Initiatives

More and more companies are recognizing their workforce as a competitive advantage in a global economy. Lester Thurow, dean of the Sloan School of Management at Massachusetts Institute Technology, says the skills of the workforce constitute "the only remaining source of competitive advantage." And according to a study by The Conference Board, more than 400 executives interviewed identified the caliber of the workforce and the availability of qualified people as some of the most dominant strategic issues for the human resources function and for top management.[2] At a national conference for the Society for Human Resources Management, employee development was identified as "a critical factor affecting an organization's success."[3] For example:

- Employees who are flexible and adaptable are more valuable.
- Organizations with demonstrated commitment to employee success are more attractive to top talent.
- Employees are more loyal to companies that provide opportunities for self-development.
- Downsizing may be mitigated with redeployment—reassigning employees rather than laying them off.
- Absenteeism and turnover are likely to decrease in an environment where employees are being challenged and fully utilized.

Sometimes employees will choose to move on, and sometimes an organization must eliminate jobs. But collaborative efforts by employers and employees can create a win-win situation that benefits both the organization and the individual. In the Harvard Business Review article "Toward a Career-Resilient Workforce," author Robert Waterman explains that "a company must help people explore opportunities, promote lifelong learning, and, if it comes to that, support no-fault exits."[4] And investment in employee career development can lift an organization's productivity. In a national workforce study by the Families and Work Institute, it was found that what helps employees seems to help employers be more productive.[5]

We were like a dinosaur: They'd whack us on the tail, and three weeks later we'd feel it in our brain . . .
Most of the industry figured they could . . . spot us a six-month head start with our own technology,
and they'd still catch up to us in the marketplace.
Bob Corrigan, IBM PC division chief, 1990-94

The Evolution of Employee Development

Secretary of Commerce Ron Brown says, "Competitive success now requires constant, sustained innovation. That means for governments and business and workers, we must constantly be re-interpreting, re-evaluating and re-inventing how we work."[6] With technological advances and emerging markets, new jobs will be created along nontraditional ways of working, with telecommuting, part-time, sabbaticals, and freelancing.

As organizations grow leaner and flatter, the traditional definition of success as upward mobility must be reexamined. According to a report by The Conference Board, only about a third of all careers in the United States are pursued as traditional, or linear, careers in large corporations. According to the authors of the report Encouraging Employee Self-Management in Financial and Career Planning, "most people have work experiences that follow less predictable paths that are likely to involve a variety of different work arrangements (including unpaid activities) over time...The new job realities have prompted corporate employers to make changes in their development, education and training programs."[7]

Career development is evolving. Authors Helen Axel and Helen Dennis explain that "Career planning and development programs are shifting away from their traditional focus on advancement. Employers...now emphasize 'career management' and 'career enrichment.'" Corporate development initiatives reflect these changes. Chevron focuses on "career enrichment," and Hewlett Packard employees participate in programs for career management. Motorola has a "Career Direction Center" and Levi Strauss incorporates training and development activities under the concept of "Life Planning."[8]

Career-development plans can help employees understand the realities of the job market—externally and internally—and help them identify ways to enhance their skills, and hence to be better prepared for changes when they come. Northern States Power of Minnesota has established a list of "Skills of Effective Northern States Power Employees" that it believes are necessary to help employees remain flexible, adaptable, and employable. Those skills are categorized in a variety of areas: Customer focus; results-driven mindset; planning; innovation and process improvement; communication; relationship and team-building; problem-solving and decision-making; business and industry knowledge; community responsibility.

Those employers and employees who are best prepared and most informed will be most successful.

Corporations should help individuals understand their personal and professional goals, and how they fit into corporate needs over time. As work changes, the economy fluctuates, globalism increases, government mandates are initiated, and technology advances, individuals must be informed and prepared to adapt to these changes. Those employers and employees who are best prepared and most informed will be most successful.

Chase Manhattan Bank:
A Model in Employee Development

"Your Success Is Our Success" is the motto of Chase Manhattan Bank's career-development initiative. Chase has recognized that organizational success depends on employees who can adapt to change. The "CareerVision" initiative is considered so important that it has been launched to over 20,000 employees in the United States, the United Kingdom, and Hong Kong.

What is CareerVision?

It is a variety of programs and services—information, tools, and resources—to assist

> *The ingrained mind-set that resists change causes self-inflicted wounds, and those are the most crippling wounds of all, because they are the hardest to cure. The bottom line is: Change is irresistible; run with it.*
> Hedrick Smith, *Rethinking America*

employees in achieving their career potential. Employees learn about themselves, their interests, values, and what motivates them. They learn how to upgrade skills and establish new career-development strategies. CareerVision helps employees by providing new career direction, revitalizing career choices, and dealing with change. Joan Gotti, Vice President, Employee Development at Chase, explains: "We have a series of integrated services for career-development education. It is not a mobility system.

We help employees identify what is an effective professional at Chase, what is happening in the marketplace, and how to prepare for and adapt to changes that impact the business." And while it is primarily up to the individual, Chase believes that career development is a shared responsibility, and defines clearly the roles of the individual employee, management, and the bank.

How Does CareerVision work?

Recognizing that people need flexibility in the way they learn, work, and access information, Chase offers a number of Career Vision resource, workshops, PC programs, business information, career forums, and tools for enhancing job skills. Career development at Chase is an ongoing process for employees." One of the challenges presented to Chase was how to get business information out to employees," says Gotti. In order to disseminate critical information, three key components were developed:

• Career Forums where unit manager discuss jobs, skills, availability, and field questions.
• CareerVision Business Network where employees from all levels and functions volunteer to provide information, interviews, or "shadowing sessions" (where employees have the opportunity to spend time on the job to gain first-hand insights); 700 employees volunteered to be a part of the network.
• Database that provides general information on the mission, strategies, products, and geography of Chase, and information on jobs and job

locations throughout the bank. The database provides employees with the opportunity to understand where the jobs are, what skills are needed, and what realistic employment options are.

Gotti explains that "CareerVision did not require building a major infrastructure. "Human resources personnel were asked to volunteer for career advising certification. Advisors are trained human resources professionals who are available upon request, and help provide linkages to other human resources services, including the career-development initiatives. To supplement human resources staff, several of the bank business managers take on CareerVision responsibilities as part of their jobs. The structure has been effective for Chase.

Is the Program a Success?

In less than a year, over 6,000 employees— one in three—have taken advantage of the initiatives. Chase is confident that the organizations that succeed will be those whose employees have the information and ability to adapt to the ever increasing pace of change. CareerVision is one of the ways in which Chase expects to remain an employer of choice, and a successful organization.

1. Summers, Lynn, "A Logical Approach to Development Planning," Training & Development, November 1994. pp. 22-30.
2. Johnson, Arlene, A., and Linden, Fabian, Availability of a Quality Work Force, The Conference Board, Report # 1010, 1992.
3. Wagel, William H., and Levine, Hermine Zagat, HR '90: Challenges and Opportunities," Personnel, June 1990, p.29.
4. Waterman, Robert H., et al., "Toward a Career-Resilient Workforce," Harvard Business Review, July-August 1994, pp. 87-95.
5. Galinsky, Ellen et al., The Changing Workforce, Families and Work Institute, New York, New York, 1993.
6. U.S. Department of Labor, "Forecasting the Future of the American Workplace," American Workplace, Vol. 1, Issue 1, September 1993, p.4.
7. Dennis, Helen, and Axel, Helen, Encouraging Employee Self-Management in Financial and Career Planning, Report Number 976, The Conference Board, 1991.
8. Dennis and Axel, p. 27.

This article originally appeared in *The Five O'Clock News.*

A Reminder of
Some Basic Career Principles

Here are a few more basic career principles—just to keep you on your toes:

1) Don't let others define you. Set your own standards. Don't measure yourself against others.

2) Know yourself and be yourself.

3) Develop a philosophy of your life as you want it. Be selective about how you spend your time. Make your own choices. Decide what you want to commit to. We each have the same amount of time.

4) Make a plan. If you don't know where you're going, chances are you won't get very far. Make a résumé of yourself five years from now, do your Forty-Year Plan, and develop a Career Plan. Identify what you will need to get there. But keep your options open, and don't stay too long in a job. Keep on developing yourself with an eye on your own future.

5) Be willing to take a risk. Make sure your next position relies on your strengths and your basic skills, and also contains a little "risk"—some new growth area. The jobs or assignments you take should have all three, and they should fit in with your Forty-Year Plan. You need the new growth areas so you will progress and advance.

6) Look for jobs that can provide quantifiable measures of your accomplishments, and look for companies that fit your style.

7) Learn how to manage or change your environment, rather than being a victim of your environment.

8) Get help. Join associations. Meet others in the company. Stay in touch. Don't go through your career alone.

9) Pick a few role models—not just one. Select the characteristics you like from each one. Observe their demeanor, dress, vocabulary, and speech patterns.

10) Don't let your guard down just because you have a new job or assignment. Always have a back-up plan in mind—just in case. Keep yourself marketable, and treat your employer as if you were a consultant. This position is not permanent.

Keep your boss's boss off your boss's back.
First Law of Corporate Survival

Can't do a lot of career planning? That's okay.
Just aim for the second job out.

When you are trying to decide on your next move, think of how that step will position you for the one after that. Even if you can't do a Forty-Year Plan—or a detailed Career Plan—you will still be better off than most people if you think at least two steps ahead.

For example, if one option is to take a position in management consulting as a sales representative, and if you think you may work for another fifteen years, what would be your next step if you lost that job—say, four years from now? If you think you would be marketable in that same kind of position, then you have developed at least a four-year career plan. If you think this job would *not* position you well for the next job, then it may not be a good move.

This kind of thinking is the start of solid career planning.

How to Keep Your Life Course in Mind

I learned three things in Zurich during the war. I wrote them down. Firstly, you're either a revolutionary or you're not, and if you're not you might as well be an artist as anything else. Secondly, if you can't be an artist, you might as well be a revolutionary.
I forget the third.
Tom Stoppard, *Travesties*

S ometimes we forget our important thoughts, or we remember them and they sound strange, or we become afraid of them. Afraid of success. Afraid of failure. Like writing this book. Some days I became nauseated at the thought of working on it. On other days, I simply "forgot" I was writing it, or I became afraid that it all sounded stupid, harsh, boring, trite. Often, I couldn't remember why I was doing it; then I was afraid I would never finish.

Writing a book is a lot like job hunting. Some days you forget why you're doing it—you just know that you must. Or you become sick at the thought of it. You can sometimes become afraid that you sound stupid, or are doing the wrong things, or will embarrass yourself, or you'll never finish.

But somehow—one day at a time—it gets done. A job hunter makes a phone call, writes a proposal, researches a company. Every day you make a new decision to do your best no matter how you feel about it. You sit down and do what you must do. That is discipline: to continue to job-hunt—or to continue to write—regardless of how you feel. And then you get into it and it flows.

You have to remember where you were trying to head. Job hunting—or writing a book—was supposed to take you somewhere.

When one lives without a clear value structure, it is both difficult to direct life in the long run and difficult to experience a sense of meaningfulness that comes from following a prescribed course.
It is possible to sail a boat, for example, without charts or a compass. However, the absence of a chart prevents the possibility of a journey. One is limited to "day" sailing, so that new destinations and new challenges are out of reach. Eventually the same seascape and circumstances will produce a tedium not unlike the absence of meaning associated with a present-centered existence.
Herbert Rappaport, Ph.D.
Marking Time

Everyone is running to and fro,
pressed by the stomach ache of business.
Frédéric-Auguste Bartholdi,
French sculptor of Statue of Liberty
Letter to his mother, June 12, 1871

It is easy to get caught up in your day-to-day activities. Your life can get off course; you become distracted. You may even discover you have veered from your true path for a number of years. That's okay. Bring yourself back and walk toward your goal. Stay with your own direction—the one that is in your heart. Deep down, you know when things are right and when things are not. Keep walking toward your goal.

Don't be bound by your past. It is important to remember that you are not whatever your jobs have been. We don't exist on a sheet of paper—a résumé. Don't identify too strongly with it. Stay fluid behind those words on the page. They are not you, but simply a sales tool.

The power is in what you are doing now and in your pull toward the future. The power is in the act of living each day to the fullest. It is the direction in which we are each heading that is important. Look to the future. We constantly gain new insights, new visions.

Taking the long view can give you satisfaction. A stonemason working on the Cathedral of St. John the Divine was asked how he could keep on cutting those stones year after year. He said he was not cutting stones—he was building a cathedral.

Of journeying, the benefits are many; the
freshness it brings to the heart, the seeing and hearing of
marvelous things . . . the meeting of unknown friends . . .
Sadi

Interviewing can soften you. It can broaden your horizons and make you realize there is a big world out there with lots of interesting things to do. In talking to people, you can see that it is not all so pat—so clearly spelled out—what a person should "be." There are endless variations, and when you realize how much variety there is, you also realize that, in the end, it is largely up to you to choose what you will be. We each have a place. Find your place. Live your part.

I have a dream that my four little children will one day
live in a nation where they will not be judged by the
color of their skin but by the content of their character.
I have a dream.
Martin Luther King, Jr.
Speech to 200,000 civil rights demonstrators,
Washington, D.C., August 28, 1963

Martin Luther King, Jr., was driven by his dream. *Your* main drives and inclinations also have power. You will come back to them again and again in your life because you are driven to do these things. They will come out. Why not harness that energy and direct it consciously rather than letting it rule you? In the right situations, your drives are a benefit and can add to your success. But in the wrong situations, they will still appear over and over, and they can harm you.

Better to find out clearly what they are, and go where they are valued. Then you will have a happy marriage between you and your environment. Then you will no longer be swimming against the tide, but will let the tide take you to new heights and a new sense of satisfaction.

They say, "Go with the flow." Go with your own flow. Go in the direction you were meant to take. Find out what it is that motivates you, and go with it.

Everyone has a talent. What is rare is the courage to
follow the talent to the dark place where it leads.
Erica Jong

. . . tendencies and aspirations are more important . . .
it is more important what people want to be than
what people actually are.
John Lukacs
A History of the Cold War

When you find out what you are inside, it will

give you great energy and a happy obsession to realize it. When this happens, people say that their jobs are fun, and not work at all. There is nothing else they would rather be doing.

There is a freedom in fulfilling your function in the world—to know you are in the right place, doing what is right for you. You are fulfilled when you know what you are, know what you are supposed to be doing on this earth, and are doing it. When what you should be doing hits you, and you make it a conscious part of yourself, you won't get easily sidetracked. You will know what's right for you, and you will care.

Accept yourself as you are and be grateful. Then go for it. Be who God made you and do it all the way. Don't hold yourself back, but turn to face the world. Take your dreams and goals seriously, and your life will be simpler and have direction.

If you don't know what your dreams and goals are, then think about yourself. Do the Seven Stories exercise and observe the real you—the you that does certain things no matter what. Ask a friend to help you, and find the threads running through your life.

> *Choose a job you love, and you will never have to work a day in your life.*
> Confucius

> *Many of us live as though the momentum in our lives is generated by others. There is often a sense of anguish when the realization emerges that we have to generate our own momentum by the images we have of ourselves and the future.*
> Herbert Rappaport, Ph.D., *Marking Time*

You have plenty of time. How many more years do you have left? Let's say you'll be very active until the age of seventy, eighty, or more. How many years is that? Perhaps I have thirty more active years—maybe forty. A lot can happen in thirty or forty years. Is it too late for me? Is it too late for you? Probably not.

Don't rush toward your dreams, but savor every step and enjoy the present. Reaching your goal is not the point. In fact, it does not matter

whether you ever reach your goal. Just live each day.

Live your life, enjoy and make the most of each day. Your goal is simply a guide—not a do-or-die phenomenon. If you can have a goal and enjoy the process of getting there, you have truly lived. It's the process that's important.

> *Why, sometimes I believed as many as six impossible things before breakfast.*
> Lewis Carroll, *Alice in Wonderland*

It's your life. Play a little. Take chances. You will succeed if you aren't too rigid about succeeding. Test things out. See what works. Don't try to hold on too tightly.

Our dreams recur. Perhaps yours are so deep and so quashed that you don't know what they are. Let them come out, then test them later to see how true they are for you. Dreams are serious things, and you might as well live them. Because, when you are old, you will find great satisfaction in having lived your dreams—in having lived your life. If you don't try to live your dreams, you may later be filled with regret.

> *One of the common themes among depressed adults who I see in my practice is the deep sense of regret for not "stretching oneself" at different stages of life.*
> Herbert Rappaport, Ph.D., *Marking Time*

> *There is only one success—to be able to spend your life in your own way.*
> Christopher Morley

Advance steadily in the direction of your goal, and don't worry about how long it will take you to get there. You will get there as soon as you can anyway. I've seen people advance steadily for many, many years. They somehow wound up doing amazing things that would have seemed impossible and frightening if they had concentrated on them earlier. By taking life one step at a time, and not getting anxious about the future, they moved ahead, taking small steps, but lots of them. The steps that followed seemed smaller still, and not frightening, and they became the persons they were meant to be. They followed their own, not completely defined dreams. As they lived each step, the next step became more clear.

Goals evolve as we test and see what feels right for us. We try a step, and sometimes step back rather than take our lives in a direction that we thought would be right but was not. And then, after a number of years, we look back, amazed at our own progress and surprised that this could happen to us—sure of our direction, still taking the steps one at a time, and testing our direction as we go.

And so our lives unfold. The excitement is in the present—the hope is in the future, and we know we are truly part of the universe as much as each star and each tree. We belong here—doing our part, full of life and living what was once a dream, and unafraid of failure.

Ah, but a man's reach should exceed his grasp,
Or what's a heaven for?
Robert Browning
"Andrea del Sarto"

There are some elemental truths about yourself that define the real you. You may have buried them over time, but now stay tuned in and see if you can uncover them. Sometimes these deep dreams of yours may shock your family and friends, and may even shock you. Better that you should know what they are.

I once had a client who had very low self-esteem, and had been doing "safe" work at a major corporation. He would sit hunched, with his head turned up toward where I was sitting, and he would meekly talk about the interviews he was going on. He didn't have a clue about what he should do with his life. There was so much confusion between what he thought he should do and what he had done in the past, it was very difficult for him to find some direction to head toward.

Then one day, as we were discussing all the usual things, this timid, hunched-over person said in a bland tone, "You can't imagine how thrilled I'd be if I could be the leader, running the entire thing

and being completely in control."

It seemed impossible that these strong words were coming out of this person's mouth. Looking at him made it seem even more unlikely, yet there was some deep, elemental truth about what he wanted for himself. I wrote down what he said because it was one of those truths that can be so easily lost—so easily dismissed with a "let's be realistic, honey."

I believe that if this person keeps his dream in mind, he will someday be an incredibly dynamic person, "in charge of the whole thing"—whatever that may be. He will learn to hold himself better, to sound more dynamic, and to look the part. And when this dynamic winner emerges, it will be the real him. I believe that the timid, play-it-safe person is not the real him, but some twisted person that emerged when the real him was submerged.

And, if this person remembers his dream, he will surely advance toward it. Ten years from now, he will look back and find it hard to believe that he is the same person. The living comes not in finally reaching his dream—the living comes in becoming the kind of person he truly is deep inside. The living comes in his day-to-day life as he simply lives it.

Those words were the most important he ever said during the many hours I spent with him. It will take him years to be the real him—that's been buried for so long. But what a happy way to spend ten years. I can't think of a better way to live them—concentrating each day on the task before him, but remembering the person he was meant to be. Finding his own place in the universe and being proud of it.

I spent a large part of my life being a loser, which I think adds an interesting dimension to my personality.
Michael Caine, *Acting in Film*

As you're the only one you can really change, the only one who can really use all your good advice is yourself.
John-Rogers and Peter McWilliams

Congratulations!

Our deepest fear is not that we are inadequate. Our deepest fear is that we are powerful beyond measure. It is our light, not our darkness, that most frightens us. We ask ourselves, "Who am I to be brilliant, gorgeous, talented and fabulous?"

❦ Actually, who are you not to be? You are a child of God. Your playing small doesn't serve the world. There's nothing enlightened about shrinking so that other people won't feel insecure around you.

❦ We were born to make manifest the glory of God that is within us. It's not just in some of us; it's in everyone. And as we let our own light shine, we unconsciously give other people permission to do the same. As we are liberated from our own fear, our presence automatically liberates others. ❦

Nelson Mandela
1994 Inaugural Speech

Dear Reader:

Congratulations on completing this program. You have just taken an important step toward achieving greater professional satisfaction and success. Because of your efforts, you have increased your understanding of yourself and your goals. This will lead to more effective career decisions.

I know this has been a very intensive process. You are to be congratulated for taking some time out of your busy schedule simply to think about yourself—what's important to you, what you want to achieve, and how you might do that.

Next Steps

What happens next depends on the goals you have set for yourself. You may choose to make improvements in your present position—to make it better suit your long-term goals.

You may want to work with an individual career counselor—to review your results and get a professional's point-of-view.

You may also wish to read the other books in the career-development series provided by The Five O'Clock Club.

Finally, you may want to join The Five O'Clock Club. Join other ambitious, intelligent people like yourself. Get our monthly magazine. Attend one of our Affiliates in your geographic area. You will receive guidance and have fun while you are learning how to manage your career.

I hope you will always be a member of The Five O'Clock Club—your Club for improving your career. We are dedicated to giving you the specific information you need to survive and thrive in this changing economy.

Here's to continued success in your career. We wish you growth—in personal satisfaction, inner peace, and financial comfort. We'd like to continue to travel along with you. I hope you feel the same.

Love and cheers!
Kate

The
Five
O'Clock
Club

PART FIVE

CAREER AND JOB-SEARCH BIBLIOGRAPHY

COMPILED AND ANNOTATED BY WENDY ALFUS ROTHMAN

The Five O'Clock Club®

Career and Job-Search Bibliography

compiled and annotated by Wendy Alfus Rothman

Introduction

During your job search there will be moments when "I don't know" may seem to be your constant refrain. You will say to yourself, "I don't know what industry to target" or "I don't know how many companies are in my target" or "I don't know what to ask my networking contacts" or "I don't know how to write a compelling letter" or "I don't know how to prepare for this interview." When you hear those words in your head, remember that the answers lie in research. Look for research resources right here in this annotated bibliography.

There are a great many books and databases listed on these next pages. Incredibly, this is only a sampling of what is available! I have organized the bibliography for easy accessibility.

Section One: Materials in Print (Some of the materials are also available on disk and I have indicated when that is the case.)

1: a guide to guides, directories and business information sources;

2: lists sources for investigating industry trends and outlooks;

3: describes guides and directories across an array of industries;

4: describes even more focused directories, geared for specific industries. They are divided into the following sections:

A. Advertising	L. Non-Profit/Fund-Raising
B. Environment	M. Public Relations
C. Finance	N. Publishing
D. Health Care	O. Sales and Marketing
E. High Technology	P. Services
F. Human Resources	Q. Small/Private Business
G. Trade	R. Events/Trade Shows
H. Information Industry	S. Transportation
I. International Markets	T. Travel and Hospitality
J. Law and Government	U. Real Estate
K. Media	V. Education

5: gives information on people and their backgrounds.

Section Two: CD-ROM Databases, using the same subcategories as **Section One.**

Section Three: On-line Databases, in the same format.

There are some universal laws to remember when conducting research:

1. **Call the library in advance of your visit.** Ask them what their hours are, the quietest times for using computer databases, and whether there is anything else that you need to know (e.g., charges for printing, time constraints for terminals). If necessary, ask to make an appointment to review how to use electronic information. You will be far better off than if you walk in at the busiest time and hope to get someone to help you.

2. **Prepare a list of questions** you want to have answered for each session. If you don't go with an agenda, it will be very easy to get distracted.

3. **When locating resources, always go to the source.** Some of these resources may not be in your local library. Call the library first and ask whether the volume or database you want is there. If it is not, perhaps the library has an alternative that would be just as valuable. If they do not, this is what I do: I call the publisher, I tell them what I want and where I am, and ask them what convenient library or facility they could refer me to. (The most prolific of these publishers is Gale Research in Detroit, Michigan. Their catalog of available resources is mind-boggling.)

4. **Use the locating of directories for a networking device.** Many people get frustrated when they can't find a particular reference book. In fact, the act of locating the information can itself be used as a powerful networking tool. For example, if you are looking for a directory of major financial institutions, you can network with someone in a financial institution, and ask if they have access to that directory. If they do, you can use it. If they don't, you can still talk about why you need it, which can lead into a discussion about your job search. Either way, you have nothing to lose.

5. **Don't just use books and databases in your own industry.** If you want to know who the experts are in your field, think about using the *Experts Contact Directory.* If you want to get a sense of a particular company, try looking it up in the *PR News Casebook.* Look up a company in *The Corporate Giving Directory* and see to which causes they make charitable contributions. Get creative!

6. **Recontact people.** As you are researching, you will come across information that will be of interest to your networking contacts. Copy the articles and send them to appreciative people. See how much that will add to the "give" part of the give and take relationships you develop.

SECTION ONE: MATERIALS IN PRINTS

1. Guide to Guides, Directories, and Business Information Sources

➜ I love this book. It is simple to use and thorough in its coverage. No matter what you need to know, this volume will help you. It also offers the most comprehensive listings and definitions of CD-ROM and on-line databases that I have seen!

➜ This is a great help when conducting out-of-town job searches.

➜ The DOT is a wonderful way to begin investigating industries, especially if you are changing careers and are not sure what jobs exist in the field you are exploring. It can really broaden your awareness of your options!

➜ NEW!!!
One stop shopping for infomrtaion on up-to-date subjects, with tables, graphs & charts and where-to-go for more info. Check it out.

• **The Business Information Desk Reference**, Macmillan Publishing Company, 1991. Melvin Freed & Virgil Diodato. BIDR is a guide to information available in almost 1,000 business information sources. The authors have devised a unique question and answer format that enables readers to identify needed information quickly, and directs them to the appropriate source.

• **Business Organizations, Agencies, and Publications Directory**. Gale Research, 7th ed., Catherine M. Ehr and Kenneth Estell, eds. This new edition tells you exactly whom to write, phone, visit, or access for facts and figures on every matter of business concern. The 26,000 entries, describing 39 types of business information sources, are arranged in five broad categories: U.S. and International Organizations, Government Agencies and Programs, Facilities and Services, Research and Education Facilities, and Publications and Information Services; directory also available on-line.

• **City and State Directories in Print 1990-91**. Gale Research, 1st edition, Julie E. Towell and Charles B. Montney, editors. This directory provides access to more than 4,500 state and city directories published in the United States. It complements the national and international coverage of Directories in Print by listing hundreds of thousands of manufacturers, chambers of commerce, exporters, minority businesses, attorneys, banks, hospitals, and other businesses, organizations, facilities, and individuals active on a local level. Entries include entry number, complete title, full address, phone number, geographic area covered, entry information, and price. Title, Keyword, and Subject Indexes.

• **Directory of Industry Data Sources**. Ballinger Publishing Company, Harper & Row Publishers, Inc. Lists 3,000 publishers of industry data sources including bibliographic and source databases, indexing and abstracting services, and market research firms; describes monographs, surveys, periodical special issues, market studies, etc., covering 65 industries. Lists company names, address and phone. Arranged alphabetically and by type of publication service. Three volumes cover the United States and Canada. Two volumes cover Western Europe.

• **Directory of Occupational Titles**. Gale Research, 4th edition. Descriptions of over 12,000 occupations. Also included: GOE (Guide for Occupational Exploration); RML (Reasoning, Math, and Language); and SVP (Specific Vocational Preparation). Alphabetical Index of Occupations.

• **Directories in Print 1995**. Gale Research, 10th edition, Charles B. Montney, editor. Contains over 13,000 detailed and up-to-date entries, including international, all conveniently arranged in 26 subject chapters. An Alternative Formats Index lists directories published in non-traditional formats, such as on-line databases, CD-ROM, diskettes, microfiche, and mailing labels and lists. It is easy to scan columns and find alternative format titles. Directories in Print is also available on-line through DIALOG.

• **Encyclopedia of Business**, Gale Research. Provides in-depth coverage on an expansive selection of business issues. Includes over 700 signed articles written by subject matter specialists, covering major business disciplines, concepts and timely topics. Subjects include: Business ethics, accounting, finance, public relations, valuation, home office, World Bank, ergonomics, robotics, family leave, and more. Most entries include a section listing sources of additional information.

• **Encyclopedia of Business Information Sources**. Gale Research, 9th ed., James Woy, ed. Wide range of business information sources listed under 1,000 alphabetically arranged business subjects. For each subject, you can quickly identify key live, print, and electronic sources of information. Provides title of the publication; database or organization; publisher of the information source; address, phone, and price/availability.

Covers basic business subjects as well as subjects of current interest, new technologies, and new industries. These include business policy trends like Aids Policy, technological developments like Facsimile Systems, current issues like Business Innovation, and health industry material like Employee Wellness Programs.

Self-respect is the fruit of discipline; the sense of dignity grows
with the ability to say no to oneself.
Abraham J. Heschel, quoted in Ruth M. Goodhill ed., *The Wisdom of Heschel*

2. General: Industry Trends, Forecasts, and Outlooks

➔ This book has been updated to provide much more accurate info that considers geographic variables as well as length of time spent in a industry.

• **American Salaries and Wages Survey.** Gale Research, 2nd ed., Arsen J. Darnay, editor. Answers salary questions for more than 4,500 occupational classifications at different experience levels, and in specific areas of the country. Salary data come from more than 300 publications issued by federal, state, and local government offices, professional organizations and other business groups, and periodicals and newspapers.

Entries are arranged alphabetically by profession and then location, and contain: occupation, specialization, and industry; location; frequency of salary ranges; and source. Occupational and Geographical Tables of Contents. Five appendices: Sources, Wage Conversions, Metropolitan Cost of Living Data, Abbreviations, and major Occupations 1986-2000.

➔ A powerful, resource. Use this!

• **Encyclopedia of Associations.** Gale Research. Guide to 22,000 national nonprofit organizations of all types, purposes and interests. Gives contact names, headquarters addresses, phone numbers, chief officials, number of members and chapters, description of membership, aims and activities. Includes lists of special committees and departments, publications, and a 4 - year convention schedule. Arranged by subject, and cross-referenced by name of chief executive, and geographic location, as well as by organization name.

➔ Though it is often overlooked, I personally love this book. It tells me exactly where to go to get concise and precise market research on any topic that I am interested in.

• **Findex: The Directory of Market Research Reports, Studies, and Surveys.** Cambridge Information Group Directories, Inc., 10th edition, edited by JoAnne DuChez and Sharon J. Marcus. An annotated bibliography of published business and market research reports, U.S. and foreign. These research reports come from many sources, and concern both domestic and foreign economies. The focus is on the operations of individual companies and on industries and their specific products. Also contains research reports on corporate management. The profile of each market report includes the title, publication date, publisher, summary, number of pages, price, and a report identification number. This is a major source for identifying commercially available market research reports and for learning where to obtain copies.

• **Manufacturing USA.** Gale Research, 3rd edition, Arsen J. Darnay, editor. Gives profiles and top company rankings for about 460 manufacturing industries, organized by 1987 four-digit SIC codes. Manufacturing USA synthesizes relevant data from the Census of Manufacturers, the Annual Survey of Manufacturers, the County of Business Patterns, the U.S. Industrial Outlook, and the Industrial-Occupational Matrix produced by the U.S. Department of Labor.

Profiles provide industry statistics: indices of change, selected ratios; product share; statistical analyses by states and regions; occupations employed by various industries; fuel and other resource consumption data; and more. Product, Company Name, Occupations Employed, and 1987 four-digit SIC indexes.

Another great way to get your hands on research reports for any field, including international areas; available on-line as well.➔

• **Market Share Reporter 1993.** Gale Research, 3rd edition, Arsen J. Darnay, editor. MSR compiles producer and product share-of-market reports from a wide range of published sources including thousands of consumer, trade, and industrial publications. It also contains reports from foreign publications to offer coverage of world trade, international products, and global competitiveness.

If you want to learn industry jargon, names of key players, hot topics, and important companies, this is your resource. Many newsletters will send you free sample copies. Ask!➔

Arranged by 4-digit SIC code, each of MSR's 2,000 entries includes: descriptive title of report; data and market description; remarks on the history, scope, and other characteristics of the study; list of producers/products along with their assigned market share; and source citation. Brand Name, Source, Place Names, Companies, Products, Services, and Issues Indexes. MSR is also available on-line through NEXIS.

• **Newsletters in Print.** Gale Research, 6th edition, John Krol, editor. Newsletters in Print details more than 10,000 authoritative sources of information on a wide range of high-interest topics.
Entries are arranged under seven broad categories comprising 33 specific subjects. Topics include business and industry; family and everyday living; information and communications; community and world affairs; science and technology; and more. Newsletters in Print is also available on-line.

• **Service Industries USA.** Gale Research, 1st edition, Arsen J. Darnay, editor. A comprehensive source of vital statistics on more than 150 U.S. service industries, along with information on more than 4,000 leading public and private corporations and nonprofit institutions active in those industries. Service Industries USA (SIUSA) organizes widely scattered and difficult-to-use federal economic information into a usable and easy-to-read graphic format.

The first part of SIUSA lists industries by SIC code and provides industry data for the U.S. and the states, using various federal statistics for service industries. The format and content of information closely follows that of MUSA (with no overlapping entries), and contains: brief industry description; general statistics; indices of change; selected ratios; statistical analyses by state and region; occupations employed; leading companies; employment; and institutional involvement within an industry.

The second part contains Metro Area Statistics, arranged alphabetically by metro area and by SIC code, for more than 600 metropolitan areas of the United States. Tables include such valuable data as: numbers of establishments, total employment, revenues, and ownership patterns for each service industry in that metro area. SIC, Services, Metro Area Index, Company/Nonprofit Organization and Occupation Indexes.

• **Standard & Poor's Industry Surveys.** Standard & Poor's Corporation. Quarterly. Two volumes of up-to-date data for all major domestic industries. Prospects for a particular industry are followed by a historical presentation of trends and problems for that industry. Tables and charts accompany the text. Sales, earnings, and market data for the leading companies in an industry are provided. This title is updated on a quarterly basis.

• **Statistical Forecasts of the United States.** Gale Research, edited by James E. Person, Jr. Population, employment, labor, crime, education, health care—all the key areas of American life are covered in SFUS.

SFUS goes beyond standard demographic data to provide in-depth coverage of "hot topics" such as the environment and health-care costs. Statistics are compiled from a diverse range of periodicals and research journals, industry reports, books, government documents, association reports, and other print sources. Data are presented in hundreds of charts, graphs, tables, and other statistical illustrations portraying both long- and short-term forecasts of future developments in the U.S.

SFUS is generously indexed to aid user access to information. In addition to the Subject Index, an Index of Forecast by Year allows users to find, for example, all predictions for the year 2005.

• **U.S. Industrial Outlook.** U.S. Department of Commerce. Annual. Describes prospects for over 350 manufacturing and service industries. An annual source of industry information, this title analyzes recent trends and forecasts for hundreds of industries. Data are presented in both narrative and tabular form. A list of additional references is included at the end of each chapter.

• **U.S. Industry Profiles,** Gale Research, 1st edition. Contains over 100 articles that analyze the most lucrative industries, including agriculture, construction, manufacturing, transportation, entertainment, wholesale and retail trade and others. Articles provide info on the size and impact of the industry, current trend and future forecasts, leading companies, size and nature of the work force, international influence, technological and legal developments, and major industry associations and publications..

3. General: Company Information Guides and Directories

• **Business Rankings Annual 1993.** Gale Research, A guide to published lists and rankings excerpted from major business publications. Has an easy-to-use subject arrangement, a listing of the top ten names in each ranking, a source list, and one master index to every name in every list. In addition to giving the top ten names in each list, each entry gives the ranking criteria; the number listed in the original ranking; and the name, date, and page of the source. The 1993 edition lists some 4,500 "top ten" businesses.

• **Dun's Business Rankings.** Dun's Marketing Services. A directory of U.S. public and private businesses that ranks companies by sales volume and/or number of employees. Rankings are at the national and state levels and by industry. There is a composite ranking for public and private firms and then separate rankings for each of these categories. Includes the names of chief executive officers, sales executives, finance executives, and purchasing officers.

• **Dun & Bradstreet's Million Dollar Directory.** Dun's Marketing Services. Annual. Information on some 160,000 private and public U.S. businesses that have indicated net worth of more than $500,000. Each company listing includes the name, address, and telephone number of the company, the titles and names of

➜ Great books, with the added benefit of being available in most libraries.

➜ Terrific source of information on industry growth projections. Particularly great for those of you with a focus on numbers, graphs, and tables.

➜ Big, fat book with short and sweet descriptions. Not too in-depth, but very useful for quick forecasts.

NEW!!!➜ This is a simply spectacular book that is a great supplement to the book of Associations and the U.S. Industry Profiles.

➜ D&B's books are all-time standbys. Use for determining the size of your target, & collecting vital statistics on the companies in your target.

key executives, a brief product or service description, approximate annual sales, and number of employees. All listings are cross-referenced geographically as well as by Standard Industrial Classification (SIC) code.

• **International Directory of Company Histories**. Gale Research. Accurate and detailed information on the development of the world's 1,200 largest and most influential companies. This multi-volume work is the first major reference to bring together histories of companies that are a leading influence in a particular industry or geographic location.

➜ What a terrific resource. Here is a description of the history and events that have shaped major companies in a variety of fields. You want to impress people with your knowledge? You need to come up with good questions for networking and/or interviewing? Look no more—here is the resource to use.

Each two- to four-page entry is meticulously detailed, with facts gathered from popular magazines, academic periodicals, books, annual reports, and the archives of the companies themselves. Entries provide information on founders, expansions and losses, labor/management actions, and other significant milestones—all prepared with statistics, dates, and names of key players.

Organized alphabetically by industry; includes Cumulative Index to companies and personal names.
Volume 1: Advertising, Aerospace, Airlines, Automotive, Beverages, Chemicals, Conglomerates, Construction, and Drugs.
Volume 2: Electrical & Electronics, Entertainment & Leisure, Financial Services, Food Products, Food Service and Retailers.
Volume 3: Health and Personal Care Products, Health Care Services, Hotels, Information Technology, Insurance, Manufacturing and Materials.
Volume 4: Mining and Metals, Paper and Forestry, Petroleum, Publishing and Printing and Real Estate.
Volume 5: Retail and Wholesale, Rubber and Tire, Telecommunications, Textiles and Apparel, Tobacco, Transport Services, Utilities, and Waste Services.
Volume 6: Service Industries.
Volume 7 and 8 will be published later on this year, thus continuing this interesting and informative series.

➜ All of Moody's books are classics, especially for financial info.

• **Moody's Industry Review.** Dun & Bradstreet. Annual weekly updates of 11 industries per issue. Ranks 4,000 companies in 145 industry categories according to revenues, price-earning ratio, net income, profit margin, return on capital. Also includes brief corporate histories, material from annual reports and 7-year income and balance sheet statistics. Classified by industry. Arranged by company name.

• **Moody's Manuals**; Moody's Investors Service. This set of eight manuals, plus index and updates, reports current financial and other information on publicly held companies, banks, utilities, and governments (federal, state, and local). The component manuals, arranged by type of organization, are: Bank and Finance Manual; Industrial Manual; International Manual; Municipal and Government Manual; OTC Industrial Manual; OTC Unlisted Manual; Public Utilities Manual; Transportation Manual.

Includes financial-statement data and narrative reviews. The information was obtained from corporations, Securities and Exchange Commission reports, reports to stockholders, and other sources. The scope includes thousands of companies and government bond-issuing agencies. There are four levels of coverage in the profiles, depending on the level that was purchased. Descriptions are arranged by coverage level and, in some of these titles, by geographic location or type of company. A blue section in the center provides special features that are usually summary statistics or special lists, depending on the manual's subject.

NEW!!

• **National Directory of Minority Owned Business Firms,** Business Research Services, 8th edition. 47,000 minority business enterprises are listed including all vital company statistics.

NEW!!

• **National Directory of Women-Owned Business Firms, Business** Research Services, 8th edition. 28,000 entries with 17 points of data including company name and contact information

➜ NEW!! Provides a terrific historical perspective on each company- established & newcomers as well.

• **Notable Corporate Chronologies,** Gale Research, 1st edition. A 2 volume set presents concise chronologies for over 1,150 of the most significant corporations currently operating in the U.S. and abroad. Coverage on both established companies, as well newcomers.
• State Rankings Reporter, Gale Research, 1st edition. 3,000 ranked lists of states under 35 subject headings derived from newspaper, magazine, & gov't reports.

• **Thomas Register.** Data on more than 140,000 specific product manufacturers, both large and small. Also lists names of officers, capital assets, and parent or subsidiary company.

The opposite of love is not hate, it's indifference. The opposite of art is not ugliness,
it's indifference. The opposite of faith is not heresy, it's indifference.
And the opposite of life is not death, it's indifference.
Elie Wiesel

This is an absolute favorite of mine, since it not only gives the standard info, it ranks companies in an industry so you can see who someone's specific competitors are. ➜

• **Walkers The Corporate Directory of U.S. Public Companies 1993**. Gale Research, 4th edition. The Corporate Directory gives you all the essential facts on more than 9,500 publicly traded firms having at least $5 million in assets. Entries are arranged alphabetically by parent company name and provide: company name and contact data; general information such as incorporation and fiscal year end, legal counsel, etc.; stock data: price range for a 52-week period, closing price at last sale; summary of the company's areas of business, primary SIC; additional SICs; major subsidiaries; and more. Eight indexes.

• **Ward's Business Directory of U.S. Private and Public Companies.** Gale Research. Annual. Profiles of some 100,000 private and public companies. The information provided for each company resembles in both style and content that which is found in the sources discussed above. All companies profiled may be accessed geographically and by SIC code. A special feature of Ward's is that companies are ranked by sales within 4-digit SIC code categories.

• **Ward's Private Company Profiles,** Gale Research. Articles from over 150 sources including investment reports and company brochures about this significant and often elusive segment of the American economy. Find big companies, recognized names, as well as cutting edge firms and small aggressive companies.

4. Specific Industry Trends and Company Information

A. Advertising and Public Relations
• **Advertising Career Directory.** Gale Research, 5th edition, Bradley J. Morgan, editor. Gives you straight talk on what it's like to work in the industry. Includes feature articles by experts on getting started as a copywriter, preparing a portfolio, radio and television advertising, direct mail, database marketing, corporate advertising, advertising outside New York City, getting started at an agency, and more.

• **Standard Directory of Advertising Agencies: The Agency Red Book.** National Register Publishing Company. An international guide to the advertising industry. Lists advertising agencies alphabetically and profiles each agency by reporting its address, telephone number, specialization, annual gross billings by media, names of accounts, names of management and account executives, and other information. Also provides a geographical index of agencies.

B. Environment

➜ Companies in this industry are listed; so are articles on trends and outlooks. A must for anyone targeting the environment.

• **Environmental Encyclopedia**. Gale Research, 1st edition, William P. Cunningham, Terence Ball, et al., editors. Comprehensive, multidisciplinary approach to the study of the environment. Over 1,200 articles provide in-depth, worldwide coverage of all aspects of the environment in a convenient encyclopedic format. Included are articles on air, water, and noise pollution, climate, prominent personalities, biology, political science, economics, organizations, legislation, regulation and compliance, and more.

Each article is written in a non-technical style by an authority from an academic or professional post and compiled under the direction of Professor William P. Cunningham, author of *Environmental Science, a Global Concern*, and associates from the University of Minnesota representing a broad spectrum of interests and experiences in environmental sciences. Articles analyze major issues and events, provide insight on current status and problems, and suggest potential solutions.

➜ A where-to-go for info in this field. Unbelievable for learning the environmental industry quickly and accurately.

• **Encyclopedia of Environmental Information Sources**. Gale Research, 1st edition, Sarojini Balachandran editor. Information on hazardous materials, acid rain, endangered species, global warming, recycling, alternative energy, and many other environmental topics. The subject-specific approach allows you to quickly identify more than 20,000 up-to-date citations to printed, electronic, and live information in more than 800 subject areas, including: abstracting and indexing services; bibliographies; directories; encyclopedias and dictionaries; on-line databases; periodicals and newsletters; associations and societies. Alphabetically arranged sections allow easy searching for specific information. This is a "source of sources," providing researchers with a convenient method to compile subject-specific lists for further research.

• **Environmental Industries Marketplace.** Gale Research, 1st edition, Karen Napoleone Meech, editor. Annual contact and descriptive directory designed to help anyone gain access to the $100-billion environmental market. An essential guide for business people, job seekers, administrators, engineers, and managers who need to know about environmental-control compliance products and services, plus much more.

Includes address, phone and fax numbers for: consultants and attorneys, land surveyors, research facilities, transportation and disposal firms, and many others. You will be able to locate specific companies in many subject areas covered, such as: air pollution, asbestos, financial services, hazardous waste, land fills, noise pollution, recycling, and more.

➜ Become an expert on the history of any topic in this industry, as seen through the print media. The info is so incredible, I wish this were my target!

• **Environmental Viewpoints.** Gale Research, Marie Lazzari, editor. This directory provides excerpts of articles that appear regularly in more than 100 popular and professional periodicals, including: *Time, Forbes, U.S. News & World Report, New Scientist, Consumer Reports, Smithsonian,* and *World Watch.*

Environmental Viewpoints excerpts articles that provide both historic and current information as well as divergent opinions. Entries are arranged to allow users to scan for background information, then explore the issue in detail.

• **Gale Environmental Sourcebook.** Gale Research, 1st edition, Karen Hill and Annette Piccirelli editors. Provides descriptive information on 8,634 environmental organizations, information services, programs, and publications involved in all aspects of the environment including advocacy and education, policy and enforcement, research and development, and consumer issues/products. Full contact data. Descriptive information may include activities, histories, affiliations, publication frequencies, meeting schedules, prices, subjects of interest, and other information that will help make research.

➜ Look! Not just info on the environmental industry, but from an international perspective.

• **World Guide to Environmental Issues and Organizations.** Gale Research, 1st edition, Peter Brackley, editor. Comprehensive, international coverage of 250 key environmental issues and organizations including government organizations, public and private research projects, and regulatory and campaign organizations. Some of the topics covered include global warming, acid rain, marine pollution, ozone depletion, forest loss, nuclear issues, water quality, and more.

C. Finance

• **American Bank Directory.** Lists over 18,000 banks. Names of executives, addresses, and phone numbers.

➜ You want banks? Here are banks.

➜ Oh, you said insurance? No problem.

• **Best's Insurance Reports, Property and Casualty.** A.M. Best Co. Annual. In-depth analyses, operating statistics, financial data and ratings, and names of officers in over 1,300 major stock and mutual property-casualty insurance companies. In addition, provides summary data on over 2,000 smaller mutual companies and on 300 casualty companies operating in Canada.

• **Business and Finance Career Directory.** Gale Research, 2nd edition, Bradley J. Morgan; editor. Insider information from industry professionals. Essays cover topics such as working as a certified public accountant; what it's like to be a securities analyst or trader; becoming a financial planner; management information consulting as a career; and the facts about banking and insurance.

➜ Venture capital firms, as well as firms that offer venture capital services as one of many financial offerings, are listed & described

• **Corporate Finance Sourcebook.** National Register Publishing Company. A directory for sources of capital funding, including firms and individuals providing financial and management services. Provides descriptive listings of venture-capital firms; major private lenders; firms that offer commercial finance and factoring; the 100 largest commercial banks with the services they offer corporations; foreign investment banks; leasing companies; securities analysts; CPA firms, and other types of organizations that offer these services. The profiles include the names and telephone numbers of individuals, and they specify the preferred investment fields, range of investments, loan criteria, and other relevant information.

• **Finance, Insurance & Real Estate USA.** Gale Research, 1st edition, Arsen J. Darnay, editor. Crucial economic and statistical data. What's happening in 50 industries listed by 4-digit SIC codes.

FIRE USA's editors consulted a wide range of sources, including the FDIC, FSLIC, SEC, the Federal Reserve System, Department of Commerce, Bureau of Economic Analysis, Ward's Business Directory, and many others. The result is a unique, easy-to-use compilation of data that will be extremely valuable to researchers focusing on industries such as: depository and nondepository institutions; mortgage bankers and brokers; foreign trade and international banks; securities and commodity brokers and services; insurance agents and brokers; real estate firms; and many other related industries.

• **Financial 1,000 Yellow Book.** Commercial banks, insurance companies, Wall Street firms, and thrifts.

• **Financial Planners and Planning Organizations Directory.** Over 4,000 planners/organizations profiled.

➜ More insurance companies, this time international as well.

• **Financial Times World Insurance 1994** Gale Research, 1994 edition. This complete guide to the insurance industry and more than 1,150 insurance companies around the world provides background information on recent developments in the insurance industry, currency tables, and definitions of key financial terms, as well as detailed summaries of individual companies.

• **Moody's Bank and Finance Manual.** Moody's Investors Service. Profiles institutions in the U.S. finance industry: banks, savings and loan associations, investment companies, insurance companies, real estate companies, real estate investment trusts, unit investment trusts, and other financial enterprises.

Includes history; location; names of officers and directors; consolidated financial statement; financial and operating ratio; debt structure; letters to shareholders; list of securities held in trust; record of income and principal distribution; and other financial information that is appropriate to the type of financial institution.

• **Morningstar Mutual Fund Service.** Provides the same information for mutual funds that Value Line provides for stocks.

• **Pratt's Guide to Venture Capital Sources.** Venture Economics, Inc., edited by Stanley E. Pratt and Jane K. Morris. Venture capital firms and individuals in the U.S. and Canada. Brief description of each source that includes address, telephone number, industry and project preferences, and other related information. Also includes a list of firms that underwrite public offerings for equity capital in small businesses.

➜ The St. James books are less well known but excellent sources of financial industry information.

• **St. James Encyclopedia of Banking and Finance.** Gale Research, 9th edition, edited by Charles J. Woelfel. Almost 4,200 entries. Defines thousands of basic banking, business, and financial terms. Provides valuable statistical data; citations to laws/regulations; background information; bibliographies; examples and analysis of product; structural and regulatory developments. These include: fiscal policy; bank failures; risk-based capital adequacy; marketing financial services; lending; customer and community service.

• **St. James Mutual Fund Directory.** Gale Research, 1st edition. More than 2,500 mutual funds operating in the U.S. Easy-to-use volume. Explains what funds are, how they are operated and regulated, and how to read a prospectus. Answers the most commonly asked questions .

Organized by mutual fund types, its 22 chapters cover virtually every mutual fund in America, providing addressees and phone/fax numbers, years in operation, names of investment advisors, asset size, minimum initial and subsequent investment requirements and where shares can be purchased.

• **St. James World Futures and Options Directory 1991-92.** Gale Research. Annual. Major world exchanges and contracts. Provides contact, membership and evaluative information on 48 exchanges. Over 350 contracts listed by exchange and alphabetically by commodity type. Includes everything brokers, investors and industrialists need to compare specific commodity contracts: administration; date of introduction; specification/basis; contract unit; quotation; tick value; delivery months; trading hours; maximum daily limit; last day of trading; delivery; method of trading; commissions; and more.

• **Standard & Poor's Bond Guide.** American and some foreign bonds, including S&P quality ratings.

• **Standard & Poor's Corporation Records.** Similar to Moody's manuals, but covers companies not listed on any stock exchange.

• **Standard & Poor's Daily Stock Price Record.** Daily and weekly records of volume, high/low and closing prices for stocks.

• **Standard & Poor's Outlook.** Weekly reports on business and stock market trends.

• **Standard & Poor's Stock Guide.** Lists 5,100 common and preferred stocks, with S&P rating, stock price range, dividends.

• **Trendline Daily Action Charts.** Nine-month trends for 750 popular and active stocks.

• **U.S. Savings and Loan Directory.** Rand McNally and Company, 7th edition. Contains an alphabetical listing, by state, of savings and loan institutions, with a profile of each institution that includes address, telephone number, names of officers, total assets, total deposits, total loans, net worth, and other financial statistics. This directory publishes information on the savings industry, including the associations and government agencies that serve the industry.

• **Value Line Investment Survey.** Lists 1,700 companies, with statistics and key investment factors. Ratings, prospects, charts and brief explanatory texts. Revised quarterly.

D. Health Care

• **Dun's Guide to Healthcare Companies.** Dun's Marketing Services. Annual. Detailed information on more than 15,000 companies which provide products or services in the health-care industry. Standard directory-type information is provided for each company. All listings are cross-referenced geographically, by SIC code, by medical/diagnostic device, and by brand name.

→ Great resource for info on topics in health care.

• **Encyclopedia of Health Information Sources.** Gale Research, 2nd edition, edited by Paul Wasserman. This subject-arranged guide contains 13,000 citations to a wide range of information sources for 450 health-related topics. Under each subject, the work provides citations for up to 14 types of sources. Citations to published works include recent publications and classics in the field. Extensive cross-referencing and a list of subjects make the work easy to consult.

• **Encyclopedia of Medical Organizations & Agencies.** Gale Research, 5th edition, edited by Karen Backus. This encyclopedia gives you instant access to the more than 12,000 public and private organizations and agencies concerned with medical information, funding, research, education, planning, advocacy, advice, and service. Entries in 69 subject chapters include the organization's name, address, telephone number, key officials, founding year, number of members, number of employees, publications and their frequency, as well as a brief description of the group's purpose.

• **Industrial Biotechnology International.** Contains an overview of major advances in biochemistry and biotechnology that are of commercial significance. Also included are financial reports of biotechnology corporations and pharmaceutical companies, discussions of specific companies involved in biotechnology, and a review of recent patents.

• **Medical & Health Information Directory.** Gale Research, 6th edition, edited by Karen Backus. A comprehensive guide to organizations, agencies, institutions, services, and information sources in medicine and health-related fields. In three volumes. Volume 1 has descriptive information on more than 16,400 organizations, agencies, and institutions. Volume 2 has contact data and descriptive details on over 9,700 libraries, publications, and institutions. Volume 3 has current data on over 23,000 health services. Also available on diskette.

E. High Technology

→ This is the where-to-go for info for high tech.

• **Computers and Computing Information Resources Directory.** Gale Research, edited by Martin Connors. A comprehensive directory of print and nonprint sources of information on all aspects of computers, computing, and data processing. It is a guide to finding sources of computer-related information. These sources include user groups, trade and professional associations, consultants, university computer facilities and research organizations, trade shows, professional exhibits, computer related association conventions, on-line database vendors and teleprocessing networks worldwide. The sources also include special libraries and information centers with an emphasis on computers or computer science, as well as journals, newsletters, and computer-oriented directories. Each entry contains the name, address, telephone number, purpose or activities, and other descriptive information for each source. Also contains a directory of some persons in the computer-information field, listing their addresses and telephone numbers.

• **Corporate Technology Directory.** Corporate Technology Information Services, Inc., 3rd edition. Public and private U.S. firms and U.S. operating units of foreign companies that manufacture or develop high-technology products, including: advanced materials, automation, biotech, chemicals, computers, software, energy, manufacturing, medical, pharmaceuticals, telecommunications, and others. Company profiles include company name, other or former company name(s), address, telephone number, telex, fax, owner-ship of the company, ticker symbol, year founded, description of the business activity, annual sales revenue, number of employees, names of executives with their titles and areas of responsibility, product descriptions, SIC codes, detailed Corp Tech product codes, and other information. Through the elaborate indexing system, companies can be identified by name, location, parent name, and their high-tech products.

➜ Global high tech! What's going on around the world in high tech and in specific industries that are related to high tech? Check it out.

➜ Very good info on all aspects of the high-growth field of telecommunications.

• **Data Sources: Data Comm/Telecomm.** Ziff-Davis Publishing Company. A guide to data communications and telecommunications hardware. Directory of data/telecommunications company profiles. Gives a description of each product. These products include network processor/network management systems, modems, multiplexors, emulation/conversion equipment, security equipment, PBX/CBX equipment, telephone call-accounting systems, facsimile machines, teleconferencing systems and services, and other telecommunication equipment. Some of the data are displayed in charts that facilitate product comparisons.

• **Telecommunications Directory.** Lists national and international organizations involved in telecommunications. Includes voice and data communications services, local area networks, teleconferencing facilities, videotex and teletext operations, and companies providing electronic mail, facsimile, telegram and telex, voice processing/response, satellite, and telecom-related associations, consultants, law firms, publishers, regulatory bodies, and seminar/training organizations.

F. Human Resources

➜ Use this directory if you need to locate headhunters who specialize in specific industries, or if you are in the search business and need to identify companies in your target. Kennedy Publications has a wide variety of guides for the staffing and consulting industries.

• **Directory of Executive Recruiters.** Consultant News, Kennedy Publications, New Hampshire, 16th edition, edited by James H. Kennedy. A directory of more than 2,500 executive search firms. These are executive recruiters who are paid by management, not job hunters. Provides the name of the executive-search firm, address, contact person, field of specialization, and other information.

• **Personnel Executives Contact Book.** Gale Research, 1st edition, edited by Cindy Spomer. Annual. Complete contact information for key personnel officers at 30,000 companies across the U.S. Arranged alphabetically by company name, listings contain information most frequently requested by job hunters: company name, address, and phone number; SIC code; number of employees; annual revenues; the name of the key personnel executive (highlighted for easy discovery); and the names of other human resources staff.

• **Training and Development Organizations Directory.** Gale Research, 5th edition, Janice McLean, editor. Guide to companies that produce workshops, seminars, videos, and other training programs that can enhance skills and personal development. Fully describes more than 10,000 such training programs.

Detailed contact information is provided for the training organization, including full name, address, phone number, fax, toll-free number, date founded, names of principals, staff size, areas of course emphasis, typical clients/target audience, course titles and fees, and packaged training programs. Geographic, Personal Name, and Subject Indexes. Directory is also available on-line.

G. Importing/ Exporting/ Trading

• **Directory of United States Importers: 1986-1987.** Journal of Commerce. A directory of importers with a profile of each firm. Cites name, address, telephone and telex numbers, cable address, year established, names of principal officers, custom-house broker, port of entry, products imported, and the source nations for the imports. Reviews the U.S. Customs Service regulations and importing procedures. Lists products that are imported and their respective importers. Also cites U.S. and foreign embassies and consulates, international banks in the U.S., trade associations, and ports of the world.

• **Exporters Directory/U.S. Buying Guide: 1987-1988**. Journal of Commerce. A directory of American exporters. Lists firms alphabetically and by product. Also contains a brand-name index. Profiles of exporting firms include name, address, telephone number, telex number, cable address, names of key officers, number of employees, year established, ports of exit, products exported, countries served, and international freight forwarder. Also describes export-related services provided by the U.S. Department of Commerce. Lists U.S. and foreign embassies/consulates, international banks in the U.S., trade associations, and ports of the world.

• **World Business Directory**. Gale Research, 1st edition, edited by Meghan A. O'Meara and Kimberley A. Peterson. Lists over 105,000 trade-oriented businesses of all sizes from more than 190 countries (even the smallest) including: top trading firms from each country or market region; small and medium-sized companies not listed elsewhere; international trade/import leaders.

Contains vital details for exploring and evaluating international markets, finding potential trading partners, identifying which firms compete internationally, and contacting executives or consultants in specific industries. The entries give readers the data they need to achieve the desired goal.

A typical entry lists: company name and contact names; contact information: address, phone, fax, telex; business activities; product details; WTC affiliation and NETWORK access code; company type (holding company subsidiary, etc.); import/export designation; revenue figures; parent company name; year est.

First three volumes contain company listings arranged geographically, then by company; fourth volume consists of three indexes (Alphabetical, Industry, and Product). Also available on CD-ROM.

→ A directory of trading firms—both big and small—across the globe. Includes their areas of specialization.

• **World Trade Resources Guide**. Gale Research, 1st edition, Kenneth Estell, ed. WTRG brings together in one convenient, easy-to-use source a wide range of resource information for anyone interested in import/export opportunities around the world. WTRG includes 80 of the world's largest trading nations as well as many smaller countries which play an important part in world trade.

Countries are arranged alphabetically in chapters, providing complete contact data for government organizations, shipping lines of registry, principal ports, free trade zones, nonprofit or trade associations, sources of foreign trade statistics, and publications concerned with foreign trade.

Each country chapter opens with a profile that provides vital statistics on that country's population, currency exchange rates, GNP/GDP, import/export/trade balance figures, major trading partners, principal commodities imported and exported, and memberships in international organizations.

H. Information Industry

NOTE: Information Industry here refers to Information Services & Retrieval. Other aspects of the broader Information & Communication industry can be found under High Technology, Publishing, & Media and Broadcasting

Use this guide in case you want to explore the incredible field of research services; you can also identify companies that, for a fee, will help you do your own research in some other target! →

• **Directory of Fee-Based Information Services**. Burwell Enterprises, edited by Helen P. Burwell. Directory of information specialists who provide services for a fee. Includes information brokers, free-lance librarians, fee-based services of public and academic libraries, and information packagers, U.S. and abroad. Includes name of the firm or individual, address, telephone number, telex and fax numbers, contact person, subject specialization areas, and types of information services provided (e.g., research, on-line retrieval, and report writing). Each profile concludes with a descriptive summary.

→ NEW!! Information retrieval comes of age with this internet guide

• Gale Guide to Internet Databases, Gale Research, 1st edition. Locate and access 2,000 authoritative databases available on the Internet. This guide focuses on major government, academic, research, and educational databases.

→ The information industry is new and wide open; this resource is full of info and ideas.

• **Information Sources: The Annual Directory of the Information Industry Association**. Information Industry Association, edited by Barbara E. Van Gorder. The membership directory of the trade association of the information industry.Company listings represent a broad spectrum of products and services in this industry, including database vendors, software producers, information brokers, and publishers of reference books and periodicals. Includes full-page company ads that describe each company, encompassing address, telephone number, products or services, and so on. Companies can be identified by the product/service index. The listing is limited to members of the Information Industry Association.

190

The only joy in the world is to begin.
Cesare Pavese, Italian writer

➜ These are great, but remember: they cost money.

• **Directory of On-line Databases.** Cuadra-Elsevier. International guide to databases, encompassing many subjects. Those related to business include accounting; advertising; management; business and industry directories (domestic and foreign); specific industries; copyrights, patents, and trademarks; corporate finance (domestic and foreign); currency-exchange rates; marketing; securities; and others.

Each database profile reports the subject and content; name, address, and telephone number of the producer and of the on-line vendor; requirements for accessing and using the database; geographic coverage; time span of the data; updating frequency; and other relevant information. Provides information on gateways in the on-line database industry.

I. International Markets

• **Asia: A Directory and Sourcebook.** Gale Research, 1st ed. Provides offices and information sources based inside and outside China, Hong Kong, India, Indonesia, Pakistan, Philippines, Singapore, South Korea, Sri Lanka, Taiwan, Thailand. Features business information sources, profiles of leading companies, comparative tables, overviews of economic trends, assessments of markets and distribution opportunities.

➜ If you are looking for information concerning companies with both foreign and domestic markets, this is an indispensable guide.

• **The Book of European Forecasts.** Gale Research, 1st edition. This unique marketing handbook maps out European development over the next decade with a series of broad-ranging social, economic, and demographic forecasts. With more than 300 pages of statistical documentation and in-depth commentary, the book explores nearly every aspect of the European way of life, including commercial activity, market development, households, media access, and services.

• **America's Corporate Families and International Affiliates.** Dun's Marketing Services. A directory of U.S. corporations and their foreign subsidiaries, arranged by corporate family. Also lists foreign parent companies with their U.S. subsidiaries. Excludes companies that are based either exclusively in the U.S. or totally outside of the U.S. Provides a cross-reference index between subsidiaries and their parent companies. Publishes a profile of corporations that reports the location telephone number, nature of business, officers, sales volume, export/import activity, and other descriptive information for each.

• **Directory of European Industrial and Trade Associations.** Gale Research, 5th edition. Describes about 6,000 industrial and trade associations (professional associations have been transferred to the Directory of European Professional and Learned Associations). Includes national associations for all European countries (except Great Britain and Ireland) and regional associations of national significance. Contains full contact information, membership data, activities undertaken by the association, publications available, and more.

➜ Will become an indispensable reference source for those seeking to track global economic trends.

• **Directory of Foreign Investment in the U.S.** Gale Research, 1st edition, edited by Nancy Garman. Data related to foreign investments in commercial property and business establishments within the U.S. Arranged into two sections: the first details foreign real estate investments in America's most fertile markets; the second describes businesses acquired or established by foreign investors.
Published with cumulative information derived from a wide variety of resources.

• **Directory of Foreign Manufacturers in the United States.** Georgia State University Business Press, 4th edition, 1990. Approximately 6,000 foreign-owned manufacturers with operations in the U.S. are listed. Information about each company includes: address, parent company, product description, and SIC code.

• **Dun's Europa.** Dun & Bradstreet Europe. Annual. Details on 45,000 leading European companies. All 12 countries of the European Community are represented, along with Austria and Switzerland. Listed alphabetically by country. Includes rankings by sales and indexing by line of business.

➜ This is a new edition, published to address a new market.

• **Eastern Europe: A Directory and Sourcebook.** Gale Research, 1st edition. Economic background information, business information sources, profiles of leading companies, and current market and consumer trends. Includes Bulgaria, Germany, Hungary, Poland, Romania, and the former states of Czechoslovakia, Yugoslavia, and the Soviet Republics. Five sections: the first gives an overview of the categories; the second discusses economics; the third lists major state-owned and private companies; the fourth provides business information sources; and the fifth gives comparative data tables in such areas as demography, energy, retail sales, and more.

Many are stubborn in pursuit of the path they have chosen,
few in pursuit of the goal.
Friedrich Nietzsche

➜ NEW!! 125 vital international industries exposed!

➜ You'll never be at a loss for facts regarding European business, regardless of which industry you're researching.

Economic outlooks; areas growing and areas declining. Think of how this can help you design really powerful questions for networking!

➜ It's simply amazing to have, in one volume, the names and special- ized markets for 5,000 European consultants. This is a great way to tap into the global market- place.

• **Eastern European Business Directory**. Gale Research, edited by Frank X. Didik. More than 7,000 companies and organizations providing close to 9,000 distinct products in the countries of Bulgaria, Hungary, Poland, Romania, the former Czechoslovakia and western Soviet Union. Arranged by product/ service, geographic location, and company name.

• **Encyclopedia of Business Information Sources: Europe**. Gale Research, edited by M. Balachandran. Covers a wide range of business information sources from 32 Eastern and Western European countries and lists them under approximately 1,000 alphabetically arranged business subjects. From Accounting to the Video Recording Industry, EBIS: Europe includes the most up-to-date topics relevant to today's researcher. Within each topic category, entries are divided geographically and then by type of resource.

• **Encyclopedia of Global Industries**, Gale Research, 1st edition. Covers industries with significant global trade and interdependence covering a broad spectrum of topics for each industry including size & eco- nomic/social impact of the industry, how it is organized and how it functions, history & development, current economic status, size & nature of the wqork force.

• **European Advertising, Marketing and Media Data 1992**. Gale Research, 2nd edition. Presents a comprehensive and detailed look at European marketing statistics such as economic indicators, demograph- ics, geographic location, and market size of 16 major Western European markets. Marketing directors, sales and export directors, corporate planners, advertising executives, media and management consultants, students, and job hunters will find this unique directory indispensable.

• **European Business Rankings**. Gale Research, 1st edition, edited by Oksana Newman and Allen Foster. Displays 2,250 business statistics and rankings from throughout Europe. Contains the top ten names in each list, and gives the ranking criteria, the total number of items listed in the original ranking, and the name, date, and page of the source. Lists the best (and sometimes worst) in hundreds of European business topics, such as advertising, insurance, law, banking, corporations, and others. Compiled from myriad sources.

• **European Business Services Directory**. Gale Research, edited by Michael B. Huellmantel. Lists approximately 20,000 European companies providing essential business services. The directory is arranged by service category, and within each category by country and city. Company names are then listed in alphabetical order under the city. Complete company entries contain contact information, annual sales, languages in which business is conducted, branch offices, SIC codes, and more. Company listings and geographic listings help to speed the information search.

• **European Companies**. Gale Research, 4th edition. Listing major sources of information on business enterprises in all countries of Europe, this useful guide is designed to help English-speaking researchers using foreign-language documents. Entries cover directories, yearbooks, newspapers, stock exchanges, commercial information and credit reporting services, magazines, databases, and other information sources, and include such details as frequency, price, size, language, and content.

• **European Consultants Directory**. Gale Research, edited by Karin Koek. Helps users find consultants to advise them in management, finance, and other business affairs as well as agriculture, engineering, educa- tion, and political and social issues. The more than 5,000 consultants are grouped by country, by broad subject terms, and then alphabetically by consulting organization. The directory also lists additional addresses for almost 2,500 branch offices, so you can contact nearly 7,500 consultants throughout Europe. Three indexes: Consulting Activities Reference List, Consulting Firms, and Personnel Listings.

• **The European Directory of Consumer Brands and Their Owners**. Gale Research, 1st edition. Up-to- date information on more than 5,000 companies in Europe. Provides an effective way to research brands across the continent. Look up brands by country, by sector, or by owning companies. Provides key financial and marketing data including key developments such as licensing and administration agreements, take- overs, and brand sales to other companies.

• **European Market Share Reporter**. Gale Research, 1st edition, edited by Oksana Newman and Allen Foster. As the planned economic alliance of the European nations creates the world's largest single market,

→ European MSR will instruct you on how to find any information in the EEC

related information needs will grow. Helps locate market share information for companies, products, industries, and markets within the European Economic Community. Coverage, format, and organization are similar to the U.S.-focused *Market Share Reporter*. 1,400 entries are arranged by 4-digit U.S. SIC codes.

• **European Wholesalers and Distributors Directory**. Gale Research, edited by Linda Irvin. Listings of approximately 5,000 wholesalers and distributors of finished consumer goods and industrial products in Western and Eastern Europe. Includes automobiles; electronic parts and equipment; construction materials; furniture; TV and radio; hardware; footwear; groceries; books, periodicals, and newspapers; and many more. Entries are arranged alphabetically by product line (based on SIC codes), and then by country, and typically provide: complete contact information; year established; territory of distribution; annual revenue expressed in local currency; products; and more. Indexes include a Directory of Company Names, a Product Key, Geographic Listings, and a Key to Territories Served.

→ You will find all the answers to the big picture questions here: international trends, forecasts and outlooks; areas growing and areas declining. Think of how this can help you design really powerful questions for netwroking!

• **International Marketing Handbook**. Gale Research, 3rd edition. Detailed marketing profiles for 141 nations. Country reports—averaging 31 pages in length and complemented by maps, tables, and charts—have been developed by the International Trade Administration of the U.S. Department of Commerce. Includes authoritative information on such areas as: foreign trade outlook; industry trends; government contracting; employment and wages; trade regulations; foreign investment; sources of economic and commercial information; and more.
Includes trade guides and international marketing briefs concerning the European Common Market, the Near East and North Africa, the Middle East situation, East-West trade, and other related topics of interest to international business.

• **Japan Trade Directory 1992-93**. Gale Research. Presents the latest information available on 2,900 Japanese companies that import or export 18,000 products and services. Locate information on specific companies by their products and services, by their location within Japan and by the company's name. Detailed company profiles provide financial data, corporate structure, full information on trade contracts, and the company's interests in importing and exporting.

• **Japanese Affiliated Companies in the U.S. and Canada 1991-92**. Gale Research. This directory lists 9,569 Japanese affiliates operating in the U.S. and Canada. Geographically arranged entries provide: company name; parent company name; North American address; year of establishment, telephone, telex, and fax number; executive officer's names; type of business and product; operating status. Six indexes.

• **Major Business Organizations of Eastern Europe and the Commonwealth of Independent States**. Gale Research, 2nd edition. Information on more than 2,000 major business organizations. Includes ministries involved in international trade, Chambers of Commerce, financial organizations, manufacturing companies, import and export trade associations and more. Arranged by country, then by business activities, entries provide contact data, names of key officials, import/export data, and descriptive information.

• **Major Companies of the Arab World 1992-93**. Gale Research, 16th edition. Gives up-to-date information about the 6,000 major companies of 20 Arab countries.Each major company profile provides: complete contact data, names of directors and management staff, principal activities, number of branch offices, principal bank, financial details, principal shareholders, date of establishment, and number of employees.

• **Major Companies of Europe 1992-93**. Gale Research, 12th edition. Three volumes cover more than 6,200 of Europe's major companies—including finance, personnel, structure, products, profitability and key executives. Arranged by country, with indexes to company names, business activities, and countries.

• **Major Companies of the Far East and Australasia 1992-93**. Gale Research, 9th edition. Three volumes provide up-to-date information on nearly 4,500 major companies. Find out about finances, personnel, structure, products, profitability, and executives. Investigate new markets, research prospective customers, plan a sales campaign, contact possible joint-venture partners, establish new business. Arranged by country, with indexes to company names, business activities, and countries.

• **Major Financial Institutions of Continental Europe 1993-94**. Gale Research, 5th edition. Profiles more than 1,100 leading financial institutions of Europe, arranged within country chapters, providing name of firm, address and telephone number, telex and fax numbers, name of chairman, name of board members, principal business activities, number of employees, and more. Company and Geographic Indexes.

• **Medium Companies of Europe 1992-93**. Gale Research, 3rd edition. A directory which describes Europe's many privately owned and growing medium-sized firms. Three volumes bring you information on over 7,000 rising European businesses.

➤ My guess is that many European job seekers don't know this information, let alone U.S. job seekers looking for international opportunities.

• **Principal International Business**. Dun's Marketing Services. The most prominent and largest businesses in countries around the world. Lists firms alphabetically within country and in a composite list for all countries. Also organizes them by line of business (SIC code). Entry profiles include address, SIC code, name of parent company, name of senior operating officer, and other information.

• **International Directory of Corporate Affiliations**. Register Publishing Company. A directory of foreign parent companies with their domestic and international holdings and of U.S. parent companies with their foreign subsidiaries, affiliates, and divisions. Lists companies by country. Also provides addresses and telephone numbers of foreign consulates in the U.S., U.S. embassies, American Chambers of Commerce abroad, and foreign trade commissions and Chambers of Commerce.

• **Japan Yellow Pages**. Croner Publications, Inc., and others. This is the yellow pages of the telephone directory for selected cities in Japan. It lists businesses by their product or service. Provides address, telephone number, cable address, telex, and fax number.

• **South America: A Directory and Sourcebook**. Gale Research, 1st edition. Lists information sources based in Columbia, Venezuela, Guyana, Surinam, Brazil, Bolivia, Paraguay, Uruguay, Argentina, Chile, Peru, and Ecuador. Divided into five sections which provide: profiles of leading companies; assessments of consumer markets; comparative tables; overview of countries; and more.

➤ How much more current could you get than a volume called "The World's Emerging Markets"? Even if this is not your target, thinking of how this kind of information could impact your target will lead to very powerful interviews.

• **The World's Emerging Markets**. Gale Research, 1st edition. This major new data book draws together a wide variety of statistics and analyses, providing a clear assessment of business opportunities in the world's fastest-growing markets.

Up-to-date, usable information about industries, regions, and particular companies. Included are market prospects, demand characteristics, and policy environment in most of the world's emerging economies. Markets are ranked by size, wealth, stability, and future potential. The World's Emerging Markets also contains an extensive compilation of up-to-date statistical data covering socio-economic activity, external trade and investment, standard of living indicators, consumer expenditures, retail distribution, advertising, marketing, and household composition.

Chapters include comprehensive information on the economies and prospects of countries within the following regions: Eastern Europe and the former USSR, Southern Europe, The Pacific Rim, Central Asia, South America, Africa, and the Middle East.

➤ Worldwide high tech.

• **World Technology Policies**. Gale Research. Offers an authoritative and comprehensive look at science and technology worldwide. Included are an overview of key trends and reviews of four key areas of growth: new materials, information technology, biotechnology, and defense. The status of science and technology in the major nations of the world is presented, including details of important national and international organizations.

• **Worldwide Branch Locations of Multinational Companies**. Gale Research, 1st edition, edited by David S. Hoopes. More than 500 top multinational companies, and nearly 20,000 plants, branches and subsidiaries located worldwide. Covers companies that are not headquartered in the U.S. in addition to those that are. Divided geographically by country. Branch, plant, and subsidiary entries are listed alphabetically within each country section. Each listing has an entry number to accommodate references for the indexes.

If I try to use human influence strategies and tactics of how to get other people to do what I want, to work better, to be more motivated, to like me and each other—while my character is fundamentally flawed, marked by duplicity and insincerity—then, in the long run, I cannot be successful. My duplicity will breed distrust, and everything I do— even using so-called good human relations techniques—will be perceived as manipulative. . . Only basic goodness gives life to technique.
Stephen R. Covey, The Seven Habits of Highly Effective People

J. Law and Government

➜ In addition to identifying opportunities for lobbyists and government-relations people, this book is a fabulous way to identify the issues particular companies are lobbying for. This provides new insight into company values and company problems. Very clever!

• **American Lobbyists Directory**. Gale Research, 1st edition, ed: Robert Wilson. A complete guide to federal and state lobbyists. Listings include 57,000 lobbyists and 25,000 organizations in state-by-state sections, 8,000 registered federal lobbyists, and 4,000 represented organizations. Descriptive entries provide completed contact information, including phone numbers, for the organizations and lobbyists involved in particular issues. Lobbyists Index, Organizations Index, and Subject/Specialty Indexes.

• **Encyclopedia of Governmental Advisory Organizations 1994-95**. Gale Research, 9th edition, edited by Donna Batten. Over 6,000 entries describing the activities and personnel of groups and committees that function to advise the President and various departments and bureaus of the federal government, as well as giving detailed information about historically significant committees.

Includes information about White House Conferences and other conferences sponsored by the federal government, groups under contract doing studies for the federal government, and congressional committees doing studies of current topical interest. Complete contact information provided when available. Five indexes provide easy access: Alphabetical and Keyword, Personnel, Publications and Reports, Organizations by Federal Department or Agency, and Organizations by Presidential Administration.

• **Law and Legal Information Directory**. Gale Research, 7th edition, edited by Steven Wassermann and Jacqueline Wasserman O'Brien. Descriptions and contact information for 30,500 institutions, services, and facilities arranged in 25 chapters, including National and International Organizations, Bar Associations, Federal Court System, Law Schools, Scholarships and Grants, Legal Periodicals, Lawyer Referral Services, Legal Aid Offices, Public Defender Offices, Small Claims Courts, and more.

Twenty-five chapters help find information on a particular area of law; discover the status of a bill in progress at the state level through a quick phone call; locate nearby law schools and schools for continuing legal education or paralegal training; and much more.

• **Worldwide Government Directory**. Gale Research, 1994 edition. This directory provides current contact information on 173 countries, their leaders, and major government offices. For each country listed, following general background facts—such as official language, capital, currency exchange rates, and telephone codes—you'll find names, titles, addresses, and telephone numbers for its head of state, cabinet members, ambassadors, key officials, state agencies, ministries, embassies, and other government offices. This new edition's comprehensive coverage includes more than 50,000 entries, and reflects recent changes in Eastern Europe, unified Germany, and the former Soviet Republics.

K. Media & Broadcasting

➜ Includes radio, TV, and cable.

• **Gale Directory of Publications and Broadcast Media 1993**. Gale Research. Julie Winklepleck, editor. Over 36,000 entries, including listings for radio and television stations, and cable companies. For each state, province, and city in the U.S. and Canada, you can quickly identify its magazines, newspapers, radio and television stations, and cable companies.

Entries are arranged by state or province, and then by city. Brief demographics are given for each city. Television and radio station entries contain: station call letters and channel; Area of Dominant Influence (ADI); name of owner network affiliation; top three local programs; advertising rates; and more. Master Alphabetical/Keyword and Classification Indexes. Also available on-line.

• **Radio and Television Career Directory**. Gale Research, 2nd edition, Bradley J. Morgan, editor. Discover on-air and behind-the-scenes opportunities in radio, TV news, broadcast meteorology, radio programming, radio marketing, writing for television, cable TV, and other specialties through insightful essays written by noted professionals within the industry.

• **Spot Radio Rates and Data**. Standard Rate and Data Service. A directory of the radio industry, with an alphabetical listing, by state and U.S. possession, of radio stations. The station profiles include address, telephone number, call letters, names of key personnel, advertising contract terms and spot rates, and other information about the station. Reports descriptions and rankings of television market areas. Contains a listing of program syndicators and firms that represent radio stations.

L. Not-for-Profit / Fund-Raising

→ ANF is a brilliant resource, especially valuable for people searching for information on smaller foundations, where much opportunity lies. It is updated annually.

• **America's New Foundations 1993**. Gale Research, 7th edition. Many new foundations are emerging every year and ANF helps fund-raisers find them. The 7th edition identifies, describes, and provides current contact information on more than 3,400 private, corporate, and community foundations created since 1987—including 250 funding organizations new to the 1993 edition.

These newly established foundations—with assets or annual giving of $100,000 or more—offer unique opportunities, as smaller foundations with brief giving histories are often overlooked. The funding organizations profiled here have combined assets of at least $4.4 billion—and total giving of more than $382 million. ANF provides a constant flow of new and changing information.

• **Charitable Organizations of the U.S.** Gale Research, 2nd edition, edited by Doris Morris Maxfield. Nearly 800 entries describe groups active in soliciting funds from the American public—their history and purpose, the nature and extent of their activities, their leadership, spokespersons, and sponsors.

Of special interest is this volume's detailed coverage of each charity's fund-raising activities and expenses. Profiles include data on sources of income; expenses for administration, fund-raising, and program payout based on total income. Geographic Location, Keyword, Subject, and Personal Name Indexes.

→ All these books— Corporate 500, Taft's, all of them— are useful not just for those in the not- for-profit sector, but for people who want to get a "fresh angle" on companies in their target area. If you want to understand what really drives a company— its values, its Board of Directors, its vision, its "behind the scenes" stuff—take a look at to whom they give money, or even *whether* they give money to anyone.

This kind of knowledge will give you an added insight and valuable understanding. And of course, very few people think to do it.

• **Corporate 500**. Gale Research, 11th edition. A convenient source of factual information on the funding programs of the 580 American corporations with the most active programs. Provides a clear picture of each corporation, including address, phone number, contact person, eligibility, number of grants made, application process, sample grants that tell who got them, why and how much, and other pertinent information. Each part of the main entry is separately indexed for quick data retrieval. Indexes.

• **Corporate and Foundation Grants**. Gale Research, 1st edition. Comprehensive guide to more than 95,000 recently awarded grants from private foundations, corporate foundations, and corporate direct-giving programs. Includes grants from hard-to-identify corporate direct givers. Awards are arranged by recipient's actual location. Provides access to grantmakers with a demonstrated history of activity in a particular geographic or interest area.

Volume One, Grants by Category, lists recipients by eight major subject areas and by the state and city in which they are located. Volume Two, Guide to Funding Organizations, lists more than 5,500 corporate and private grantmakers, and includes application procedures, deadlines, and restrictions for the programs listed. In addition, grant recipients are indexed alphabetically by name, and funding organizations are indexed alphabetically by recipient type and by grant recipient location.

• **Taft's Corporate Giving Directory 1993**. Gale Research, 14th edition. A classic reference that identifies 607 companies that collectively donate $2.75 billion in cash and non-monetary support annually—more than 50 percent of all corporate giving. Provides up-to-date contact names, deadlines, total assets, average grant size, and names of recent front recipients. The new edition profiles 35 corporate givers never before featured.

Approximately 60 percent of the profiles in this edition cover difficult-to-find corporate-giving programs—information not available from the IRS, corporate annual reports, or similar directories. Also provides practical insights—biographical data on decision makers, analyses of priorities, corporate philosophy, etc.

• **Corporate Giving Yellow Pages 1993**. Gale Research, 8th edition. An easy-to-use guide to the people to contact at the leading corporate-giving programs and corporate foundations in America. More than 3,900 listings that provide contact name, title, address, and phone number. The directory provides the most current contract data available.

→ International giving.

• **Taft's Directory of International Corporate Giving in America and Abroad 1993**. Gale Research, 4th edition. In this age of global markets, a great many of the world's most powerful multinational corporations have begun to set up international philanthropies. Profiles more than 450 companies that give in the U.S. and overseas.

Section 1 provides fund-raisers with the most current information available on the funding activities in the U.S. of 350 companies; Section 2 provides up-to-date information on international funding activities of 105 U.S.-head-quartered companies.

This is the only directory on U.S. companies that give internationally and the only one that profiles foreign multinationals giving in the United States. More than 75 percent of the entries profiled maintain direct giving programs, providing information not available from public records. All profiles have been updated since the last edition—and 30 new profiles have been added. Multiple indexes allow you to uncover networks and connections between companies, countries, and philanthropic interests.

➜ Job hunters, career changers, and career counselors, take note of this surprising statistic: as of 1987, employment in the nonprofit sector totaled 12,449,000—almost 10 percent of total U.S. employment.

• **Finding a Job in the Nonprofit Sector**. Gale Research, 1st edition. A combined career advisory guide and employment directory, this volume helps experienced nonprofit professionals as well as newcomers to the nonprofit field assess their potential and find their niche within this vast and potentially lucrative job market. In addition, career counselors, librarians, recruiters and others seeking information on employment opportunities in the "third sector" would be wise to tap into this useful publication.

Finding a Job in the Nonprofit Sector first presents two insightful essays on job hunting, an analysis of employment trends in the sector, and detailed listing of nonprofit employers. The essays, "Forty-Two Action Steps for Seeking NPO Jobs" and "What If? Approaching NPOs from Where Your Are," give job seekers tips on search strategy, interview preparations, skills inventory, and more. An additional feature, "The Nonprofit Sector: An Overview of Employment Trends," summarizes facts from recent annual National Nonprofit Wage and Benefit Surveys published by the Technical Assistance Center in Denver.

The guide also lists nearly 5,000 nonprofit organizations from across America, all with estimated annual incomes of more than $10 million. Approximately 1,000 full descriptive profiles are provided.

➜ If you live in New York City, use the Center as well as their directory. It is dedicated to the not-for-profit industry. If you don't live in the city, call them and ask for help. The people are terrific and incredibly knowledgeable.

• **The Foundation Directory**. Foundation Center, 11th edition, edited by Loren Renz and Stan Olson. Lists foundations alphabetically by state. Reports for each foundation its address, telephone number, purpose, types of projects funded, financial data, application information, whom to write, and the names of officers and trustees. Foundations are indexed by subject area of giving, geographical location, type of support awarded, and alphabetically. Specifies the geographical scope of a foundation's activities.

• **National Directory of Nonprofit Organizations 1993**. Gale Research, 4th edition. Provides the annual income figures, names, addresses, and phone numbers of more than 256,000 organizations—175,000 of which have incomes in excess of $100,000. An indispensable aid to professionals who search in the nonprofit sector. Volume 1 (in two parts) lists organizations with annual revenues of $100,000 or more. Volume 2 covers organizations with annual reviews between $25,000 and $99,999.

In addition, two step-saving indexes—Geographic/Income and Activity-allow users to access organizations by the state and the ZIP codes in which they are located, and by their principal areas of activity.

NEW!!
Inside stories on managing image under siege. ➜

Here is another example of creative use of research tools. Don't just use this book if you are in advertising! It is like a window into major faux pas that companies have had to handle. You learn a lot by seeing how firms have dealt with problems and/or public perceptions of those problems. This is a <u>fantastic</u> book. ➜

M. Public Relations

• **Crisis Response, Visible Ink Press, 1st edition. 25 chapters written by media professionals who handled crises such as Love Canal or the Perrier recall. Summaries provided of the crisis and understanding of each incident.**

• **O'Dwyer's Directory of Public Relations Firms**. J.R. O'Dwyer Co. Found here are directory entries of over 1,900 U.S. and Canadian public relations firms, listed alphabetically, including their overseas offices, clients, and billings. Indexed by firm specialty, client and geography, including a list of the top 50 public relations firms.

• **Public Relations Career Directory**. Gale Research, 5th edition, Bradley J. Morgan, editor. In this resource, the pros offer advice to you on international public relations, the differences in beginning your career at a large vs. a small PR firm, opportunities in corporate communications, community affairs, media relations, and public relations for associations, financial and sports organizations.

• **The PR News Casebook**. Gale Research, 1st edition, edited by David Bianco. From the pages of *PR News*—the world's most widely read public relations weekly—comes this collection of 1,000 case studies covering major PR campaigns and events from the publication's nearly 50-year history. Based on personal interviews conducted by *PR News* founder and former publisher Ms. Denny Griswold, each case study analyzes how the most important businesses, government agencies, and other organizations from around

We're a society that's not about perfection, but about rectifying mistakes.
We're about second chances.
Harry Edwards, in "Hardline," *Detroit Free Press*, May 1988

the world have handled issues such as: boycotts, downsizing, industrial achievements, minority relations, new product introductions, plant closings, product tampering, stockholder relations, and many others.

Each one-page entry begins with a brief overview of the background leading up to the campaign, then deals with the company's planning for the event, reaction to it, and the methods they used to respond to it. The analysis includes a review of how effective the company was (or was not) in handling the event.

N. Publishing

• **Book Publishing Career Directory.** Gale Research, 5th edition, Bradley J. Morgan, editor. Offers insider's advice and job leads. Specific areas of coverage include working for a university press, independent publishing, religious publishing, book clubs, electronic publishing, sales and marketing, book publicity, and trade publishing.

• **Magazines Career Directory.** Gale Research, 5th edition, Bradley J. Morgan, editor. Here you will find essays discussing some of this industry's many varied career paths: art, editorial, sales, and business management functions at consumer publications. Also includes company listings and career resources, associations, the business press, and much more.

➔ NEW!!   • National Directory of Catalogs 1995, Oxbridge Communications. Organizes and describes over 7,000 catalogs and their producers, products, printers, circulation lists, and list managers. Organized by product within 78 different areas.

➔ NEW!!   • **National Directory of Magazines 1995**, Oxbridge Communications. Information on 20,000 North American magazines. Entries include details on staffing, advertising, and production details.

➔ NEW!!   • National Directory of Mailing Lists 1995, Oxbridge Communications. Organizes & describes magazines, journals, newsletters, catalogues, directories, newspapers, tabloids, looseleafs, bulletins, indices, and all other periodically produced publications-over 15,000 lists. Entries are arranged within specific subject categories.

• **Newspapers Career Directory.** Gale Research, 4th edition, Bradley J. Morgan, editor. Newspaper professionals discuss their specialties including classified and retail advertising sales, national account sales, art and graphics, circulation, starting out as a reporter, breaking into editorial at a large paper, newspaper research, photo-journalism, internships, and openings for minorities.

• **Publishers Directory 1993.** Gale Research, 13th edition, Linda S. Hubbard, editor. Information on nearly 18,000 currently active U.S. and Canadian book publishers, and 600 distributors, wholesalers, and jobbers. Makes it easy for you to research or contact virtually all the publishing firms listed in *Literary Market Place* as well as the independent and hard-to-find firms.

In one soft-cover volume, Publishers Directory 1993 gives you such key facts on each publisher as: complete contact information, founding date, ISBN, discounts and returns policies, description of subject specialties, imprints, a breakdown of sales to libraries, bookstores, non-book retail outlets, and individuals, a list of representative titles, and more. Publishers, Subject, and Geographic Indexes.

O. Sales and Marketing

➔ Here they are: International market research companies.   • **The GreenBook: International Directory of Marketing Research Companies and Services.** American Marketing Association. Names firms in 53 countries that provide market research services. Lists address, telephone number, names of principal officers, and a description of services offered. Indexed by service, geographically, and alphabetically, including advertising research, concept development and testing, consumer research, interviewing service, name development, package development, and product testing.

• **Marketing and Sales Career Directory.** Gale Research, 4th edition, Bradley J. Morgan, editor. Tells effective ways to reach customers and consumers. Specific areas discussed include direct sales, industrial sales, business-to-business marketing, consulting, services marketing, retail marketing, database marketing, and market research.

Change does not roll in on the wheels of inevitability, but comes through continuous struggle.
And so we must straighten our backs and work for our freedom.
A man can't ride you unless your back is bent.
Martin Luther King Jr., "The Death of Evil upon the Seashore,"
sermon given at the Cathedral of St. John the Divine, New York City, May 17, 1956

P. Services

➜ Everyone says they want to be a consultant—check it out with the pros.

• **Consultants and Consulting Organizations Directory 1993.** Gale Research, 13th edition, edited by Janice McLean. Here you can find important details, like services offered, typical clients, full contact information, date founded, principals, and more.

The nearly 18,000 firms and individuals listed in the new edition are arranged alphabetically under 14 general fields of consulting activity ranging from Agriculture to Marketing. Over 400 specialties are represented including finance, computers, fund-raising, job hunting, and more. Location, Specialization, Personal Name, and Company Name Indexes enable users to pinpoint the best source for expert advice. Consultants and Consulting Organizations Directory is available on-line.

• **Dun's Directory of Service Companies.** Dun's Marketing Services. Annual. Profiles of some 50,000 companies, both public and private, deriving their primary revenue from a service activity and employing 50 or more people. Very little overlap exists between this and other titles. Indexing by geography and by industry.

Q. Small / Private Business

➜ Here's a tool for those hard to research smaller companies where opportunities abound.

• **Small Business Sourcebook.** Gale Research, 6th edition, edited by Carol A. Schwartz. Look to SBS to find 30 new small business profiles as well as broader coverage of audiovisual media; expanded listings of newsletters; increased coverage of Canadian resources.

SBS's convenient arrangement and special features, such as an appendix of Standard Industrial Classification (SIC) codes used to profile small businesses, as well as a glossary of small business terms, make locating information easy.

• **MacMillan Directory of Leading Private Companies.** Lists 12,500 companies and wholly-owned subsidiaries with sales of $10,000,000.

• **Over the Counter 1,000 Yellow Book.** Has the leading growth companies quoted on NASDAQ; comprehensive directory introducing leading, dynamic, younger growth companies in the U.S. Gives address, phone, titles of 20,000 executives who manage these smaller companies on the cutting edge of innovation.

• **The Top 1,500 Private Companies.** Listing with brief information and ranking by sales, products, employees, and number of locations.

• **Small Business Administration.**

• **Small Business Development Corporations.**
• **Chambers of Commerce.**

Following are lists from magazines. Updated annually.
• **Business Week 100 Best Small Companies.**

• **Business Week Top 1,000.**

• **Forbes 200 Best Small Companies in America.**

• **Forbes 400 Largest Private Companies in the United States.**

NEW!! Find the information you seek on that elusive segment of industry in the private arena. ➜

• **Inc. Magazine's 500 America's Fastest Growing Private Companies.**

• **Inc. Magazine's 100 Fastest Growing Small Public Companies.**

• **Ward's Private Company Profiles,** Gale Research. Articles from over 150 sources including investment reports and company brochures about this significant and often elusive segment of the American economy. Find big companies, recognized names, as well as cutting edge firms and small aggressive companies.

➜ NEW!! For people investigating starting their own business, this is a terrific resource.

• **Small Business Profiles,** Gale Research, Vol.1. A guide to top opportunities for Entrepreneurs. Covers start up business issues and opportunities. Issues include marketing, advertising, licensing and insurance, computer systems and programs, costs and profits, financing, location, lay-out, staffing, and more.

Passion costs me too much to bestow it on every trifle.
Thomas Adams

R. Special Events / Trade Shows

➜ I talk to so many people who are interested in this field, but have no idea how to find out names of possible companies.

• **Trade Shows and Professional Exhibits Directory**. Gale Research, 2nd edition, edited by Robert J. Elster. A directory of exhibitions, trade shows, conventions, and other types of meetings designed to foster direct sales/trade contacts. Lists these meetings by general subject categories. Each entry includes such information as the name, address, and telephone number of the sponsor; name of the exhibits manager; co-sponsors; expected attendance; targeted participants; charges to exhibitors; and dates and locations of the meetings.

• **Trade Shows Worldwide 1995**. Gale Research, 7th edition, edited by Valerie J. Webster. TSW provides profiles of 5,796 trade shows—2,400 more than competing directories and over 700 more than the previous edition. TSW lists more than 4,600 trade show organizers and sponsors throughout the world and provides complete contact information and events descriptions.

This new edition covers 723 convention centers worldwide and provides listings of 431 exhibit builders, transportation firms, and other industry suppliers. Information about professional associations, consultants, and published sources of industry information is also included in this essential reference source.

S. Transportation

• **Directory of Consultants**. National Association of Regulatory Utility Commissioners. Annual. Lists 190 consultants and consulting firms active in utility and transportation industries. Includes firm or individual name, address, and phone; names of regulatory agencies by which engaged in the past; purpose and dates of past engagements; areas of specialization; qualifications and experience.

➜ Here's a guide to trends, forecasts, and histories of companies in the transportation industry. Something for everyone!

• **Moody's Transportation Manual**. Moody's Investors Service. One of the eight Moody's Manuals, it profiles companies in the transportation industry. These include railroads, airlines, trucking, steamships, automobile/truck leasing and rental companies, oil pipelines, and bridge companies. The level of coverage for each company depends on the coverage purchased.

The information usually includes corporate history, company business activities, annual report to stockholders, address and telephone number, names of officers and directors, consolidated income account, consolidated balance sheet, notes to financial statements, structure of long-term debt and bond ratings, and other information. For some of the major companies, a map of their routes is displayed. A "Special Features" section presents summary statistics of the transportation industry.

T. Travel and Hospitality

• **Travel and Hospitality Career Directory**. Gale Research, 2nd edition, Bradley J. Morgan, editor. Find out about the wide variety of career options this industry has to offer. Essays discuss breaking into the hotel and motel industry, working for a local travel and tourism board, becoming a travel agent, getting started in car rental, convention and meeting planning, working for an airline, and more.

• **Financial Times International Yearbook: World Hotel Directory 1993**. Gale Research, 18th edition. Directory of over 3,200 hotels in 140 countries around the world. Lists hotels by geographic region, allowing users to quickly identify business in an easy-to-use country-by-country format.

Entries include the hotel address; telephone, fax, and telex number; reservation system; style; location; and manager's name. Information on rooms, fees, service, and facilities is also available. Additional sections list hotel incentive programs, foreign currency exchange rates, major airports worldwide, and airlines.

U. Real Estate

• **The Directory of Real Estate Investors**. National Register Publishing Company. An international directory of brokers, investors, and developers of commercial property who have at least $1 million of equity funds to invest. Reports the kind of income-producing properties in which they are interested and the geographic region(s) of their preference. Each company is also described by reporting the address, telephone number, names of contact persons, size of portfolio, investment structure, total funds available, and other relevant information.

As a splendid palace deserted by its inmates looks like a ruin, so does a man
without character, all his material belongings notwithstanding.
Mohandas Gandhi

V. Education

• **The World of Learning.** An international directory of educational, cultural, and scientific institutions with contact information of over 150,000 people—chief personnel involved in higher education worldwide. Also provides information on over 400 international organizations.

5. Information on Executives and Management

• **Experts Contact Directory.** Gale Research, edited by Nora Paul. This directory is a compilation of contact information for 25,000 academics in the U.S. who are recognized authorities in their fields. This comprehensive and timely reference is designed to help users locate speakers, expert witnesses, network contacts, interview subjects, and others.

➜ This is simply a brilliant and novel approach to networking and asking true experts about their field. Even if you don't talk to them, knowing who they are is in itself pretty impressive knowledge.

Arranged by subject with names of experts listed alphabetically under appropriate subheadings, each entry contains the expert's name, title, position, university, specialty, and phone number(s). Geographic, University Name, and Personal Name Indexes.

• **How to Find Information About Executives.** Washington Researchers Publishing. A guide to how and where to find information about executives in the business community. Explains procedures and places. Targets may be the competitor's business manager, plant manager, or others. Useful for locating information about prospective customers or clients, prospective employees, suppliers, the CEO of a company in which an investment is being considered, and other persons.

The sources of information are governmental agencies, the Securities and Exchange Commission, courts, trade and professional associations, labor unions, publications, databases, and other references. Also explains how to conduct telephone interviews when seeking information about people.

• **International Who's Who.** Europa Publications Ltd. Biographical dictionary profiles notable persons from around the world and in most areas of endeavor. Biographical sketches include the biographee's nationality, birth date, education, names of parents, marriage, career information, awards, publications, office address, home address, telephone number (home and/or office), and other biographical data.

• **Medical Sciences International Who's Who.** Gale Research, 5th edition. Turn to this global resource when you need to get in touch with medical scientists and researchers from around the world. Detailed professional biographies are provided for approximately 8,000 senior biomedical scientists and their researchers in over 90 countries worldwide. All subject areas are covered, including biochemistry; dental sciences; immunology and transplantation; clinical medicine; molecular biology; neoplasia; pharmacology and therapeutics; psychiatry; clinical psychology; and surgery and anesthesia. Entries include full contact data, education, career information, memberships, publications, and more. Fully indexed.

• **Taft's Owners and Officers of Private Companies 1993.** Gale Research, 3rd edition. An annually updated source of hard-to find data on the people who form the backbone of American business.

Volume 1 provides entries on more than 105,000 owners and officers of private American companies with annual sales over $5 million. Volume 2 contains Personal Name, Company Name, Standard Industrial Classification (SIC) and Geographic Indexes.

• **Reference Book of Corporate Managements.** Dun's Marketing Services. Annual. Biographical data and work history for tens of thousands of people who are officers and directors of more than 12,000 companies.

➜ If you want to be in corporate America, it surely would be important to know who owns what. Talk about seeing the connections and links...

• **Who Owns Corporate America 1993.** Gale Research, 1st edition. WOCA offers comprehensive listings of "insider" stockholders-the officers, directors and 10 percent principal stockholders who own securities registered with the U.S. Securities and Exchange Commission (SEC). WOCA lists approximately 75,600 stockholders by last name—along with detailed information on the list's stock ownership—thus facilitating biographical research.

WOCA provides a cost-effective, easy-to-use alternative to the expense of on-line services. Annual updating will ensure that you get the latest information on wealthy stockholders.

Entries in WOCA include the following: insider's name; name of the security/issuing company; stock symbol; number of shares held by the listee; date of last transaction within the filing period; class of "type" of security held; ownership; and market value in dollars of the insider's holdings.

• **Who's Who in Business and Industry in the UK 1991.** Gale Research, 1st edition, edited by Juliet Margetts. Provides biographies of the 10,000 most important people in British industry, including managers, executives and directors of Britain's top 1,000 companies as well as those involved in distribution, advertising, consulting, civil service, trade associations, unions, journalism, and academic pursuits.

Each entry includes details on the entrant's responsibilities, career, education and recreations, as well as biographical facts on birth, marriage nationality, etc. The book concludes with three indexes: the Company Index is a directory unto itself, providing address and telephone information as well as names of top managers; the Business Sector Index arranges company names by 80 subject categories; and the Geographic Index lists companies by nearly 100 areas, from Aberdeen to York.

• **Who's Who in Finance and Industry.** Marquis Who's Who/Macmillan Directory Division. Biographical dictionary of notable persons in finance and industry. Biographies are of corporate executives and people from professional and trade associations, business research, stock exchanges, labor unions, government agencies, and other organizations. The biographical profiles include occupation, home and business addresses, date and place of birth, parents' names, marriage data, education, professional certifications and memberships, avocations, and other descriptive information.

➜ *Pretty interesting reading!*

• **Taft's Who's Wealthy in America 1993.** Gale Research, 3rd edition. Gives you access to more than 100,000 of America's most prosperous people; listings are based solely on wealth. Each new edition contains information on hundreds of new prospects, plus new information on previous listees—such as political contributions made in the 1992 elections. A treasure chest of up-to-date, valuable prospect information, designed to put you in touch with new donors—America's top-tier wealth holders and consumers. You'll find all the contact information, plus critical data on political contributions, insider stock holdings, education, and lifestyle indicators (Rolls Royce owner, art collector, etc.). Plus, additional references will lead you to further information.

• **Who's Who in Venture Capital.** John Wiley & Sons. A directory of venture capitalists that reports their address, telephone number, investment interests, names of principals with their educational and business experience, and size of the investment fund along with the average amount per investment. Includes venture capitalists in the U.S., U.K., and Canada. Discusses the criteria often used by venture capitalists when contemplating an investment decision.

• **Standard & Poor's Register of Corporations, Directors and Executives.** Directors and Executives volume. Annual. An alphabetical list of over 70,000 individuals serving as officers, directors, trustees, partners, etc. Provides principal business affiliations with business addresses, residence addresses, and where available, year and place of birth, and college.

SECTION TWO: CD-ROM Databases

General Reference Information / General Financial Information

• **Gale Globalaccess: Associations.** Gale Research. Provides information from the *Encyclopedia of Associations: National Organizations of the U.S.; Encyclopedia of Associations: Regional, State and Local Organizations; Encyclopedia of Associations: International Organizations;* and the *Encyclopedia of Associations: Association Periodicals Database* on non-profit membership organizations of international, U.S., state, regional, or local interest. Includes professional societies, labor unions, cultural and religious organizations, etc. For each organization the record includes the name, acronym, address, telephone number, and further information on the organization. Corresponds in part to the on-line version. **Coverage:** Updated biannually.

Both Globalaccess and the Encyclopedia of Associations are simply unparalleled when you are browsing for industry ideas.

• **Encyclopedia of Associations.** Gale Research. Thirteen print volumes on one disk. The same 22,000 Associations found in print version.

• **Thomas Register of American Manufacturers;** Directory of products and manufacturers in the U.S. and Canada. Covers more than 152,000 public and private companies. Current year. Updated semi-annually.

*The price one pays for pursuing any profession or calling is
an intimate knowledge of its ugly side.*
James Baldwin, *Nobody Knows My Name*

➔ If you want to
check annual reports
& don't have time to
send away for
them...

• **Corporate Text.** Provides copies of annual reports for companies traded on the NYSE, AMEX, NASDAQ, and OTC. **Coverage:** Current. Updated monthly.

• **Dun's Million Dollar Disc.** Provides a wide range of marketing information, including data on more than 180,000 firms with a net worth of more than $500,000 and information on approximately 500,000 decision makers at these firms. **Coverage:** Current. Updated quarterly.

• **LaserDisclosure.** A full text database of exact reproductions of original SEC filings, including graphs and photographs, from more than 6,000 companies traded on the NASDAQ, OTC, AMEX, and NYSE. **Coverage:** Current. Updated weekly.

• **Standard & Poor's Corporations.** Contains financial data for public and private companies and biographical data on their executives. **Coverage:** Current year. Updated bimonthly.

• **Statistical Masterfile.** Indexes citations and provides abstracts to statistical publications published in the United States and worldwide. Contains the *American Statistical Index,* indexing statistical information published by more than 500 U.S. federal agencies; *Statistical Reference Index* covering statistical information from more than 1,000 associations, businesses, state governments, universities, and research centers; and the *Index to International Statistics,* covering 95 major intergovernmental organizations since 1983. **Coverage:** 1984 to the present. Updated quarterly.

• **General Business File Database.** A database covering topics in business. Includes corporate profiles of public and private companies, industry reports, investment analysis reports, and company rankings. Depending on the topic, citations, abstracts, or full-text is available. **Coverage:** Most recent four years. Updated monthly.

• **Predicasts F&S Plus Text** (U.S. and Abroad). Contains facts and figures about companies, products, markets, and applied technology in all manufacturing and service industries worldwide. Contains one-and-two line summaries, abstracts from PROMT *(Predicasts Overview of Markets and Technology)* and full text articles when available. **Coverage:** Current year. Updated monthly.

• **Social Sciences Citation Index.** Contains citations to articles from 1,400 international social science journals, as well as social sciences articles from journals in the natural, physical, and biomedical sciences. These citations include all works cited in the articles. Searches by citation can be performed to determine when a work has been cited. **Coverage:** 1980 to the present. Updated quarterly.

• **Social Sciences Index.** Indexes over 300 English-language periodicals published worldwide in all areas of the social sciences, including anthropology, economics, international relations, political science, and women's studies. **Coverage:** February 1980 to the present. Updated quarterly.

Newspaper Articles and Abstracts
• **British Newspaper Index on CD-ROM.** Indexes major British newspapers: *The Times, Sunday Times, Financial Times, Independent, Independent on Sunday, Times Literary Supplement, Times Higher Education Supplement,* and *Times Educational Supplement.* **Coverage:** 1990 to the present. Updated quarterly.

➔ I use this all the
time.

• **National Newspaper Index.** Offers combined, in-depth indexing of five major newspapers: *The New York Times, The Wall Street Journal, Christian Science Monitor, Washington Post,* and *The Los Angeles Times.* **Coverage:** Most recent four years. Updated monthly.

• **The New York Times.** Contains the full text of *The New York Times.* **Coverage:** 1991 to the present. Updated monthly.

• **Newspaper Abstracts OnDisc:** Provides comprehensive indexing of 20 major newspapers, including *The New York Times, The Boston Globe, The Los Angeles Times,* and *The Chicago Tribune.* Brief article abstracts are included for most of the newspapers. **Coverage:** 1985 to the present. Updated quarterly.

• **The Wall Street Journal.** Full text of *The Wall Street Journal.* **Coverage:** One year. Updated monthly.

Magazines, Trade Journals, and Abstracts

• **Periodical Abstracts OnDisc** - Offers comprehensive indexing, with short abstracts, of over 950 general-interest periodicals from the United States, Canada, and the United Kingdom. **Coverage:** 1986 to the present. Updated bimonthly.

• **Readers' Guide to Periodical Literature.** An index to over 190 of the most popular general-interest periodicals published in the United States and Canada. Corresponds to the printed and on-line indexes of the same title. **Coverage:** 1983 to the present. Updated quarterly.

➡ Outstanding coverage, particularly for international publications.

• **Ulrich's Plus.** Contains citations to approximately 145,000 international publications (such as magazines, journals, annuals, and irregular publications, but not daily newspapers) well as over 25,000 publications discontinued since 1979. Corresponds to the printed and on-line versions of the same title. **Coverage:** 1979 to the present. Updated quarterly.

• **PAIS.** Public Affairs Information Service is an index to more than 900 periodicals in addition to books, directories, reports, and government documents. Coverage is of all aspects of public affairs including business, government, economic and social issues, with an emphasis on statistical and factual information. Indexes material in English, French, German, Italian, Portuguese, and Spanish. Corresponds to the printed and on-line indexes of the same title. **Coverage:** 1972 to the present. Updated quarterly.

• **Business Periodicals Index.** An index to 304 of the most important English-language business periodicals covering all areas including management, marketing, economics, transportation, and specific industries. **Coverage:** 1984 to the present. Updated monthly

➡ ABI/Inform:
I don't feel prepared until I have accessed this database. A word of warning: the synopses are only as good as the person who writes them: sometimes the author does not really capture the true nature of the article.
BPO is actually more powerful than ABI, but it is not as commonly accessible.

• **ABI/Inform.** Indexes and abstracts 800 business and management journals, appearing worldwide, covering a wide variety of topics including management, accounting, finance, economics, advertising, labor relations, and real estate. **Coverage:** 1987 to the present. Updated monthly.

• **Business Dateline.** Contains the full text of articles appearing in more than 180 U.S. and Canadian regional business publications. Covers information on companies of regional as well as national importance. **Coverage:** 1990 to the present. Updated monthly.

• **Newspaper Abstracts OnDisc.** Provides comprehensive indexing of 20 major newspapers, including *The New York Times, The Boston Globe, The Los Angeles Times,* and *The Chicago Tribune.* Brief article abstracts are included for most of the newspapers. **Coverage:** 1985 to the present. Updated quarterly.

• **Business Periodicals OnDisc.** BPO combines the ABI/Inform database of article references and abstracts of more than 800 business and management periodicals with the ability to view or print the complete text from many of the periodicals. **Coverage:** 1987 to the present. Updated monthly.

• **Ethnic Newswatch CD-ROM.** Ethnic newspapers and magazines in full text, access in English and Spanish. **Coverage:** 1991 to the present. Updated quarterly.

Science, Engineering, and Technology

• **Applied Science and Technology Index.** An index to articles in 390 of the key English-language periodicals in applied sciences and technology. Covers engineering, computer technology, mathematics, physics, energy-related topics, chemistry, and data processing. Corresponds to the printed index of the same title. **Coverage:** 1983 to the present. Updated monthly.

• **Compendex.** An index to citations from journal articles, conference papers, and other literature in the field of engineering. Corresponds to the on-line COMPENDEX and *Engineering Index* providing full bibliographic citations and abstracts encompassing all fields of engineering. **Coverage:** 1985 to the present. Updated quarterly.

• **Computer Select.** Information on computers and software. Includes articles or abstracts from over 150 journals, 70,000 hardware, software, and communication product specs, information on 12,000 companies in the field, and definitions of 9,000 terms. **Coverage:** 1989 to the present. Updated monthly.

• **General Science Index.** Indexes articles in 109 English-language science periodicals of general interest. Includes astronomy, biology, botany, chemistry, earth sciences, food and nutrition, genetics, mathematics, physics, and zoology. **Coverage:** 1984 to the present. Updated monthly.

• **INSPEC.** A citation index with abstracts to periodicals in technical literature dealing with physics, electrical engineering, telecommunications, computers, and information technology. **Coverage:** 1989 to the present. Updated quarterly.

• **Mathsci Disc.** Indexes and abstracts literature on mathematics, statistics, and computer science, and their application in several fields. Corresponds to the printed *Mathematical Reviews* and *Current Mathematical Publications.* **Coverage:** 1981 to the present. Updated semi-annually.

• **Science Citation Index.** Contains citations to the literature of science, technology, medicine, and related disciplines from 3,300 science journals worldwide, as well as science articles from journals in the social sciences. These citations include all works cited in the articles. Searches by citation can be performed to determine when a work has been cited. **Coverage:** 1980 to the present. Updated quarterly.

• **NTIS (National Technical Information Service Documents).** Contains bibliographic citations and abstracts to unrestricted technical reports of both U.S. government and non-U.S. government sponsored research. Compiled from the *Government Reports Announcements and Index.* Includes a wide range of topics in the physical, natural, and social sciences. Includes information on energy from the U.S. Department of Energy. **Coverage:** 1990 to the present. Updated quarterly.

• **ICP Software Directory.** A directory of descriptions of more than 15,000 publicly available business applications software from over 5,000 vendors for microcomputers, minicomputers, and mainframes. Includes proprietary software products and vendor contact information. Current. Updated three times a year.

Health Care (also check Science, Engineering, and Technology)
• **Medlinc.** Indexes the world's medical periodical literature in biomedicine, dentistry, nursing, and related topics. Abstracts are provided for some entries. Includes MESH (Medical Subject Headings). **Coverage:** 1966 to the present. Updated annually.

• **CD Plus/Health.** A bibliographic index to non-clinical aspects of health-care delivery, such as administration and planning of health-care facilities, health insurance, personnel, HMO's, and related topics. Data are supplied from the National Library of Medicine, the American Hospital Association, and the printed Hospital Literature Index. **Coverage:** 1982 to the present. Quarterly.

Government and Law
• **CIS—Congressional Masterfile.** Provides citations and abstracts of publications issued by the U.S. Senate, House, and joint committees and subcommittees. Includes bills, reports, debates, hearings, and committee prints covering a wide range of topics and interests. **Coverage:** 1970 to the present. Quarterly.

• **GPO Monthly Catalog.** Indexes the publications of the Government Printing Office since 1976, providing full bibliographic descriptions of federal government documents. Based on the printed *Monthly Catalog,* coverage is of a wide range of media and topics. **Coverage:** 1976 to the present. Monthly.

• **Legaltrac.** Index to four areas of law: subjects, titles and authors, cases, and statutes, interfiled in a single alphabetical listing. The index is sponsored by American Association of Law Libraries. **Coverage:** 1980 to the present. Updated monthly.

Academia
• **Education Index.** Contains citations to articles, interviews, selected editorials, letters to the editor, and reviews of books, educational films, and software from 350 English-language periodicals, monographs, and yearbooks in the field of education. Covers school administration, pre-school, elementary, secondary, higher and adult education, and teaching methods. Covers a wide variety of individual curriculum areas. **Coverage:** June 1983 to the present. Updated quarterly.

I found that values, for each person, were numerous. Therefore, I proposed to write my value names and to annex to each a short precept—which fully expressed the extent I gave to each meaning. I then arranged them in such a way as to facilitate acquisition of these virtues.

Benjamin Franklin

• **ERIC**. An index to the literature of education, ERIC includes Resources in Education and the Current Index to Journals in Education, indexing over 775 journals. Provides bibliographic citations and abstracts. **Coverage:** 1966 to the present. Updated quarterly.

• **Petersen's College Database.** Full-text database containing profiles of all accredited degree-granting colleges and universities in the U.S. and Canada. **Coverage:** Most recent four years. Updated monthly.

Services

• **Training and Development Organization Directory.** Gale Research, 5th edition, Janice McLean, editor. Guide to companies that produce workshops, seminars, videos, and other training programs. Describes over 10,000 such programs and includes complete contact information for each company. This on-line service allows searches with any combination of the following fields: course emphasis, subject classification, organization, state/province, city, zip code, area code, and principal executives and title. Available through HRIN database.

➜ This directory contains information on a host of topics, not just consulting: e.g., staffing, health care, high technology.

• **Consultants and Consulting Organizations Directory.** Profiles consulting firms in more than 400 different fields and describes over 17,000 companies and their services. Subject areas include employee assistance programs, strategies for corporate growth, installation of computer equipment. Each entry contains: name, address, phone, fax, toll-free numbers, principal executives, staff size, industries served, founding date, branch offices, seminars and workshops, special services, publications, and videos. Database is reloaded every year and supplemented every six months.

Miscellaneous Creative: Music, Art, Architecture, Graphics, and Religion

• **Religion Indexes.** Contains citations to articles, books, theses, and book reviews on all aspects of religion and theology. Updated quarterly.

• **Art Index.** Indexes articles in over 200 domestic and foreign periodicals, yearbooks, and museum publications that address important developments in art, art history, architecture, graphic art, and design. Also indexes reproductions of works of art. Corresponds to the printed and on-line indexes of the same title. **Coverage:** September 1984 to the present. Updated quarterly.

• **Muse.** An international database of over 300 journals and all significant literature on music history, theory, analysis, performance, instruments, voice, liturgy, acoustics, psychology, ethnomusicology, and related disciplines. Updated annually.

SECTION THREE: On-Line Databases

The real benefit to using on-line databases is the immediacy of the information. The downside is that they are often more difficult to access, and they cost money—both in computer to phone connect time, and in charges for the actual information. Most people can function more than adequately using CD-ROM databases that are typically updated quarterly. For that reason, I have included more of the former, and am limiting my listing for on-line services. Please be aware that this is only a sample of what is available. There are hundreds of on-line databases. I am also not including those databases that are available in CD-ROM versions. If you need a more complete listing, consult the Directory of On-Line Databases (in this bibliography).

Big Picture / Trends

➜ Access to the most current trade show sponsors and schedules.

• **Fairbase.** An international directory of planned and past conferences, conventions, exhibitions, expositions, trade fairs, trade shows, and other such meetings of interest to business and industry. Indicates date, location, and organizers of the meeting, and, sometimes, the number of visitors expected and the amount of space available for exhibitors.

• **Arthur D. Little Online.** Market research reports from Arthur D. Little on industries, products, and services. Most of the reports are in full text. Contains abstracts.

206

→ CIRR is like CIA access to corporate news.

- **Corporate and Industry Research Reports** (CIRR). JA Micropublishing. An index to intelligence reports on companies and industries. Some abstracts.

- **Econbase: Time Series and Forecasts.** WEFA Group. Time series of economic data in tables arranged by year, quarter, or month. Expenditures, production, sales, and wages in various industries; personal-consumption expenditures and personal income; consumer price indexes, interest rates, and stock-market indicators. Tables list only several recent years or extend back 20 or more years. Some include two years of forecast data.

→ Great information on trends in different industries

- **Industry Data Sources.** Information Access. 1979-present. An index to reports on financial, marketing, and statistical data for 65 industries. Typical data cover economic forecasts; industry profits, earnings, and growth; manufacturing-plant sites and closings; market-research reports; and market share. Abstracts. Includes address and telephone number of the producer of each report

General News/Trade/Business Articles

- **Business Wire.** Business Wire. The full text of press releases from corporations and other organizations.

→ Business Wire, Financial Times, and AP News are all up-to-the-moment and superb.

- **Financial Times Abstracts.** 1982-present. Financial Times Business Information. Indexes articles about companies that have appeared in the *Financial Times* newspaper. Abstracts. The whole text given for short articles. A special access point is product codes.

- **Associated Press News Highlights.** Associated Press. The Associated Press's hourly full-text news reports, including business topics. Dow Jones Industrial Average reported every half-hour.

→ Great information for those in the Midwest in particular, or for those doing a long-distance search with the Midwest as the target.

- **Chicago Tribune.** 1988-present. Chicago Tribune. The full text of news stories published in this newspaper, a major source of Midwest and national business news. Some statistical tables from the business section of the paper are not available in the database. A special access point is the ability to restrict a search to specific editions of the paper.

- **Management Contents.** 1974-present. Information Access. An index to articles in over 120 management periodicals. Emphasizes management topics in accounting, advertising, banking, finance, marketing, personnel, and general management. Contains abstracts.

→ This is where most database articles first appear. If up-to-dateness is critical to you & you can't find what you're looking for—check here.

- **Newsearch.** Information Access. Contains daily updates to other Information Access databases: COMPUTER DATABASE, LEGAL RESOURCE INDEX, MANAGEMENT CONTENTS, NATIONAL NEWSPAPER INDEX, NEWSWIRE ASAP, and TRADE & INDUSTRY INDEX . A very up-to-date index to newspapers, magazines, and other periodicals. References from *The New York Times* and *The Wall Street Journal* usually appear within 48 hours after publication.

- **Pts Newsletter Database.** 1988-present. Predicasts. The full text of articles appearing in over 170 business and industry newsletters. Emphasis is on industry analysis, new products and technologies, company activities, and government regulations and programs. Provides directory information about the newsletter's publisher plus subscription prices and frequencies.

→ Both Pts databases are great. Pts Promt can access both magazines <u>and</u> newspapers articles.

- **Pts Promt.** 1972-present. Predicasts. A major index to business articles from over 1,200 periodicals, as well as to information from annual reports, news releases, and other sources. Provides abstracts. Wide variety of topics, with an emphasis on product and company information. "PROMT" stands for Predicasts Overview of Markets and Technology.

- **UPI News.** 1983-present. United Press International. The full text of stories from this newswire. Stories appear in the database about two days after being on the newswire.

Engineering

- **Compendex*Plus.** 1969-present. Engineering Information. An index to engineering applications and research articles, books, papers, and reports. Contains abstracts.

- **Pts Aerospace/Defense Markets & Technology.** 1982-present. Predicasts. An index to articles about 75 aerospace and defense periodicals. Contains abstracts, some with statistical tables.

Finance Industry

➜ If you need financial articles 24 hours within their publication, check in here.

- **American Banker**. 1981-present. Published by American Banker-. Contains full text articles published in this financial newspaper. Online articles often appear within 24 hours after their print publication.
- **Finis: Financial Industry Information Service**. 1982-present. Published by the Bank Marketing Association. An index to articles from over 200 periodicals and to case studies gathered by the publisher. Emphasizes marketing articles on banks, thrift institutions, and financial services companies.

Financial Information about Companies

- **D & B—Dun's Financial Records Plus**. Published by Dun's Marketing Services. Directory and financial information on private and public companies. Data on assets, liabilities, profits, ratios, and sales for the given company and for its industry. Narrative on company history and operation.

➜ Disclosure is widely available, and quite outstanding. Also published for CD-ROM.

- **Disclosure**. Published by Disclosure. Financial data and directory information on over 12,000 public companies. Sources include 8K, 10K, 10Q, and 20F reports as well as annual reports. Extensive data for each company, such as annual and quarterly balance sheets; five-year financial summary; ratio analysis covering about 30 ratios; dividends; earnings; share figures; a listing of directors and officers; subsidiaries; narrative from president's letter and "management discussion"; address; telephone number.

General Company Information

- **Business Dateline**. 1985-present. Published by UMI/Data Courier. Full text of articles from over 180 regional business periodicals, at least 10 daily newspapers. Business activities, executives, products.

- **Corporate Affiliations**. Published by National Register Publishing. Provides a corporate family directory for a company, listing its parent company, distribution centers, divisions, plants, subsidiaries, and so forth. Directory information, including names of directors and officers. Brief financial information (net worth, liabilities, sales, and total assets) for parent companies. Covers private and public companies.

- **D & B—Million Dollar Directory**. Published by Dun's Marketing Services.. Directory information for private and public companies, including names of directors and officers. Some sales data.

- **Moody's Corporate News**—U.S. Published by Moody,'s Investors Service. News about public U.S. companies gathered from annual reports, news releases, newswires, and periodicals.

- **Moody's Corporate Profiles**. Published by Moody's Investors Service. Directory and financial information on thousands of public companies, including address, telephone number, balance-sheet data, and price/earnings ratio. Some companies have a brief narrative evaluation by Moody's.

➜ New product announcements are particularly important on a current basis.

- **Pts New Product Announcements**. 1985-present. Published by Predicasts. Announcements of new products in full-text news-release style. Directory-type information for the announcing companies.

- **Standard & Poor's Corporate Descriptions Online**. published by Standard & Poor's. Detailed directory, strategic business, and financial information on public companies. Covers balance-sheet data, bond descriptions, corporate-background narrative, names of officers and directors, stock data, and subsidiaries.

- **Standard & Poor's Register**—Corporate. Published By Standard & Poor's. Directory information on more than 40,000 private and public companies. Lists officers and directors. Narrative description of market territory, products, and services. Some sales data.

- **Thomas New Industrial Products**. Published by Thomas Online. For recently introduced products and technologies, provides name and telephone number of manufacturer, product specifications, trade names, model numbers, and SIC codes.

Advertising

- **Pts Marketing & Advertising Reference Service**. 1984-present. Predicasts. An index to articles on advertising from about 75 periodicals and other sources. Includes abstracts. Special access points include advertising slogans, agency spokespersons' names, CUSIP numbers, modified SIC codes.

Health Care
• **Health Industry Research Reports** (HIRR). JA Micropublishing. An index to intelligence reports on health-care companies and in-depth studies of the industry. Includes abstracts. Reports provided by investment and securities firms and by periodicals in the health profession.

• **Pni: Pharmaceutical News Index.** 1974-present. UMI/Data Courier. An index to more than 20 periodicals that cover pharmaceuticals, cosmetics, and medical devices. Includes news on acquisitions and mergers, drug approvals and recalls, research, and other health-related issues.

High Technology
• **Computer Asap.** 1983-present. Information Access. The full text of articles on computers, electronics, and telecommunications from over 130 business and technical periodicals. Covers hardware and software evaluations .

• **Computer Database.** 1983-present. Information Access. An index to articles on computers, electronics, and telecommunications from more than 130 business and technical periodicals. Contains abstracts and the full text of some articles. Covers hardware and software evaluations. Daily updates first appear in the NEWSEARCH database.

• **Inspec.** 1969-present. Institution of Electrical Engineers. An index to articles and papers on research and applications in computers, electronics, information technology, and physics. Includes abstracts.

Insurance
• **Bestlink Online Database.** A. M. Best. Financial and operating data on life/health and property/casualty insurance companies. Major data sources are each company's quarterly and annual statements to the National Association of Insurance Commissioners.

• **Insurance Periodicals Index.** 1983-present. NILS Publishing. An index to articles in about 45 insurance periodicals. Provides abstracts. Ability to search for directory information in these periodicals, such as directories of agencies, agents, annuities, brokers, consultants, policyholder-owned facilities, and software products.

International Markets
• **D & B—International Dun's Market Identifiers**. Dun's Marketing Services. Directory information on private and public U.S. and foreign companies. Some sales data expressed in both foreign and U.S. currency.

• **Infomat International Business**. 1984-present. Infomat. An index to articles on companies, markets, and products outside the U.S. Covers more than 425 journals and newspapers, with emphasis on European publications. Includes abstracts.

• **Moody's Corporate News—International.** Moody's Investors Service. News about companies in approximately 100 countries. A news report may be narrative or statistical.

Law
• **Legal Resource Index.** 1980-present. Information Access. An index to over 750 legal periodicals, including bar-association journals, law reviews, and legal newspapers. Also, selective indexing of legal articles from more than a thousand general publications. Daily updates first appear in the NEWSEARCH database.

PART SIX

JOIN THE
FIVE O'CLOCK CLUB

"FOR BUSY, CAREER-MINDED PEOPLE"

The Five O'Clock Club:

- **Job-Search Strategy Groups**
- **Private Coaching**
- **Membership Information**

The Five O'Clock Club was founded by Kate Wendleton in 1978 to provide thoughtful career-development help for busy people of all levels. The programs and materials have helped thousands take control of their careers and find good jobs fast.

The original Five O'Clock Club was formed in Philadelphia in 1886. It was made up of the leaders of the day, who shared their experiences "in a spirit of fellowship and good humor."

For a listing of local Affiliates, or more information on becoming a member, please fill out the Membership Application Form in this book, or call:
1-800-538-6645, ext. 600

The Five O'Clock Club Search Process

The Five O'Clock Club process, as outlined in Kate Wendleton's three books, is a targeted, strategic approach to career development and job search. Five O'Clock Club members become proficient at skills which prove invaluable during their *entire working lives*.

We train our members to *manage their careers*, and always look ahead to their *next* job search. Research shows that an average worker spends only four years in a job—and will have 12 jobs, in as many as 5 career fields—during his or her working life.

Five O'Clock Club members find *better jobs, faster*. The average job search for a managerial position is now estimated at 8.1 months. The average Five O'Clock Club member who regularly attends weekly sessions finds a job by his or her tenth session. Even the discouraged, long-term job searcher can find immediate help.

The keystone to The Five O'Clock Club process is in teaching our members an understanding of the entire hiring process. A first interview is only a time for exchanging critical information. The real work starts after the interview. We teach our members *how to turn job interviews into offers*, and to negotiate the best possible employment package.

The Five O'Clock Club is *action-oriented*. <u>We'll help you decide what you should do this very next week to move your search along</u>. By their third session, our members have set definite job targets by industry or company size, position, and geographic location, and are out in the field, gathering information and making the contacts which will lead to interviews with hiring managers.

Our approach evolves with the changing job market. We're able to synthesize information from hundreds of Five O'Clock Club members, and come up with new approaches for our members. For example, we now discuss temporary placement for executives, how to handle voice mail, and how to network when doors are slamming shut all over town.

Note: The following pages are taken from brochures and handouts of The Five O'Clock Club.

Let us consider how we may spur one another on toward love and good deeds.
Let us not give up meeting together, as some are in the habit of doing, but let us encourage one another.

Hebrews 10:24-25

The Job-Search Strategy Group

The Five O'Clock Club meeting is a carefully planned *job-search strategy session*. We provide members with the tools and tricks necessary to get a good job fast—even in a tight market. Networking and emotional support are also included in the meeting.

The first part of the meeting is devoted to a forty-minute *main group presentation* on a particular aspect of job search; another part, to *small group strategy sessions* led by trained career consultants.

The *main group presentations* are given on a rotating schedule, so a job searcher can join The Five O'Clock Club at any time. Members are encouraged to attend ten sessions in a row, after which they are free to stay with the main group or switch to the *advanced discussion group*, if one is offered.

Your *small group strategy session* is your chance to get feedback and advice on your own search, listen to and learn from others, and build your business network. All groups are led by trained career consultants, who bring years of experience to your search. The small group is generally no more than eight to ten people, so everyone gets the chance to speak up.

The first fifteen minutes of every meeting are given over to *informal networking*; the fifteen minutes between the main lecture and the small group strategy sessions are set aside for members to report on new jobs. The meetings are information-packed and action-oriented, move rapidly, and give you the tools and incentive to keep your search going.

Private Coaching

Your local Affiliate can give you a list of career consultants available between group meetings for *private coaching*. Individual sessions help you answer specific questions, solve current job problems, prepare your résumé, or take an in-depth look at your career path. Please pay the consultant directly, as *private coaching is not included in The Five O'Clock Club seminar or membership fee.*

From the Club history, written in the 1890's

At The Five O'Clock Club, [people] of all shades of political belief—as might be said of all trades and creeds—have met together. . . The variety continues almost to a monotony. . . [The Club's] good fellowship and geniality—not to say hospitality—has reached them all.

It has been remarked of clubs that they serve to level rank. If that were possible in this country, it would probably be true, if leveling rank means the appreciation of people of equal abilities as equals; but in The Five O'Clock Club it has been a most gratifying and noteworthy fact that no lines have ever been drawn save those which are essential to the honor and good name of any association. Strangers are invited by the club or by any members, [as gentlepeople], irrespective of aristocracy, plutocracy or occupation, and are so treated always. Nor does the thought of a [person's] social position ever enter into the meetings. People of wealth and people of moderate means sit side by side, finding in each other much to praise and admire and little to justify snarlishness or adverse criticism. People meet as people—not as the representatives of a set— and having so met, dwell not in worlds of envy or distrust, but in union and collegiality, forming kindly thoughts of each other in their heart of hearts.

In its methods, The Five O'Clock Club is plain, easy-going and unconventional. It has its "isms" and some peculiarities of procedure, but simplicity characterizes them all. The sense of propriety, rather than rules of order, governs its meetings, and that informality which carries with it sincerity of motive and spontaneity of effort, prevails within it. Its very name indicates informality, and, indeed, one of the reasons said to have induced its adoption was the fact that members or guests need not don their dress suits to attend the meetings, if they so desired. This informality, however, must be distinguished from the informality of Bohemianism. For The Five O'Clock Club, informality, above convenience, means sobriety, refinement of thought and speech, good breeding and good order. To this sort of informality much of its success is due.

The
Five
O'Clock
Club®

Questions You May Have About the Weekly Job-Search Strategy Group

The Weekly Job-Search Strategy Group

is a Professional Career-Counseling Program
presented by Affiliates of The Five O'Clock Club
"For busy, career-minded people"

Job hunters are not always the best judges of what they need during a search. For example, most are interested in lectures on answering ads or working with search firms. We will cover those topics, but, strategically, they are relatively unimportant in an effective job search.

At The Five O'Clock Club, you get the information you really need in your search—such as how to target more effectively, how to get more interviews, and how to turn job interviews into offers.

What's more, you will work in a small group with some of the best counselors around. In these strategy sessions, your group will help you decide what to do, this week and every week, to move your search along. And you will learn by coaching and being coached by others in your group.

Here are a few other points:

• For best results, attend on a regular basis. Your group gets to know you and will coach you to eliminate whatever you may be doing wrong—or refine what you are doing right.

• Those who think they need to come to a session only to ask a quick question are usually wrong. Often the problem started weeks before the job hunter realized it. Or the problem may be more complex than the job hunter realizes and require a few sessions to straighten out.

• You must be a member to attend the strategy group sessions. Some Affiliates will allow you to have a sample session, after which you must become a member before continuing in the group.

• Most Affiliates charge for multiple sessions at a time to make administration easier. If you miss a session, you may make it up at any time. You may even transfer unused time to a friend.

• Although many people find jobs quickly (even people who have been unemployed a long

time), others have more difficult searches. Plan to be in it for the long haul and you'll do better.

• Carefully read all of the material in the Beginner's Kit that you got with your membership in The Five O'Clock Club. It will help you decide whether or not to attend.

The first week, pay attention to the strategies used by the others in your group. Soak up all the information you can.

• Read the books before you come in the second week. They will help you move your search along.

To register

1. Call 1-800-538-6645 ext. 600 for the current list of Affiliates.

2. After you become a member and get your Beginner's Kit, call your local Affiliate to reserve a space for the first time you attend. If there is a waiting list, preference is given to current members of The Five O'Clock Club.

3. Read the books ahead of time, or purchase them at your first meeting.

To assign you to a counselor, your Affiliate liaison needs to know:

• your current (or last) field or industry,

• the kind of job you would like next (if you know),

• your desired salary range in general terms.

If you would rather see a private counselor before starting, call for suggested names.

What Happens at the Meetings?

Each week, job searchers from various industries and professions attend. Some Affiliates specialize in professionals, managers and executives; others in recent college graduates, specific minority groups, or those over fifty years of age.. Usually, half are employed; half unemployed.

The two-hour weekly program is in two parts. First, there is a lecture on a job-hunting topic appropriate to those in the audience. In the second hour, job hunters meet in small groups headed by senior full-time, professional counselors.

> *We find ourselves not independently of other people and institutions but through them.*
> *We never get to the bottom of our selves on our own. We discover who we are face to face*
> *and side by side with others in work, love, and learning.*
> Robert N. Bellah, et al, *Habits of the Heart*

The first week, you get the text books, hear the lecture, are assigned to your small group, and listen to the others in your group. You learn a lot by listening to how your peers are strategizing their searches.

By the second week, you will have read the materials. Now we can start to work on your search strategy and help you decide what to do next to move your search along. For example, we'll help you figure out how to get more interviews in your target area, or how to turn an interview into a job offer.

In the third week, you will see major progress in the other members of your group, and you may notice major progress in your own search as well.

By the third or fourth week, most members are conducting a full and effective search. Over the remaining weeks, you will tend to keep up a full search rather than go after only one possibility. You will regularly aim to have six to ten things "in the works" at all times. These will generally be in specific target areas that you have identified, will keep your search on target, and increase your chances of getting multiple job offers to choose from.

Those who stick with the process find that it works.

Some people prefer to just observe for a few weeks before they start their job search, and that's okay, too.

How Much Does it Cost?

The fees vary by location. Although each Affiliate may charge what they want, an average fee is 5 sessions for $200: 10 for $350. For administrative reasons, most Affiliates charge for 5 sessions at a time. This avoids having a large number of people paying each week.

You must have the materials so you can look at them before the second session. That's why it is important for you to buy the books provided at the seminar. Otherwise, you will tend to waste the time of the others in the group by asking questions that are covered in the texts.

Is The Club right for me?

The Five O'Clock Club process is for you if:
• You are looking for a job or consulting work.

• You have some idea of the kind of work you want.
• You fit the salary profile of the Affiliate.
• You want to participate in a group process on a regular basis.
• You realize that finding or changing jobs and careers is hard work . . . which you are absolutely willing and able to do.

If you have no idea about the kind of job you want next, you could see a counselor privately for one or two sessions, develop tentative job targets, and then join the group. On the other hand, some job hunters prefer to start the group program and see a counselor individually later if they still haven't come up with some-thing. The choice is yours. Your Affiliate liaison will be happy to provide you with the names of counselors you can see privately.

How long will it take me to get a job?

Although our members tend to be from difficult fields or industries, the average person who attends regularly finds a new position within ten sessions. Some take less time, and others take more. One thing we know for sure: *those who get regular coaching during their searches get jobs faster and at higher rates of pay than those who search on their own or simply take a course.* This makes sense. If a person comes only when they think they have a problem, they are usually wrong. They probably had a problem a few weeks ago, but didn't realize it. Or the problem may be different from what they thought. Those who come regularly benefit from the observations others make about their searches. Problems are solved before they become severe, or are prevented altogether.

Those who attend regularly also learn a lot by paying attention and helping others in the group. This "vicarious" learning can cut weeks from your search. When you hear the problems of others who are ahead of you in the search, you can avoid those problems completely. People in your group will come to know you, and will point out sub-tleties you may not have noticed and interviewers will never tell you.

The Five O'Clock Club is plain, easy-going and unconventional. . . .
Members or guests need not don their dress suits to attend the meetings.
(From the Club History, written in the 1890's)

Will I be with others from my same field/industry?

Probably, but it's not that important. If you were a salesperson, for example, would you want to be with seven other salespeople?

Probably not. The search techniques are the same for the level handled by your Affiliate. You will learn a lot and have a much more creative search if you are in a group with people who are in your general salary range but not exactly like you. Our clients are from virtually every field and industry. The process is what will help you.

We've been doing this since 1978, and understand your needs. That's why the mix we provide is the best you can get.

How can you charge such a small session fee?

1. We have no advertising costs because 90% of those who attend have been referred by other members.

We need a certain number of people to cover expenses. When lots of people get jobs quickly and leave us, we could go into the red. But so long as members refer others, we will continue to provide this service at a fair price.

2. We focus strictly on job search strategy, and encourage our clients to attend free support groups if they need emotional support. We focus on getting jobs, which reduces the time clients spend with us and the amount they pay.

3. We attract the best counselors, and our clients make more progress per session than they would elsewhere, which also reduces their costs.

4. We have expert administrators and a sophisticated computer system that reduces our overhead and increases our ability to track your progress.

May I change counselors at my local Affiliate?

Yes. Some care is taken in assigning you to your initial counselor. However, if you want to change once for any reason, you may do it. We don't encourage group hopping: it is better for you to stick with a group so that everyone gets to know you. On the other hand, we want you to feel comfortable. So if you tell your Affiliate liaison you prefer a different group, you will be transferred immediately.

What if I have questions outside of the group?

Some people prefer to see their group counselor privately. Others prefer to meet with a different counselor to get another point-of-view. Whatever you decide, remember that the group fee does not cover counselor time outside of the group session. Therefore, if you want to be able to ask a counselor a "quick question" in between sessions, you would normally meet with the counselor first for a private session so he or she gets to know you better. "Easy, quick questions" are often more complicated than they appear on the surface. After your first private session, some counselors will allow you to establish an account by paying in advance for one hour of counseling time, which you can then use for quick questions (usually a 15-minute minimum is charged). Since each counselor has an individual way of operating, find out how the counselor arranges these things.

What if I want to start my own business?

The process of becoming a consultant is essentially the same as job hunting, and lots of consultants attend regular Five O'Clock Club meetings. However, if you want to buy a franchise or an existing business or start a growth business, you should see a private counselor, or attend the entrepreneurial program that is offered by a few of our Affiliates.

What if I'm still not sure what to do.

Some Affiliates allow you to take a sample session before you become a member, for a modest fee. Then you can experience for yourself how we operate.

Whatever you decide, just remember that it has been proven that those who receive regular help during their searches get a job faster and at higher rates of pay than those who search on their own or simply attend a course. If you get a job just one or two weeks faster because of this program, it will more than have paid for itself. And you may transfer unused sessions to anyone you choose. However, the person that you choose must attend the Affiliate from which you purchased your sessions.

The
Five
O'Clock
Club®

The Way We Are

Just like the members of the original Five O'Clock Club, today's members want an ongoing relationship. George Vaillant, in his seminal work on successful people, found that "what makes or breaks our luck seems to be . . . our sustained relationships with other people." (George E. Vaillant, *Adaptation to Life*)

Five O'Clock Club members know that much of the program's benefit comes from simply showing up. Showing up will encourage you to do what you need to do when you are not here. And over the course of several weeks, certain things will become evident that are not evident now.

Five O'Clock Club members learn from each other: the group leader is not the only one with answers. The leader brings factual information to the meetings, and keeps the discussion in line. But the answers to some problems may lie within you, or with others in the group.

Five O'Clock Club members encourage each other. They listen, see similarities with their own situations, and learn from that. And they listen to see how they may help others. You may come across information or a contact that will help someone else in the group. Passing on that information is what we're all about.

If you are a new member here, listen to others to learn the process. And read the books so you will know the basics that others already know. When everyone understands the basics, this keeps the meetings on a high level, interesting, and helpful to everyone.

Five O'Clock Club members are in this together, but they know that ultimately they are each responsible for solving their own problems with God's help. Take the time to learn the process, and you will become better at analyzing your own situation, as well as the situations of others. You will be learning a method that will serve you the rest of your life, and in areas of your life apart from your career.

Five O'Clock Club members are kind to each other. They control their frustrations—because venting helps no one. Because many may be stressed, be kind and go the extra length to keep this place calm and happy. It is your respite from the world outside and a place for you to find comfort and FUN. Relax and enjoy yourself, learn what you can, and help where you can. And have a ball doing it.

The
Five
O'Clock
Club®

Lexicon Used at
The Five O'Clock Club

Use The Five O'Clock Club lexicon as a shorthand to express where you are in your job search. It will focus you and those in your group.

I. Overview and Assessment

How many hours a week are you spending on your search? Spend 35 hours on a full-time search; 15 hours on a part-time search.

What are your job targets?
Tell the group. A target includes industry or company size, position, and geographic area.

The group can help assess how good your targets are. Take a look at "Measuring Your Targets."

How does your résumé position you?
The summary and body should make you look appropriate to your target.

What are your back-up targets?
Decide at the beginning of the search before the first campaign. Then you won't get stuck.

Have you done the Assessment? If you have no specific targets, you cannot have a targeted search. You could see a counselor privately for two or three sessions to determine possible job targets.

II. Getting Interviews

How large is your target (e.g., thirty companies)? How many of them have you contacted? Contact them all.

How can you get (more) leads?
You will not get a job through search firms, ads, networking or direct contact. Those are techniques for getting interviews—job leads. Use the right lexicon, especially after a person gets a job. Do not say, "How did you get the job?" if you really want to know, "Where did you get the lead for that job?"

Do you have six to ten things in the works?
You may want the group to help you land one job. After they help you with your strategy, they should ask, "How many other things do you have in the works?" If "none," the group can brainstorm how you can get more things going: through search firms, ads, networking, or direct contact. Then you are more likely to turn the job you want into an offer because you will seem more valuable. What's

more, five will fall away through no fault of your own. Don't go after only one job.

How's your Two-Minute Pitch?
Practice a *tailored* Two-Minute Pitch. Tell the group the job title and industry of the hiring manager they should pretend they are for a role-playing exercise.

You will be surprised how good the group is at critiquing pitches. Make sure your pitch separates you from your competition.

You seem to be in Stage One (or Stage Two or Stage Three) of your search. Know where you are in the process. See our book *Job-Search Secrets*.

Are you seen as insider or outsider?
See "How to Change Careers" for becoming an insider. If people are saying, "I wish I had an opening for someone like you," you are doing well in meetings. If the industry is strong, then it's only a matter of time before you get a job.

III. Turning Interviews into Offers

Do you want this job?
If you do not want the job, perhaps you want an offer, if only for practice. If you are not willing to go for it, the group's suggestions will not work.

Who are your likely competitors and how can you outshine and outlast them? You will not get a job simply because "they liked me." The issues are deeper. Ask the interviewer: "Where are you in the hiring process? What kind of person would be your ideal candidate?"

What are your next steps? What are *you* planning to do if the hiring manager doesn't call by a certain date, or what are you planning to do to assure that the hiring manager *does* call you?

Can you prove you can do the job? Don't just take the "Trust me" approach.

Which job positions you best for the long run? Which job is the best fit? Don't decide only on the basis of salary. See which job looks best on your résumé, and will make you a stronger candidate next time.

In addition, find a fit for your personality. If you don't "fit," it is unlikely you will do well there. The group can give feedback on which job is best for you.

The Five O'Clock Club®

Dear Prospective Five O'Clock Clubber:

The Five O'Clock Club has helped thousands find jobs, change, or manage their careers!

At The Five O'Clock Club, we focus your search with real-world information that tells you exactly what you need to get more interviews . . . **and turn those interviews into offers.**

As a member, you also get—

❑ An attractive **membership card** and a **Beginner's Kit** containing information based on 12 years of research regarding who gets jobs and why, that will enable you to improve your job-search technqiues . . . immediately.

❑ A **subscription to *The Five O'Clock News*,** ten issues filled with information on career development and job-search techniques— information to help you thrive in your career.

❑ **Access to reasonably priced weekly seminars** featuring individualized attention to your specific needs in small groups supervised by our senior counselors.

❑ Access to **one-on-one counseling**.

❑ The opportunity to exchange ideas, experiences, and even role-play with other job searchers and career changers.

All that access, all that information, for the nominal membership fee of only $35.

The sooner you become a member, the sooner you can begin working on having a career that truly meets your financial, emotional, creative and intellectual needs.

Believe me, with self-examination and a lot of hard work with our counselors, you **can** find the job . . . you **can** have the career . . . you **can** live the life you always wanted!

The best of luck, whatever you may decide.

Sincerely,
Kate Wendleton, President

❑ Yes! I want access to the most effective methods for developing and managing my career, as well as for finding jobs.

. . . .

I enclose $35.00. I will receive a Beginner's Kit, a membership card, a one-year subscription to *The Five O'Clock News*, a listing of current Affiliates of The Five O'Clock Club, access to a network of career counselors and to reasonably priced seminars at Affiliates of The Five O'Clock Club in the U.S. and Canada.

Name _____

Address _____

City _____ State/Prov. _____ Zip/Postal _____

Work Phone _____

Home Phone _____

Today's Date: _____

Referred by: _____

Targeting the Job You Want

. . . .

Method of payment:

❑ I enclose my check for $35.00 U.S., made out to The Five O'Clock Club, 300 E. 40th St., Suite 6L, NY, NY 10016.
❑ MasterCard or VISA:
    (This form can be faxed to 212-286-9571)
Account Number:_____
Exp. Date:_____Signature: _____

. . . .

The following information is for statistical purposes. Thanks for your help.

Age: ❑ 20-29   ❑ 30-39   ❑ 40-49   ❑ 50+

Sex: ❑ Male   ❑ Female

Salary range:
❑ under $30,000   ❑ $30-$49,999   ❑ $50-$74,999
❑ $75-$99,999   ❑ $100-$125,000   ❑ over $125,000

Current or most recent position/title: _____

_____

. . . .

The original Five O'Clock Club® was formed in Philadelphia in 1886. It was made up of the leaders of the day, who shared their experiences "in a spirit of fellowship and good humor."

Index

A

A journey   95
Academia   205
Accomplishment statements
    67, 68, 126
Accomplishments
    difficulty of writing   113
    early in your career   126
    how to state   111
    negative   113
    process-oriented   112
    project-oriented   112
Accountants   7
Actor   13
Adams, Henry   189
Ads, answering   126
Advanced planning
    strategies   155
Advertising   185, 208
Advertising, traditional field of
    17, 19, 164
African-American freedom song   95
Agase, Alex   34
Aging population, growth target
    22
Agricultural services   21
Allaire, Paul   55
Allen, Gracie   41
Anderson, Hans Christian   66
Animals   35
Architecture   206
Arnold, Matthew   95
Art   22, 206
Artists   7, 23
Ashe, Arthur   153
Asimov, Isaac   46
Assessment   218
    example   26
    purpose of   59
    results of   28
Associations   182, 202
    for meeting people   26
Atwater, Lee   62

B

Babe Ruth   10
Bacon, Francis   187
Balanced life   151
Baldwin, James   108, 203
Banking   17, 21
Barriers to achieving goals   110
Bartholdi, Frédéric-Auguste   174
Bates, Marston   139
Bellah, Robert N.   15, 215
Bennis, Warren   16
Bible   20, 54, 152, 139, 213
Blackwell, Elizabeth   9
Blanchard, Kenneth   44
Bliss, Edwin C.   151
Blount, Jr., Roy   36
Bond, Edward   146
Bookkeeping   37
Bosses   73, 76, 77
    managing relationships with   161
    revolving   8
    your relationship with   76
Bowman, C.B.   166
Brainstorming possible jobs
    99, 115, 116
Bridges, William
    24, 31, 106, 160, 161, 162
Brilliant, Ashleigh   24
Broadcasting   195
Bronte, Lydia   45
Brown, Deborah
    head of Workforce America   153
Brown, Ron   170
Browning, Robert   176
Brussell, Shirley   46
Burke, Edmund   79
Burnham, Daniel   58
Business articles   207
Business information sources   181
Butler, Samuel   17
Byrne, Robert   153

C

Cable stations   18
Caine, Michael   176
Camus, Albert   110
Canin, Ethan   60, 88
Career
    management   57
    parallel   168
    planning   11
    principles   172
    scenarios   153
    vs. "work"   151
Career change   10, 25, 26, 166
Career counselor   51, 79
Career Plan   159, 160
    detailed   153
Career plan
    second job out   172
Carlyle, Thomas   54, 167
Carroll, Lewis   8, 55, 175
Carter, David M.   34
Casals, Pablo   45
Casino industry   9
CD-ROM   136
CD-ROM databases   202
Chagall, Marc   45
Chambers of Commerce   136
Chanel, Coco   95
Change   6, 51
    as opportunity   8, 51
    careers   9
    technological   7
Changing careers   166
Charles, Ray   78
Chewning, Thomas   31
Chief financial officer   11
Child, Julia   47
Churchill, Winston   44, 151
Clinton, Bill   12, 13, 39, 83
Clinton, Hillary   99
Commitment   118
    impact on job search   118
    to a target   26
Company
    style or environment   119
Company information   183, 208
Compensation, fair   15
Competition   126, 218
    outshine and outlast   218
Compton, Ronald   52, 133
Computer field   20, 21, 23
Computers   7, 23
Confucius   175
Connelly, Julie   39
Consumer goods   20
Controller   11
Corporate career-development
    initiatives   169
Corrigan, Bob   170

Cosmetics 40
Cousins, Norman 47, 48
Covey, Stephen R. 11, 59, 157

D

Databases 136
de Geus, Arie P. 145
Deadlines
  in planning 157
Decision-making, objective vs.
  subjective 14
Desiderata 51
Developing scenarios 106, 108
Directories 181
Disraeli, Benjamin 155
Drucker, Peter F.
  16, 23, 25, 133, 134, 147
Dubuffet, Jean 42
Durant, Will 59

E

Eastern Europe 18
Education 21, 99, 201
Education, field of 14, 20, 22
Educational film maker 14
Edwards, Harry 198
Ehrlichman, John 30
Einstein, Albert 23
Electric power industry 29
Eliot, George 99
Eliot, T. S. 8
Ellis, Larry 31
Emerson, Ralph Waldo
  17, 52, 61, 142
Emotions
  overcoming negative 87
Employers 5
Employment
  non-traditional 6
Engineering 18, 21, 204, 207
Environment 185
Environmental 21
Epictetus 28
Executives
  retraining of 28
  unskilled 18
Exercises
  Analyzing Your Seven Stories 69
  Bosses 76
  Brainstorming Possible Jobs
    101, 107

Career Plan 159
Feedback 78
Forty-Year Plan 83
Ideal Scene 86
Interests 74
List of Companies to Contact
  137
Satisfiers and Dissatisfiers 75
Stating accomplishments 111
The Seven Stories 67
Values 72
Expand search, geographically 19

F

Fashion 42
Faulk, Bruce
  13, 77, 85, 90, 115, 117, 119
Feedback
  form 80
  from others 77
Fields 17
Finance 186, 208
Financial information
  on CD-ROM 202
Financial services 21
Foreman, George 93
Forty-Year Plan 11, 13, 83, 87
  a case study 106
  example of 27, 91
  my own 87
  the exercise 83, 84
Fowles, John 181
France, Anatole 42, 186
Franklin, Benjamin 113, 206
Freud, Sigmund 48
Fromm, Eric 17

G

Gandhi, Mohandas 201
Garcia, Jerry 165
Gardner, John W. 47
Garfield, Charles 58
Gendron, George 105
Geographic location
  as part of target 60
Getting credit 161
Getting interviews 218
Gide, André 19, 57
Glasow, Arnold H. 24
Goal-setting 57, 81

Goals 12, 13, 153
  and happy people 61
  balanced 151
  barriers to achieving 110
  life 152
  long-range 99
  stretch 151
  written 12
Goldberg, Whoopi 14
Goldwyn, Samuel 165
Goleman, Daniel 13, 95
Gotti, Joan 171
Government 195, 205
Gramsci, Antonio 143
Graphics 206
Gray, E. M. 127
Greisser, Harriet 6, 21, 29
Grove, Andrew S. 38

H

Haley, Alex 53
Halper, Jan 77, 103, 109
Handy, John 16
Harvard study 12, 81
Hastie, William 87
Hawking, Stephen M. 55
Health care
  11, 17, 21, 25, 188, 205, 209
Hedrick, Smith 171
Hemingway, Ernest 188
Henderson, Bruce 126
Herbert, Bob 158
Herodotus 26
Heschel, Abraham J. 182
High technology 188, 209
Highlighting in résumés
  industries 127
Homemaker 37
Hope, high levels of 13
Human Resources 189

I

Ideal Scene, the exercise 86, 89
Importing / Exporting / Trading
  189
Industries 17
  growing 20, 21
  retrenching 18, 20
Industry or company size
  as part of target 60

Industry trends 182
Information industry 190
Information on executives and
    management 201
Information systems 20
Insurance 20, 209
Interests 73, 74
Interests exercise 27, 73, 74
International 17, 21, 184, 191, 209
Interviews
    turning them into offers 218
Irving, John 183
Irving, Washington 127

J

James, Henry 122
James, William 12, 109
Japanese saying 194
Job hunting, definition of 7, 23
Job satisfiers and dissatisfiers,
    exercise 75, 77, 80, 161
Job search
    how to organize 116
Job security 7
Job target, definition of 25
Job targets 218
    selection of 59
Jobs, of the future 17
Jobs, Steven 57
Johansen, Robert 16
John-Rogers 176
Johnson, Samuel 141
Jong, Erica 174
Jung, Carl 92

K

Kafka, Franz 109
Keillor, Garrison 109
Keller, Helen 6
Kennedy, John F. 9, 52
Khruschev, Nikita S. 184
Kier, Richard 33
Kiev, M.D., Ari 82
Kimbro, Dennis 156
King Jr., Martin Luther 199
King, Jr., Martin Luther
    82, 83, 174
Kitchen, Patricia
    17, 32, 33, 37, 40, 43
Korda, Michael 111

Korn, Lester 58
Kuhn, Maggie 47

L

Landy, Frank 48
Lao-tzu 168
Law 195, 205, 209
Law, the field of 18
Law, William 117
Lawrence, D.H. 190
Leads, serendipitous 117
Lerner, Max 47
Lewis, Michael 62
Life, balanced 151
Life expectancy 45
Lincoln, Abraham 5
List of Companies to Contact,
    worksheet 137
Long-range goals 99
Longfellow, Henry Wadsworth
    25, 193
Lukacs, John 95, 174
Lustig, Barry 52
Luther, John 62, 133
Lynberg, Michael 120

M

Maguire, Jack 25, 110
Managing bosses 162
Mandela, Nelson 177
Manufacturing 21, 182
Market, ahead of the 18
Marketing 198
Maugham, Somerset 202
May, Rollo 59
Mays, Benjamin E. 197
McFarlane, Colleen 40
McWilliams, Peter 176
Measuring Your Targets 124
Media & Broadcasting 195
Merton, Thomas 51, 116, 121
Meyer, Michael 57
Miller, Arthur 91, 99, 151
Miller, Henry 91
Miller, Irwin 114
Money 12
Montagu, Ashley 207
Morley, Christopher 175
Morrow, Lance 55
Mother Teresa 88

Motivated skills 111
Multiplier effect 155
Murray, Diane 35
Music 206
Musicians 7

N

Nash, Ogden 24
Nef, Evelyn 45
New media, the 18, 19, 21
Newman, James W. 205
Newsday 32
Next steps, after an interview 218
Nietzsche, Friedrich 192
Nobel, Alfred 82
Noble, Charles C. 100
Not-for-profit 12, 14, 17, 54
Not-for-profit / fund-raising 196
Nursing 18

O

O'Hara-Devereaux, Mary 16
Old Testament 53
Older workers 14, 45
Oliver, Betty 37
On-Line databases 206
O'Neill, Nena 125
Optimism 13

P

Paderewski, Ignace 112
Pasternak, Boris 62
Patton, Forrest H. 81
Pauling, Dr. Linus 46
Pavese, Cesare 191
Pavlova, Anna 27
Peale, Norman Vincent 44, 70
Peers 77
Personality, in résumés 127
Peterson, Esther 48
Pharmaceuticals 21
Phases, of a job search 116
Photographer 23
Picasso, Pablo 45
Pitch 126
Plan
    deadlines 157
    detailed career 153
Poe, Edgar Allen 20
Pope John Paul II 125

Position or function
   as part of target   60
Positioning
   for the long run   11, 19, 218
Possible jobs, how to brainstorm
   99
Preliminary Target Investigation
   100, 114
Present situation
   how to benefit from   160
Pritchett, Price   163
Private business   199
Public Relations   185, 197
Publishing   20, 198

Q

Quisenberry, Dan   209

R

Rappaport, Ph.D., Herbert
   173, 175
Read, Leonard E.   25
Real Estate   200
Real estate   18
Reeve, Christopher
   93, 95, 125, 153
Reeve, Dana   93, 125
Reference information
   on CD-ROM   202
Relationships, work-related   78
Religion   206
Research   87
   creative   148
   for assessment   141
   for better networking   143
   for career change   145
   for expanding your targets;
      identifying companies   142
   for interview preparation   143
   for salary negotiation   144
   how I do it   133
   how to   139, 172
   identifying targets   140
   importance of   133
   in the library   133
   primary   139
   secondary   139
   The Encyclopedia of Associa-
      tions   140
   through associations   135

through networking   136
to become an insider   144
using university libraries   136
Researching
   the environmental field   145
   the health-care field   141
   the international market   147
   to uncover small companies   146
   your job targets   133, 173, 177
Resolving internal conflicts   106
Résumé
   case study   126
   sample   126
Retail industry   20, 22, 25
Ries, Al   135
Right Associates   6, 29
Rilke, Rainer Maria   65
Ross, Steven J.   99
Rothman, Wendy Alfus   139

S

Sadi   174
Saint-Exupéry, Antoine de   18, 139
Sales and marketing   198
Salespeople   7
Salk, Dr. Jonas   46
Salter, James   88
Santayana, George   91
Sarnoff, David   140
Satisfiers and dissatisfiers   73, 75
Satisfying work   58
Schaefer, Jack   24
Schaen, Robert   154
Schundler, Russ   6, 29
Schwartz, Peter   86, 136
Science, engineering, and technol-
      ogy   204
Sculley, John   57, 104
Search   116
   an organized   116
   inside your present company   5
   out-of-town   122
   phases of   116
Secretary   54
Self-assessment, summary of
   94, 95
Senge, Peter   9
Serenity Prayer   55
Services   199, 206
Setting goals   81

Seven Stories Exercise
   26, 63, 67, 99, 113, 126, 127
   background of approach   64
   case study   103
   demonstration of the   65
   example of   91
   how to analyze   69
   importance of   59
   the exercise   67
Shakes, Ronnie   24
Shakespeare, William   82, 122
Shaw, George Bernard   7, 125
Sherman, Stratford   21
Singer, Isaac Bashevis   208
Six to ten things in the works   218
Skills, enjoyable   57
Skills, hard   23
Sloan School of Management   169
Small business   37, 40, 199
Smaller companies, job creation in
   19
Smith, Hedrick   24, 160
Smith, Raymond   17
Smith, Walter ("Red")   196
Snyder, Dr. Charles R.   13
Sondheim, Stephen   158
Spark, Muriel   64
Speaker, Tris   10
Special events   200
Spiritual, African-American   99
Sports   33
Stages
   of a job search   218
Statistics, employment   6
Statistics, labor   21
Stein, Gertrude   57
Steinbeck, John   22
Stoppard, Tom   144, 173
Subordinates   77
Suburbs, job creation in   19
Success, predictor of   13
Successful managers   58
Summary statement(s)   127, 218
Szent-Gyorgyi, Albert   139

T

Target
   selection   121, 123
Target elements
   geographic area   118

industry or company size 118
position or function 119
Target selection 118, 123, 134
Targeting 116
benefit of 25
the steps for 54
Targets
adding new 117
aiming too low 53
back-up 218
brainstorming 115
defining job 118
expanding your 122
measuring 122, 124
narrowing down 116
ranking of 123
sample 120
selecting job 118
serendipitous 117
Teacher 14
Technological change, affecting
jobs 20
Technology
7, 17, 20, 188, 204, 209
Telecommunications 21
Television, interactive 18
Television, network 17
Tetzel, Rich 16
The Conference Board 170
The Five O'Clock Club
6, 8, 212, 217, 218
environment 217
lexicon 218
membership information 212
search process 212
Thoreau, Henry David 66
Thurow, Lester 110, 169
Todd, Mike 62
Tolstoy, Leo 151
Tomlin, Lily 118
Trade shows 200
Training 126
Training and development 206
Transportation 200
Travel and Hospitality 200
Trends 206
Trout, Jack 135
True, Herb 136
Truman, Harry S. 5
Tueli, Celebra 25
Two-Minute Pitch 218

V

Values 14, 72
Values Exercise 27, 72
Ventura, Michael 86
Viorst, Judith 151
Vision 154
Volunteer experience 112

W

Walters, Barbara 153
Webb, Dennis R. 86
Wheeler, Michael 169
White, E. B. 109
Whitman, Walt 11
Wiesel, Elie 185
Wilde, Oscar 164
Wilkerson, Isabel 14
Wilson, August 55
Work experience 99
Worker, older 23
Workers, unskilled 18
Workforce America 93

About the Author

Kate Wendleton is a nationally recognized authority on career development. She has been a career coach since 1978, when she founded The Five O'Clock Club® and developed its methodology to help job hunters and career changers of all levels in job-search-strategy groups. This methodology is now used by Affiliates of The Five O'Clock Club, which meet weekly in the United States and Canada.

Kate also founded Workforce America™, a not-for-profit Affiliate of The Five O'Clock Club, serving adults in Harlem who are not yet in the professional or managerial ranks. Workforce America helps each person move into better-paying, higher-level positions as each improves in educational level and work experience.

Kate founded, and directed for seven years, The Career Center at The New School for Social Research in New York. She also advises major corporations about employee career-development programs, and coaches senior executives. A former CFO of two small companies, she has twenty years of business-management experience in both manufacturing and service businesses.

Kate attended Chestnut Hill College in Philadelphia and received her MBA from Drexel University. She is a popular speaker with groups that include The Wharton Business School Club, the Yale Club, The Columbia Business School Club, and Workforce America in Harlem.

While living in Philadelphia, Kate did long-term volunteer work for The Philadelphia Museum of Art, The Walnut Street Theatre Art Gallery, United Way, and the YMCA. Kate currently lives in Manhattan.

Kate Wendleton is the author of *Through the Brick Wall: How to Job-Hunt in a Tight Market*, the *What Color Is Your Parachute?* of the nineties, and The Five O'Clock Club's three-part career-development and job-hunting series: *Targeting the Job You Want, Job-Search Secrets (that have helped thousands of members)*, and *Building a Great Résumé*.

The original Five O'Clock Club was formed in Philadelphia in 1886.
It was made up of the leaders of the day, who shared their experiences
"in a spirit of fellowship and good humor."

Get the Best Job-Search/ Career-Development Books on the Market

For Job Hunters, Career Changers, Consultants & Freelancers

Targeting the Job You Want
(Five O'Clock Books, 240 pp., ISBN 0-944054-08-0, $15.)

Finally, the best way to figure out what to do with your life in this tumultuous economy.

- Where are the jobs of the future?
- Where do you fit in?
- How can you have job security?

"Kate breaks the process into do-able steps that are easy to understand."
— Albert Prendergast, sr. vp, Mastercard International

The Five O'Clock Club® Job Search Secrets
(Five O'Clock Books, 304 pp., ISBN 0-944054-10-2, $15.)

Learn the secrets of the renowned career counseling and job-hunting organization that has helped thousands of people find their dream jobs.

- Getting and handling interviews
- Beating out the competition
- Negotiating the best salary whether you're full-time, a consultant or a freelancer

"I have doubled my salary during the past five years by using The Five O'Clock Club techniques. Now I earn what I deserve."
— M.S., entertainment industry attorney

Building a Great Résumé
(Five O'Clock Books, 256 pp., ISBN 0-944054-09-9, $15.)

The only book on the market with a case study approach, *Building a Great Résumé* is a step-by-step guide for career changers, consultants and freelancers, as well as job hunters, who want to develop the best possible résumé.

"A person who follows Kate's formula would certainly get my attention, even if I'd already rejected his or her résumé."
— Carole F. St. Mark, president, Pitney Bowes Logistics Systems & Business Services

Available at most major bookstores, or call
1-800-888-4945